Islam in Foreign Policy

Islam in
Foreign Policy

EDITED BY
ADEED DAWISHA

Published in association with
The Royal Institute of International Affairs

Cambridge University Press

CAMBRIDGE

LONDON   NEW YORK   NEW ROCHELLE

MELBOURNE   SYDNEY

Published by the Press Syndicate of the University of Cambridge
The Pitt Building, Trumpington Street, Cambridge CB2 1RP
32 East 57th Street, New York, NY 10022, USA
296 Beaconsfield Parade, Middle Park, Melbourne 3206, Australia

First published 1983

Printed in Great Britain at the University Press, Cambridge

Library of Congress catalogue card number: 83-7458

British Library Cataloguing in Publication Data
Islam in foreign policy.
1. Islam and politics 2. Islamic countries——
Foreign relations
I. Dawisha, Adeed I.
327.17′671   DS39

ISBN 0 521 25815 4

NP

Contents

Contributors   vii

Preface   ix

1   Islam in Foreign Policy: Some Methodological Issues   1
ADEED DAWISHA

2   Khumayni's Islam in Iran's Foreign Policy   9
R. K. RAMAZANI

3   Islamic Values and National Interest: The Foreign Policy
of Saudi Arabia   33
JAMES P. PISCATORI

4   Libyan Loneliness in Facing the World: The Challenge
of Islam?   54
B. SCARCIA AMORETTI

5   In Search of an Identity: Islam and Pakistan's Foreign
Policy   68
SHIRIN TAHIR-KHELI

6   The Limits of Instrumentalism: Islam in Egypt's Foreign
Policy   84
ALI E. HILLAL DESSOUKI

7   Explaining the Nearly Inexplicable: The Absence of
Islam in Moroccan Foreign Policy   97
I. WILLIAM ZARTMAN

8   Invoking the Spirit of Arabism: Islam in the Foreign
Policy of Saddam's Iraq   112
ADEED DAWISHA

CONTENTS

9 Islam and Nigerian Foreign Policy: Tradition and Social
   Criticism   129
   SAM C. NOLUTSHUNGU

10 The Islamic Factor in Indonesia's Foreign Policy: A Case
    of Functional Ambiguity   144
    MICHAEL LEIFER

11 Islam in the Foreign Policy of the Soviet Union: A
    Double-Edged Sword?   160
    KAREN DAWISHA and
    HÉLÈNE CARRERE D'ENCAUSSE

12 Conclusion   178
    ALBERT HOURANI

    Index   183

Contributors

HÉLÈNE CARRERE D'ENCAUSSE, *Professor at the University of Paris 1, and Director of the Post-Graduate Programme on the USSR and East Europe at the Institut d'Études Politiques de Paris*

ADEED DAWISHA, *Deputy Director of Studies at the Royal Institute of International Affairs*

KAREN DAWISHA, *Rockefeller International Relations Fellow at the London School of Economics, and Lecturer in Politics at the University of Southampton*

ALI E. HILLAL DESSOUKI, *Professor of Political Science at the University of Cairo*

ALBERT HOURANI, *Emeritus Fellow of St Antony's College, Oxford, and Emeritus Reader in the Modern History of the Middle East at Oxford University*

MICHAEL LEIFER, *Reader in International Relations at the London School of Economics*

SAM C. NOLUTSHUNGU, *Lecturer in Government at the University of Manchester*

JAMES P. PISCATORI, *Research Fellow at the Royal Institute of International Affairs*

R. K. RAMAZANI, *Edward R. Stettinius Professor of Government and Foreign Affairs at the University of Virginia*

B. SCARCIA AMORETTI, *Professor of Islamic Studies at the University of Rome*

SHIRIN TAHIR-KHELI, *Associate Professor of Political Science at Temple University*

I. WILLIAM ZARTMAN, *Professor and Director of African Studies at the School of Advanced International Studies, The Johns Hopkins University*

Preface

The essays in this book grew from papers delivered initially at the international conference held by the Royal Institute of International Affairs at Chatham House in July 1982. The conference was meant to follow on and complement the work of another conference, held at Chatham House a year earlier, which examined the role of Islam in domestic politics, and which resulted in a book edited by James P. Piscatori, entitled *Islam in the Political Process* (Cambridge University Press, 1983). The two conferences are part of a larger research project on the impact of Islam on the international system, which is funded by the Ford Foundation. As the organizer of the conference and the editor of the resulting volume, I am thankful to the Foundation and the officers of its international relations programme for providing the funds, and to the Royal Institute of International Affairs for making available its excellent facilities and support services for the conference.

From conference to book, a number of people have been a great help to me. I am particularly grateful to Albert Hourani whose advice was always invaluable, and to James Piscatori who helped me throughout the whole process, not least through chairing many of the conference's sessions. Along with the other contributors to the book, I owe a great deal to all the members of the conference, who provided many pertinent comments on earlier drafts of the essays that follow. At the Institute, I am thankful to Elizabeth Watson, Patricia Louison and Ann De'Ath for typing various drafts of the book efficiently and patiently.

As far as the transliteration of Arabic words is concerned, I have followed the form in *Islam in the Political Process*. I have, therefore, indicated the 'ayn (') and the medial hamza ('), but omitted the hamza when it occurred at the beginning or at the end of a word, and deleted all diacriticals. In the case of Arabs mentioned in the text who themselves have written in European language, I tried to use their own spelling of their names.   A.D.

February 1983

1 Islam in Foreign Policy: Some Methodological Issues

ADEED DAWISHA

The revolution in Iran, the Muslim virulent resistance to the Soviet invasion of Afghanistan, the assassination of Egypt's President Sadat by an Islamic fundamentalist group, the attempted takeover of the Grand Mosque in Mecca, and the clear Islamic dimensions and manifestations of the Iran–Iraq war were some of the more dramatic events that focussed the world's attention on Islam as a potent agent of domestic transformation and international change.

The Ayatollah's takeover of power in Iran, perhaps the first mass-based, non-communist uprising this century, gave rise to fears in the West that neighbouring countries, most of whom were of vital economic and strategic importance to the Western world, might fall victim to the same forces that so radically changed the structure of Iran's domestic politics and the direction of its foreign policy. And from observing political and social developments in the Islamic world in the seventies, the Iranian case ranks as only one indicator (albeit a most dramatic and consequential one) of Islam's seeming universal revival as a major internal and international political force.

A major research project was mounted by the Royal Institute of International Affairs to examine the impact of Islam on the international system; an exercise which has already produced one volume concentrating on the influence of Islam on the domestic political activities of states with predominantly Muslim populations.[1] Whatever the conclusions regarding the potency of Islam's influence on domestic policies, its role in determining, constraining and/or justifying foreign policy is a different intellectual exercise because the focus of the analysis is different. The object of this volume, therefore, is to shift the attention from the domestic to the external arena, examining in the process the role of Islam in the foreign policies of a number of states in which all, or a considerable part, of the population is Muslim.

Foreign policy and domestic politics

Unlike in domestic politics, where political leaderships exercise relative control over their environment, in foreign policy political decisions are aimed at an environment over which political leaders have very little, if any, control. In national systems, individual members of society are inculcated from childhood with roughly the same values, and as such national society tends to acquire, generally speaking, a common and unifying value system, which in turn generates a common set of rules and laws that become binding on individuals. Governments, who are perceived as 'those organs involved in the authoritative allocation of values',[2] are therefore accorded the authority by their societies to initiate legislation, pass laws and, most importantly, to ensure compliance.

Beyond the nation-state, however, no common value system exists, and consequently there is a lack of a common set of rules and laws. There exists a system of international law, which in theory is supposed to regulate the activities of states and national governments; in reality, the conduct of states in the international arena is constrained 'by the decisions of the states themselves, not by any authority external to them'.[3] In other words, the basic feature of international society is its 'anarchical nature'.[4] Thus, while societal values can be translated into governmental decisions within the nation-state itself, in dealing with 'foreign' states and other international entities, lack of control means that governmental decisions are apt to be frustrated, or at least compromised, unless a particular government is powerful enough, or aims its policies at a friendly international environment, to be able to ensure foreign compliance with its decisions.

The structure of foreign policy

From the discussion so far, it is apparent that foreign policy is being defined as 'the actions of a state toward the external environment and the conditions under which these actions are formulated'.[5] Within this context, the term 'policy' is conceived of as 'the decisions that define goals, set precedents, or lay down courses of action, and the actions taken to implement those decisions'.[6] Foreign policy is thus a process, and it unfolds in three distinct, yet interrelated, areas of analysis. The influences on foreign policy, the making of foreign policy and the implementation of foreign policy.[7]

The influences on foreign policy usually include such factors as the culture and religion of the society; the geography of the country and its military and economic capability; and the role of pressure groups and public opinion. These factors influence foreign policy not only in an objective sense, but also in the way they make an impact on the perceptions of decision-makers. In the Muslim world, one expects that Islam would constitute a significant influence on policy.

The making or formulation of foreign policy refers to the processes, procedures and personalities whose task it is to make policy decisions. This area of analysis usually encompasses the constitutional and institutional structure of the state, the composition and circulation of the decision-making elite, the interactions and relationships that exist among the members of the elite, the role of 'personality' in foreign policy behaviour, and the values of the policy-making elite. Again, Islam should play a role in the perceptions and images of the political elites generally, and of the decision-makers particularly, thus forming an important input into the formulation of policy.

The final area of analysis is the implementation of foreign policy, which, as stated earlier, occurs outside the national boundaries of the states, thus separating foreign policy, intellectually as well as in a practical sense, from domestic politics. The emphasis here is first on the instruments of policy – how and by what means are decisions translated into action; and second on the impact of the foreign policy action on the other actors in the international system and the responses of these actors to the action in question. In this area of analysis, one can expect the Islamic institutions, diplomatic, economic and cultural, to play some part in the implementation of the foreign policy of states with significant Muslim populations.

Islam in foreign policy

Islam, unlike Christianity, does not prescribe the separation of religion from politics. Indeed, devout Muslims argue that Islam is a complete social, political, legal and cultural system. In the *shari'a*, the Muslims have a law that deals with all constitutional and legal matters, and as such is treated, in orthodox Islamic theory, as the only legally acceptable code. Consequently, to the devout Muslim, there can be only one legitimate rule, and that is through Islam, and there can be no disjunction between political and religious discourse. Thus, for example, the world congress of Friday Imams, held in Tehran on 2 January 1982, resolved among other things that the contents of the Friday sermons should

stress the coordination and indivisibility of religion and politics and clearly praise them ... should make the people aware of the active role played by

3

religion in all aspects of social life ... should prepare the ground for the creation of Islamic Governments in all countries, under the precise and active supervision and leadership of committed clergymen and Islamic experts ... should be rich in content from the point of view of ... encouraging the people to take part in political and social activities ... [and] should explain all aspects of the policy of 'neither East nor West' to the people.[8]

The importance of Islam as an *influence* on policy, therefore, needs to be considered carefully by the analyst. As an influence,[9] it can act as a capability when it functions as an integrative force, creating consensus on foreign policy objectives; when it provides *l'esprit de corps* or the *'Asabiya* of Ibn Khaldun to a population, and when it helps in mobilizing external resources in support of the state. In the case of the Wahhabi movement and revolutionary Iran, Islam bestowed on its followers a sense of mission. In other cases, Islam can be a constraint on policy: whatever the real interests of Saudi Arabia are, because of the special position of Islam in the country, the Saudi rulers cannot but adopt an inflexible position on the Islamic status of Jerusalem.

However, is there really something specifically definable called Islam, or indeed, when we refer to the Muslim world, are we pointing to a phenomenon that is understood by all to be a monolith both in terms of structure and behaviour? These are methodological questions that have vexed many analysts of Islam and the Islamic world. In the conclusion to a recent perceptive book on Islam, the author concedes this methodological difficulty; he asserts:

I can only define Islam as 'the religion of the Muslims', and a Muslim, for me, is simply one who calls himself that. For me, in my condition of *jahiliya*, there is no Islam, in the sense of an abstract, unchangeable entity, existing independently of the men and women who profess it. There is only what I hear Muslims say, and see them do.[10]

And if that were the method by which Islam is defined, then one is struck by the variety of Islamic thought and practice, and by the bewildering number of political interpretations of Islam. Indeed, the historical, social and economic differences existing between the various Muslim countries have given Islam 'a different colouring', a different resonance in each of them; so that even groups with ostensibly similar programmes find themselves playing a different political role.[11] In this volume, therefore, no author has attempted the almost impossible task of defining Islam. It is simply taken for granted that, notwithstanding the variety of interpretations, there still exists an ideological force called Islam that has a symbolic value, ranging from nebulous to significant, among people who call themselves Muslims.

If this is true, then one should expect that in the actual *making* of foreign policy, decision-makers of countries, a substantial part of whose population is Muslim, must take Islam into consideration when formulating their policies. At this level of analysis, therefore, one can legitimately assume that Islam must constitute a part (how significant a part is another matter) of the images and perceptions, even attitudes and value-systems, of decision-makers. However, this does not explain how relevant Islam is to particular policies, for 'to identify factors is not to trace their influence. To uncover processes that affect external behaviour is not to explain how and why they are operative under certain circumstances and not under others.'[12] In other words, to say that Islam is an important force in Saudi Arabia does not necessarily mean that it was relevant, say, to the Saudi decision to give Iraq massive economic aid in the latter's war with Iran.

One reason for this methodological ambiguity is the difficulty involved in determining whether Islam acts as a motivator, legitimator or simply a justifier for a particular foreign policy. In his chapter on Islam in Iran's foreign policy, for example, R. K. Ramazani concludes that Ayatollah Khumayni's interpretation of Islam motivates Iran's foreign policy decisions, commitments and strategies. Ramazani adds that Islam is also used to communicate, rationalize and justify foreign policy behaviour. And indeed this statement could be true in the case of most of the Muslim states examined in this book, and most particularly in the case of Saudi Arabia, Libya and Pakistan. Beyond this general statement, however, lies a conceptual and empirical difficulty: how can the analyst, examining a specific policy option, distinguish between Islam's various functions? The question with which the analyst is repeatedly faced is the following: was a particular policy pronouncement or decision motivated by Islam, or was it motivated by some other value or consideration (for example, personal interest), whereby Islam would be used simply to bestow credibility and legitimacy on the policy? In other words, the methodological problem is twofold; namely how to separate the perceived influence of Islam from other motivating values; and how to distinguish between, on the one hand Islam as a motivator of policy, and on the other hand its other functional roles. Unfortunately, the disciplines of political science, international relations and foreign policy analysis are not, and are not likely to be, sufficiently 'scientifically' precise for the analyst to be able to surmount these analytical difficulties.[13] It is therefore largely left to the analyst to use his own judgement, derived from his own expertise and knowledge, to arrive at specific conclusions that he sees fit with regards to these difficulties.

The effort to isolate Islam from other values and to determine its precise (or at least probable) functional role is usually undertaken by reference to the articulated images of the decision-makers. But this immediately raises a further problem, for, as I. William Zartman contends in his chapter on Islam in Moroccan foreign policy, with a little interpretation nearly anything can be justified through reference to Islam, and as such its power to explain and unravel ambiguities can be questioned. Therefore, the best that can be done, according to Zartman, is simply to locate Islam in the language and symbolism used by decision-makers. But even here the analyst needs to take these political leaders at their word – a particularly risky endeavour.

This is not to suggest (as some analysts have in the past) that there is no reason to believe that Islam had ever motivated Muslim regimes, but that it had been cynically used by these regimes to legitimize their rule and to mobilize support for their policies. Such statements suffer from logical inconsistency, since they presuppose a priori the prevalence of Islam as a consequential value of society. If this were not the case, then evidently Islam would not be able to engender the public support and legitimization desired by the political leaders. Since these leaders have to have, and consciously covet, public support, and as they themselves are members of that society, and are likely to have been inculcated by the same values, it stands to reason that Islam, as an important societal value, would in one way or another motivate the policies of Muslim regimes.

The authors of the various chapters, thus consciously endeavour to look at the declaratory as well as the operational aspects of foreign policy. They try to draw inferences from both in order to arrive at a plausible explanation of the potency of Islam in the various countries' foreign policies. Within this context, foreign policy is treated as a process and a continuum, which, as has been stated earlier, includes the formulation as well as the implementation of foreign policy. Each author therefore was asked to delve into the domestic roots of foreign policy; to describe and explain the environment, social, political and organizational, in which policy is made; to look at the policy-making structure and determine not only the key political actors, but their attitudes, images and perceptions; and finally to see how all this results in the final stage of the foreign policy process – the implementation of policy. Beyond these general guidelines, the authors were not asked to adhere to a rigid framework or 'model' when writing their various contributions. It was decided at the outset that it would be more productive to allow the various authors a free hand in approaching the subject matter in question, than to artificially impose on them an intellectually restrictive framework simply for the purpose of uniformity. What follows, therefore, is a number of original essays, written by specialists who were allowed to research and write their various contributions in their own individual way. However, the general guidelines communicated to them before they began writing their chapters, and the discussions of the various papers during the conference, ensured a general consistency with regards to the analytical and empirical questions that they asked and attempted to answer. Naturally, the relevance of the questions, and the style in which they were posed and answered, differed from one chapter to another; but that is only as it should be. The style and emphasis of the various contributions are, consequently, eclectic. The consistency that runs throughout the book lies in the authors' attempt to answer, in one way or another, similar sets of questions about the role and influence of Islam in the foreign policy process of countries in which all, or a considerable part of, the population is Muslim.

Notes

1. James P. Piscatori (ed.), *Islam in the Political Process* (Cambridge, Cambridge University Press, 1983).
2. David Easton, *A Framework for Political Analysis* (Englewood Cliffs, Prentice-Hall, 1965), p. 50.
3. P. A. Reynolds, *An Introduction to International Relations* (London, Longman, 1971), pp. 9–10.
4. The classic work on this is Hedley Bull, *The Anarchical Society: A Study of Order in World Politics* (London, Macmillan, 1977).
5. K. J. Holsti, *International Politics: A Framework For Analysis* (Englewood Cliffs, Prentice-Hall, 1972), p. 21.
6. *Ibid.*
7. Different terminology is used by different authors to describe the three areas of analysis. See James N. Rosenau, 'Comparative Foreign Policy: Fad, Fantasy or Field?', in James N. Rosenau, *The Scientific Study of Foreign Policy* (New York, The Free Press, 1971), pp. 67–94; James N. Rosenau, 'The Study of Foreign Policy', in James N. Rosenau *et al.* (eds.), *World Politics: An Introduction* (New York, The Free Press, 1976), pp. 15–35; Howard H. Lentner, *Foreign Policy Analysis: A Comparative and Conceptual Approach* (Columbus, Ohio, Merrill Publishing, 1974); Joseph Frankel, *The Making of Foreign Policy: An Analysis of Decision-Making* (London, Oxford University Press, 1963); and M. Brecher *et al.*, 'A Framework for Research on Foreign Policy Behaviour', *Journal of Conflict Resolution*, 13 (1969), pp. 75–101.
8. British Broadcasting Corporation, *Summary of World Broadcasts, Part 4: The Middle East, Africa and Latin America* (hereafter cited as *SWB*), ME/7222/A/3, 4 January 1983.
9. The following paragraph draws heavily on the comments made by Dr Ali E. Hillal Dessouki during the Conference on Islam in Foreign Policy at the Royal Institute of International Affairs, 13–15 July 1982.

10. Edward Mortimer, *Faith and Power: The Politics of Islam* (London, Faber and Faber, 1982), p. 396.
11. *Ibid.*, p. 404.
12. James N. Rosenau, 'Pre-Theories and Theories of Foreign Policy', in R. Barry Farrell (ed.), *Approaches to Comparative and International Politics* (Evanston, Northwestern University Press, 1966), p. 31.
13. It is a measure of the lack of progress in the efforts to instil scientific rigour into the study of politics and international relations that a celebrated debate on the subject between Morton Kaplan and Hedley Bull, which was conducted in 1966, is still relevant today. See Hedley Bull, 'International Theory: The Case for a Classical Approach', *World Politics*, 18 (April 1966), 363–77; and Morton Kaplan, 'The New Great Debate: Traditionalism versus Science in International Relations', *World Politics*, 19 (October 1966), 1–20.

2 Khumayni's Islam in Iran's Foreign Policy

R. K. RAMAZANI

The 'Islamic Republic of Iran' celebrated its third anniversay on 1 April 1982. The Iranian revolution has gone through three major stages of development in three years, and is still evolving. It has been marked by international crises and war with other states as well as by domestic political chaos, economic paralysis, acts of terrorism, armed insurrection, ethnic insurgency, summary executions, and generally a basic lack of internal cohesion. It has also been marked by a sensational record of governmental changes; revolutionary Iran has had three presidents, four prime ministers, and seven foreign ministers in the span of only three years.

The primary purpose of this paper is to inquire into the influence of Ayatollah Khumayni's Islam on the foreign policy of revolutionary Iran. This study is not intended to be an analysis, or a survey, of Iran's foreign relations since the seizure of power by revolutionary forces. Nor is it intended to be a complete discussion of Khumayni's theory of international politics. Nevertheless, it is intended to provide a preliminary understanding of both. Toward that end, the chapter will begin with a brief inquiry into the interaction between revolutionary politics and foreign policy in Iran since the fall of the Shah's regime in 1979.

Domestic politics and foreign policy

The interaction between domestic politics and foreign policy has been intense throughout the three stages of Iran's revolutionary development. The eruption of the revolution itself significantly reflected the effects of that interaction. It was a 'twin revolution'.[1] The Shah's foreign policy, particularly his American policy, contributed over the decades to the revolutionary process, as did his misguided domestic politics. Revolutionary forces destroyed his regime as much out of a conviction that he was an 'American king' as that he was a tyrant monarch.[2]

The first stage of Iran's revolutionary politics began with the seizure of power by the opponents of the Shah's regime (11 February 1979) and ended with the fall of the provisional Bazargan government (6 November 1979). It was marked by an incessant struggle for power between his largely secular and technocratic government with what Bazargan called a 'gradualist' policy, and the militant Shi'i clerics and their lay supporters within and outside the Revolutionary Council. At the beginning it appeared that the important understanding of 5 November 1978 reached in Paris between Ayatollah Khumayni, Bazargan and Sanjabi would provide a basis for the new political order. They had agreed that the revolution embodied both the 'national and Islamic movements'.[3] Bazargan was appointed prime minister and Sanjabi foreign minister but, as Bazargan boldly protested, Iran had a 'thousand chiefs'. Khumayni sacked Sanjabi from two of his ambassadorial appointments, and Yazdi was appointed foreign minister in his place.

Domestic political divisions were reflected in the diverse approaches of Bazargan and Khumayni to foreign policy. Bazargan was intent on establishing a semblance of 'equal' relationship with the United States, which Khumayni denounced as the 'Great Satan'. Khumayni did not see why Iran should have any relationship with the United States. He charged that Iran's relationship with the United States was that of a 'tyrant' (*zalem*) with an 'oppressed' (*mazlum*) people, that of a 'plunderer' (*gharat-gar*) with a 'ravaged victim' (*gharat-shodeh*), and declared, 'We don't need America; it is they who need us. They want our oil.'[4] Bazargan's Foreign Minister Yazdi as well as the prime minister himself were suspected by leftist extremists of pro-American sentiments. Yazdi was pressured by right-wing as well as leftist extremists to reverse his decision on receiving Walter Cutler as the new American ambassador in place of William H. Sullivan. The meeting between Bazargan and Yazdi with the American national Security Adviser Brzezinski played into the hands of militant Muslim students led by Hojatulislam Kho'eniha, who later became the head of the Foreign Affairs Committee of the Majlis (Parliament). They seized the American Embassy on 4 November 1979, forcing the fall of the Bazargan government, which was accused by the student militants of trying, together with other liberals, to invite the Americans and the Israelis into Iran through the back door. The fall of the Bazargan government put an end to any attempt at normalization of Iran's relations with the United States on an equal footing.

The second stage of Iran's revolutionary politics, having thus begun with the fall of the Bazargan government and the onset of the hostage crisis, lasted until the dismissal in June 1981 of Bani-Sadr, who had been elected in January 1980 as the first president of the republic. Revolutionary politics during most of this period were marked primarily by a power struggle between Bani-Sadr and Ayatollah Beheshti, the leader of the Islamic Republican Party (IRP) and the head of the Supreme Court. With the fall of the Bazargan government, the Revolutionary Council moved to a central power position. Although Bani-Sadr chaired the Council, he was unable to influence its decision significantly; the Council was dominated by hardline Khumayni supporters. Furthermore, Bani-Sadr, the romantic, and as Iranians dubbed him 'talkative' (*Bani-Harf*), leader was not much helped by either his landslide electoral victory, nor by the earlier support of Khumayni. Above all, his failure to establish a political party made him a poor rival of the shrewd and cunning Beheshti, whose IRP focussed the power of the Muslim militants against Bani-Sadr, and whose friends Rafsanjani and Raja'i formed an informal but powerful triumvirate with him against Bani-Sadr. Fundamentalist clerics and their lay supporters, who had presumably helped establish a 'purely' Islamic republic, which was not contaminated by the 'democratic' designation that many had unsuccessfully demanded, and which had shaped a constitution that accorded the *faqih* ('jurisprudent') the leadership of the republic during the first phase of the revolution, now established their control through the IRP over the newly-elected Majlis.

Bani-Sadr's power struggle with the Beheshti–Rafsanjani–Raja'i triumvirate increasingly estranged him from the Muslim fundamentalists. Even his attempted exploitation of Iran's setbacks in the war with Iraq, which he blamed on his opponents, failed to make up for his ineffective leadership. Bani-Sadr's power rivalry with Muslim fundamentalists and their political arm, IRP, focussed at this particular time on an open clash with Prime Minister Raja'i, whose appointment had been practically forced on Bani-Sadr. The president and the prime minister attacked each other over a wide variety of issues, including the conduct of the Iran–Iraq war, the hostage crisis, and the appointment of several cabinet members, especially the foreign minister.

The disturbances at the University of Tehran on 5 March 1981 marked the beginning of the end for Bani-Sadr. The scuffles, assaults, beatings and knifings between the supporters of Bani-Sadr and Raja'i[5] played into the hands of the Muslim militants. They castigated Bani-Sadr, and tried to pressure Khumayni to strip him of his position as the commander-in-chief of the armed forces. Although Khumayni confirmed Bani-Sadr in this position, he appointed a three-man committee to pass judgement on Bani-Sadr's conduct. Meanwhile, his opponents joined in a chorus of denunciation of the beleaguered president. Raja'i's Minister of State for Executive Affairs, Behzad Nabavi, for example, accused Bani-Sadr of being involved in a movement to weaken and overthrow the Raja'i government; Ayatollah Sadeq Khalkhali urged the Majlis to try and dismiss him on the ground that he had 'committed treason against constitutional law'; and 130 judges and prosecutors from all over the country sent a letter to Khumayni asking him to deliver a judgement on Bani-Sadr's behaviour, which they claimed had created national disunity. The handwriting was on the wall. The story of Bazargan was repeated. Muslim militants once again managed to out-manoeuvre their relatively 'moderate' opponents. On 10 June Bani-Sadr was stripped of his post as commander-in-chief of the Iranian armed forces. While in hiding, he was also dismissed as president on 22 June 1981.

The domestic power struggle and its resolution in favour of right-wing Muslim militants in the second stage, as in the first stage, were also reflected in the overall direction of the republic's foreign policy. The taking of American hostages, which had brought down the Bazargan government and terminated its attempted policy of normalization of relations with the United States, was now used by the right-wing Muslim militants to consolidate their power, and foil any attempt by the United States to forge a new relationship with Iran. The hostage crisis, to use Behzad Nabavi's characterization, had been squeezed dry like an orange, and had to be finally discarded once it was no longer useful. Muslim militants held the hostages, while Bani-Sadr unsuccessfully pressed for their release, and once the Muslim militants decided to release them Bani-Sadr opposed the terms of the hostage settlement. The decision to release the hostages was actually reached before the outbreak of war between Iran and Iraq, as evidenced by the Iranian initiative to approach American officials secretly in Germany before the four-point proposal of Khumayni was declared in his message to the pilgrims to Mecca on 12 September 1980. The Iranians told the Americans in advance to anticipate the Khumayni proposal as a means of indicating to the sceptical American officials that the Iranians meant business this time.[6] The Iran–Iraq war, and the prospects of a hardline position by the United States in the event of the success of Ronald Reagan's candidacy, no doubt added impetus to the settlement of the crisis, but they did not cause the Khumayni decision to release the American hostages. That decision was influenced primarily by the felt impact of the Western economic sanctions, and the success of the Muslim militants in capturing the seats of power by September 1980.

The prolonged hostage crisis did more than destroy the prospects of normalization of Iran's relations with the United States; it isolated Iran in the international system in general, and estranged it from the West in particular. The unanimous Provisional Order (29 November 1979), and the Judgement (15 May 1980) of the International Court of Justice; the Security Council's Resolution 457 (4 December 1979), and Resolution 461 (31 December 1979); and the resolutions of the Organization of the Islamic Conference in January and May 1980, for example, all disapproved the taking of the American hostages, and called for their release. The estrangement of Iran from the United States was intensified as a result of American economic and diplomatic sanctions against Iran. President Carter's imposition of a ban on US imports of Iranian oil on 12 November 1979 and of a freeze on $8 billion of Iranian assets were subsequently followed by such other measures as the American break in diplomatic relations with Iran; the ban on all American exports to Iran, except food and medicine, and on all American imports from Iran.

The West European decision to impose phased economic and diplomatic sanctions against Iran on 22 April 1980, to be sure, was half-hearted. The European countries and Britain had larger stakes in Iran as compared to the United States, but the fact still remains that their symbolic actions antagonized Iran. Even the failed American rescue mission on 24 April 1980, which was denounced by most states, failed to engender any real or durable sympathy for Iran. For example, after the Iraqi invasion of Iran on 22 September 1980 there was a clear reluctance on the part of many states, both within and outside the United Nations, to contemplate any serious action against Iraq.

Besides the fall of President Bani-Sadr, the bombings which killed first Beheshti and 70 other IRP leaders in June 1981, and then President Raja'i and Prime Minister Bahonar in August 1981, marked the start of the third phase of the Iranian revolution. The so-called alliance between Bani-Sadr and Rajavi, the leader of the Mujaheddin in exile in France, has been paralleled by continuous acts of terrorism against the Khumayni regime. The regime's counter-measures have included mass arrests, imprisonment, torture and executions of many thousands of members of the Mujaheddin organization, their sympathizers, and others suspected of 'counter-revolutionary' activities. There is little doubt that in this violent political process innocent people have also been the victims of terrorist and counter-terrorist acts. Furthermore, this latest and most violent phase of the Iranian revolution has far-reaching implications for domestic policies and foreign policy.

On the domestic level, two implications in particular deserve brief mention. First, the acts of assassination by the opponents of the regime have taken a heavy toll among the more 'moderate' IRP leaders. The new leadership, as a result, is perceived to be more anti-Western. Since October 1981 Hojatolislam Sayed Ali Khamenei – formerly the *imam* of the Friday prayers in Tehran and the victim of an attempted assassination – has been Iran's president. He is reputedly a Turkish-speaking hardline cleric who is reportedly supported by other hardline anti-Western elements both within and outside the IRP. Second, despite the decimation of IRP leaders, the supporters of Khumayni have continued to consolidate their power. As a matter of fact, a year after the bombing of IRP headquarters, and despite other acts of terrorism against its leaders ever since, the Khumayni regime appears to have tightened its control on the reigns of power. Events have so far disproved the forecasts by its opponents of the regime's imminent demise.

On the international level, the ability of the Khumayni regime to implement Iran's foreign policy appears to have increased. The regime seems determined to break away from its isolation in international politics that followed the taking of American hostages. It has stepped up its ties with a wide variety of countries, largely by using its oil in barter deals with such Third World countries as Syria, Turkey, Pakistan, North Korea, India, and others. It has expanded its transit, trade and economic ties with the Soviet Union, despite continued political, ideological and other differences. Above all, the consolidation of power domestically increased the capacity of the regime to successfully defend Iran against Iraq until Tehran blundered into the invasion of Iraq on 13 July 1982. The first real break in the stalemated war in favour of Iran occurred in September 1981, only a few months after the fall of Bani-Sadr. Subsequently, successful Iranian offensives led to the expulsion of the bulk of the Iraqi troops and the recovery of Khuramshahr. Iran's conduct of the war was greatly aided by Khumayni's effective use of Islamic symbols as long as Iran appeared to wage a defensive war against the Iraqi invaders on its own territory, but once Iran repeated the blunder of Iraq by deciding to invade, Khumayni's use of Islamic symbols failed to make up for logistical and other pragmatic problems facing the revolutionary regime.

Proliferation of ideological conflicts

Interaction between Iranian domestic politics and foreign policy during all the three stages of the Iranian revolution outlined above has invariably contained ideological factors. The struggle for power between Bazargan and the Muslim fundamentalists in the first stage, between them and Bani-Sadr in the second stage, and between them and the Mujaheddin in the third stage have all included ideological conflicts of various kinds and degrees of intensity: Khumayni's fundamentalist Islam clashed first with Bazargan's libertarian Islam in the first stage, then with Bani-Sadr's socialist Islam in the second stage, and finally with Rajavi's Marxist Islam in the third stage.

This portrayal, however, reveals only the clash of ideologies between predominant political actors and their supporters. In every stage of the Iranian revolution other ideological conflicts have also prevailed. Khumayni's interpretation of Islam, for example, has been challenged by the secular liberal democratic ideology of the National Front, by the social democratic ideology of the National Democratic Front, by the Marxist–Leninist ideology of the Fedayeen-e Khalq, by the communist ideology of the Tudeh Party and by the ideologies of a myriad other disparate groups and individuals who banded together under the leadership of Khumayni in their common opposition to the Shah's regime, but who have split up since its fall.

Ideological conflicts exist even among the present supporters of Khumayni both within and outside the IRP. The most prominent example is the division between the *Maktabi* and *Hojati* clerics. Both schools of thought believe in the establishment of a political order shaped by Islam, but the *Maktabi* school of thought believes in the choice of a single man to succeed Khumayni in the role of *Velayat-e Faqih*, while the *Hojati* school of thought envisages a collegiate group – not just one man – to exercise religious leadership, and leave government in secular, not exclusively religious, hands.[7]

Diversity in ideological perspectives, both religious and secular, is reflected in ideas not only regarding the shape of the polity, but also of foreign policy. For example, with respect to the hostage crisis, Khumayni declared: 'This is not a struggle between the United States and Iran; it is a struggle between Islam and blasphemy,' while Bani-Sadr viewed it as a struggle for Iran's political independence. He considered the taking of hostages as contrary to the law of nations, and wished to settle the matter through the United Nations, which Khumayni decried as an instrument of American foreign policy. To cite another example, the current ideological perspectives of the *Maktabi* and *Hojati* schools of thought have different foreign policy implications. The *Maktabis* believe in the export of the 'Islamic Revolution', as a prime goal, while the *Hojatis* do not. The *Maktabi* school of thought is, of course, closer to Khumayni's Islam. Raja'i made the *Maktabi* orientation the supreme test of qualification for holding posts in government; merit was only a secondary test.

Granted all these and other ideological differences, we should now turn to Khumayni's Islam and Iran's revolutionary foreign policy. Despite the challenge of all other ideologies, his interpretation of Islam has so far prevailed. This chapter, therefore, will examine first his world view, and then consider its practical effects on the conduct of Iran's foreign policy. In attempting the latter, analytical difficulties involved will be pointed out, and three major issues in particular will be closely examined.

Khumayni's world view

Compared to his political thought, Khumayni's world outlook has been remarkably consistent over the decades. There are some observers who seem to have read their own predispositions into Khumayni's view of the desirable political order. One observer, for example, seems to read Khumayni's rejection of the monarchy in the late 1960s and early 1970s into his early criticism of Reza Shah's rule.[8] But my own comparison of Khumayni's political thought during World War II with his view of 'Islamic government' (*Hokomat-e Islami*) in the early 1970s reveals that earlier he seemed to accept the idea of limited monarchy, but he rejected it altogether after his long exile in Iraq. He did not at first reject the constitution of 1906–7, which included the institution of monarchy. Rather in his *Kashf-e Assrar* ('Discovery of Secrets'), published in 1944, he demanded the implementation of the constitutional provision for clerical supervision of all laws enacted by the Majlis.[9]

In any event, compared to his political thought, Khumayni's ideas about the international system have undergone little change. They deserve closer attention than they have received so far. Given the limited scope of the chapter, however, only four major aspects of Khumayni's world outlook will be analysed. In doing so, the related outlooks of other leaders of the republic will also be examined as a means of showing how Khumayni's precepts and guidance are interpreted by those who use them in practice.

First, Khumayni has consistently rejected the contemporary international system. Seen against the background of his world outlook, he would find the Westphalia conception of the nation–state and the international system to be flawed. The earliest indication of this strong view is found in his *Kashf-e Assrar*, in which he stated categorically as early as 1944 that modern states 'are the products of man's limited ideas', and the world is 'the home of all the masses of people under the law of God'.[10] Populism, millenarianism, Shi'ism, and revolutionism converge in Khumayni's world outlook. For example, in a statement to Iranian students abroad, he declared:

Iran's Islamic Revolution, with the support of the gracious Almighty, is spreading on a worldwide scale and, God willing, with its spread the satanical powers will be dragged into isolation and governments of the meek will be established; the way will be opened for the world government of the imam mahdi (12th imam), may the exalted God hasten his noble advent and may our lives be sacrificed to the dust of his path.[11]

As applied to revolutionary Iranian foreign policy, the 'satanical powers' are the enemies of Islamic Iran, and the 'governments of the meek' are its true friends. For example, in a meeting with the Lebanese Shi'i Amal delegation, he said:

Even if America and Israel were to shout: 'There is no god but God', we would not accept it from them, because they wish to deceive us ... Do you expect us to be indifferent to America and Israel and the other superpowers that wish to swallow the region? We will not agree to be dominated by America or by the Soviet Union. We are Muslims and wish to live. We want that kind of progress and civilization which would make us reach our hands out to aliens. We want that civilization which is based upon honour and humanity and which would preserve peace upon this basis. The superpowers wish to dominate human beings. We, you and any other Muslim, are dutybound to remain steadfast against them, not to compromise with them and to reject plans such as those of As-Sadat and Fahd. It is our duty to condemn these plans which are not in the interest of the oppressed people.[12]

Second, Khumayni's world outlook calls for Islamic universalism. The passages quoted above include this notion but, it should be emphasized, Khumayni neither advocates pan-Shi'ism, nor pan-Islamism; he calls for the establishment of Islam throughout the world. In the words of Mir-Husayn Mussavi, Iran's former foreign minister and present prime minister, the ultimate goal of Iran's foreign policy is the 'liberation of mankind'. The context of his statement is important. As Iran's foreign minister, he told the CBS television network:

The fact is that values have been greatly transformed in Iran and new values have been presented to our society. Correct understanding of the values will show that our nation regards recent events in Iran as salutary, not that our nation is fond of killing. Rather they regard this as a prerequisite to the liberation of mankind in the region and those struggles will continue until the region and the world are rebuilt upon new foundations ... All over the world, today, Islam is reviving. What is being formed in the Islamic world now is the return to an Islamic human identity and the Islamic Revolution of Iran is a prerequisite for the transformation of the Islamic countries and the world.[13]

Khumayni's Islamic universalism is sometimes portrayed by his supporters as what is in fact expected of Iran by other Muslim people. For example, one revolutionary reporter claims that during the *hajj* rituals, when he met with 'people of all nationalities and politico-religious personalities from different countries', he learned that 'now people expect everything from Iran alone'. He then adds that 'what is to be said is that the Moslem nation of Iran has risen for the obliteration of tyranny throughout the world and will not seize [*sic*] its struggle until a global Islamic government is established'.[14]

Third, it is more than implicit in Khumayni's own world outlook as well as those of his supporters that Iran is considered uniquely qualified to exert worldwide leadership for the realization of the ultimate goal of the establishment of an Islamic world order. In his own words, 'Islam is a sacred trust from God to ourselves and the Iranian nation must grow in power and resolution until it has vouchsafed Islam to the entire world'. Khumayni's disciples consider the Iranian leadership as a 'divine obligation'; they also point to the uniqueness of the present form of government in Iran as the special leadership qualification that Iran alone enjoys as compared to all the nations of the world. Only in Iran is the *faqih* the head of the state, and presumably this feature of the Islamic Republic of Iran entitles the followers of Khumayni to expect that other Muslim-populated states should emulate the same form of Islamic government. For example, one Khumayni disciple states:

Today if we want the establishment of Mohammad's Islam, we should entrust the political leadership of our societies and countries to one who is also a religious leader. And this magnificent fact has only come to reality in the Islamic country of Iran and Imam Khumayni as a person who studies Islam for 70 years as the religious Marj'a and the religious leader of the Moslems, had accepted the responsibility for the political leadership, formation of the Islamic Government as well as the Commander in Chief of the Armed Forces.[15]

Fourth, given the universalist, populist, and millenarian features of Khumayni's world outlook, the important leadership role of Iran for the export of the 'Islamic Revolution' to the rest of the world becomes self-evident. In a major speech to the Iranian people on the occasion of the Iranian New Year in 1980, he declared unequivocally:

We should try hard to export our revolution to the world. We should set aside the thought that we do not export our revolution, because Islam does not regard various Islamic countries differently and is the supporter of all the oppressed peoples of the world. On the other hand, all the superpowers and all the powers have risen to destroy us. If we remain in an enclosed environment we shall definitely face defeat.[16]

An important practical question about such an advocacy is how the 'Islamic Revolution' is supposed to be exported. This question has been of great concern to the leaders of most states of the Middle East, especially the Gulf states, as we shall see. At this point, however, it is necessary to consider what policy guidelines, if any, are provided by the Iranian leaders themselves for the export of the 'Islamic Revolution'. The best way to start is with Khumayni himself. For example, he told a group of young Iranians going abroad:

Today we need to strengthen and export Islam everywhere. You need to export Islam to other places, and the same version of Islam which is currently in power in our country. Our way of exporting Islam is through the youth, who go to other countries where a large number of people come to see you and your achievements. You must behave in such a way that these large gatherings are attracted to Islam by your action. Your deeds, your action, and your behaviour should be an example; and through you the Islamic Republic will go to other places, God Willing.[17]

Iranian leaders have taken pains to stress to Iranian foreign service personnel on numerous occasions that the export of the 'Islamic Revolution' must be accomplished by example and propaganda. For example, Khumayni told a group of ambassadors and chargés d'affaires who had been recalled to Tehran for consultation:

It does not take swords to export this ideology. The export of ideas by force is no export. We shall have exported Islam only when we have helped Islam and Islamic ethics grow in those countries. This is your responsibility and it is a task which you must fulfill. You should promote this idea by adopting a conduct conducive to the propagation of Islam and by publishing the necessary publications in your countries of assignment. This is a must. You must have publications. You must publish journals. Such journals should be promotive and their contents and pictures should be consistent with the Islamic Republic, so that by proper publicity campaigns you may pave the way for the spread of Islam in those areas.[18]

The theme that the export of the Islamic Revolution must be effected by the example of Islamic behaviour of Iranians abroad in general and of Iranian diplomats in particular has been taken up by other Iranian leaders as well. For example, Hojatolislam Ali Khamenei, the president of the republic, stated that the Iranian

Foreign Ministry's officials abroad are the apostles of the revolution. The nature of an official despatched abroad by a government demonstrates the nature of his government. If our diplomatic representative in all his dealings, including with people and government officials of the country to which he is despatched, adopts an Islamic approach, then he will be utilizing the best method to demonstrate the role of the Islamic Republic of Iran.[19]

Theoretically, subversion as well as armed aggression for exporting the 'Islamic Revolution' seem to be ruled out by Iranian leaders. For example, former Foreign Minister Mir-Husayn Mussavi asserts,

We have declared time and again that we have no intention of interfering in other countries' internal affairs, but what is shaking the Islamic world is a movement springing from this revolution among the Moslem masses of the world and, naturally, each people will shape their movement according to their own peculiar circumstances. They will force their governments to tread this path and, if not, naturally they will be confronted by the peoples' moves.[20]

Khumayni's Islamic world order and Iranian foreign policy

The effects of ideological influences in the foreign policy of any state present formidable intellectual and methodological challenges, let alone in the foreign policy of a country like Iran which is caught in the pangs of a revolution. For example, Soviet specialists debate inconclusively the relative weight of communism and the legacy of Russian imperialism in the foreign policy of the Soviet Union. The debate on the relative importance of democratic ideals and pragmatic considerations has never ceased among specialists on American foreign policy either. Former President Carter's human rights crusade, for example, is still faulted by some observers for the failure of American policy, including the Carter administration's policy toward Iran before, during, and after the seizure of power by revolutionary forces.

Examination of the role of Khumayni's Islamic world order in Iran's foreign policy presents its own particular problems. Two of these must be faced at the outset. First, it is not always possible to say what pronouncements, decisions, and courses of action in foreign affairs, unambiguously represent official policy of the revolutionary regime. For example, in 1979 a cleric's renewal of the Iranian claim of sovereignty to Bahrain aroused a deep and widespread sense of outrage not only in Bahrain, but also in all other Arab states of the Gulf region. In response, however, Foreign Minister Yazdi and other Iranian officials joined in a chorus of denials. They denied that Ayatollah Ruhani's threats, to the effect that Iran would annex Bahrain unless its rulers adopted an Islamic political order, represented the official position of Iran.

Second, the same revolutionary disarray that underpins the official–unofficial division just mentioned, creates another problem that also complicates analysis, namely, the problem of the administration of Iranian foreign policy. The Shah's Ministry of Foreign Affairs, like his military and other institutions, is undergoing drastic changes as a result of repeated purges, resignations, and exile. Furthermore, revolutionary leaders want to overhaul both the ministry and the Iranian diplomatic mission abroad in keeping with the emerging ideological tenets, direction and priorities of the Islamic Republic. According to former Foreign Minister Mir-Husayn Mussavi, for example, the Iranian foreign ministry 'is disorganized ... it seems the various units are not working in harmony'. It is thus crucial 'to create a united and coordinated organization inside the ministry, by making use of devoted people, specialists and others devoted and faithful to the revolution ...' This and other organizational changes envisaged will include the creation of a committee or a unit that 'will determine the basis of the foreign policy from an ideological perspective, and the principle of rule of theocracy ...'[21]

Despite such general statements about the changing nature of Iran's revolutionary foreign policy, it is still too early to speak with certainty about what it will mean in practice. For example, various Iranian foreign ministers, including the present Foreign Minister Ali Akbar Velayati, have said that in establishing relations with other states Iran accords the highest priority to Muslim states, followed by other Third World states, and then others. Meanwhile, the present Iranian President Ali Khamenei states: 'We have divided the world into groups – brotherly countries, friendly countries, neutral countries, and enemy countries. Enemies are governments which launch aggression against us and have an anti-Iranian posture. The rest are either brothers, friends or neutral.'[22] Are these revolutionary leaders talking about the same ideas regarding Iran's foreign policy priorities? It is difficult to say.

In the light of the ideological stance of Iranian leaders discussed above, and of their pronouncements, however, the main guiding principles for the conduct of Iranian foreign policy seem to include at the present time: (1) rejection of 'dependency' on either the West or the East; (2) identification of the United States as the 'principal enemy' (*doshman-e asli*) of the Islamic Revolution; (3) struggle against superpowers and the 'Zionist power'; (4) close relations with all oppressed peoples, especially those in Muslim countries; (5) liberation of Jerusalem, and opposition to pro-Israel states; (6) anti-imperialism; and (7) support everywhere for oppressed people (*Mustaz'afeen*). These 'principles' represent a total break with those that guided the foreign policy of the Shah's regime. For example, for the first three principles listed above one could easily substitute: (1) reliance on the West, especially the United States, as a means of maintaining the Shah's regime and the territorial integrity and political independence of Iran; (2) identification of the Soviet Union and communism as the main sources of threat; and (3) friendship with pro-Western and anti-Soviet states.[23]

Revolutionary leaders take pains to emphasize a total break with not only the principles and priorities of the Shah's foreign policy, but also with those of the former nationalist leader Dr Muhammad Musaddeq. Nowhere does this appear more clearly than in their insistence that their overriding principle, 'Neither West, nor East', is not only a question of 'negative balance'. In other words, they reject the central principle of Musaddeq's foreign policy, that is, 'negative equilibrium' (*muvazeneh-ye manfi*). For example, Mir-Husayn Mussavi says that the slogan 'Neither West, nor East' should also include the phrase 'Islamic Republic' denoting that the people of Iran will not, under 'any circumstances', allow Iran to slip 'toward the East or the West'. Furthermore, they 'want to establish a new system of values, independent of East and West in their own country; to expand it and under the all-round cover of this new system of values – which stems from ideology, Islam – to continue their own way; organize their lives; organize their relations with other countries, nations and liberation movements'.[24]

The central analytical difficulty in specifying the weight of Islamic influence in the formulation and execution of Iran's revolutionary foreign policy is not helped by examining Iran's actual practice any more than by analysing the policy statements of its leaders. The principal reasons for this are two. First, the unreliability and contradictory nature of the available data. Secondly, the fact that few, if any, decisions, commitments, or courses of action can be said to reflect, purely or predominantly, the influence of Khumayni's Islamic ideology. Even the Iranian policy-makers themselves admit that the overriding principle 'Neither West, nor East' only in part reflects the influence of their Islamic ideology; it also derives, they say, from Iran's own unhappy historical experience with the hegemonic policies of the superpowers. Because of this mixture of ideological with non-ideological considerations in Iran's foreign policy, observers may alternatively emphasize pragmatic or ideological influences in Iran's foreign policy behaviour.

A few examples will suffice. It may well be argued that the Iranian decision to settle the hostage crisis was made purely for political and economic, or other pragmatic, reasons. Ideologically it should have been unacceptable for Muslim leaders to compromise with the 'Great Satan'. Examples of the controlling effect of pragmatic considerations may be easily cited for other Iranian actions as well. In order to advertise its success, Iran did not hesitate to invite the ideologically distasteful 'imperialist media and purveyors of Satanic untruth' to visit Iran's warfront after the March offensive. Nor did Iran hesitate to charge that the Muslim Brothers who rebelled in Hama and paid with their lives were the agents of Iraq and Zionism. It was expedient to maintain friendship with Syria, the enemy of Iran's enemy, Iraq. Despite vehement denials, there is evidence of Iranian oil sales to the 'Great Satan', arranged through a Geneva-based trading company named Gatoil International.[25] Also, despite Iran's ferocious denials, Israeli arms have indirectly arrived in Iran. But any such judgements about the influence of pragmatic considerations on Iran's foreign policy must be balanced against a different interpretation that would emphasize ideological considerations.

Now, it may well be argued that the compromise with the 'Great Satan' over the hostage crisis was a lesser evil than the weakening of the 'Islamic Revolution' that would have resulted from dragging out a crisis that was no longer useful to the Islamic Republic. The indirect oil sale to the United States, and round-about military purchases from Israel, one may argue, were justified by the higher good of defending the interests of the *Dar al-Islam*.

Granted all these and other analytical difficulties, the influence of Islam with respect to several other issue areas deserves closer attention. Three of these issues will be discussed below.

The Gulf war

No matter what personal, historical, racial, political, legal and other factors are influential in the war between Iraq and Iran, the influence of Khumayni's Islam has been manifest in a variety of ways. First, the universalistic, millenarian, legitimistic, and populist 'Islamic Revolution' was perceived before the war in Baghdad as posing a major threat to the secular Ba'thist ideology and the regime of Saddam Husayn. The Iraqi revolution did not enjoy, the Iranians claimed, any popular support comparable to that of the Iranian revolution. Furthermore, the Ba'thist ideology did not possess the same legitimacy as did the Islamic ideology; the authentic indigenous Islam challenged the imported ideas of nationalism and socialism that underpinned the Ba'thist secular ideology, and as such it was inevitable that the Ba'thist regime would be provoked.

Saddam Husayn, for example, rejected in an interview with *Al-Mustaqbal* the charge that the Ba'thist ideology was a foreign product. He then claimed that the 'Arab revolution' has the task of effecting 'a qualitative change in the society in all fields'. It also has the task of placing the Arab nation in a position in which it can defend and reconstruct itself, and achieve justice. This is an Arab revolution whose formula is not the same as a religious one; it derives 'its central values from its history', and Husayn added that 'The Islamic Revolution and any other revolution should be friendly to the Arab Revolution; and any revolution calling itself Islamic should not contradict the Arab Revolution, otherwise it would not be Islamic at all.'[26]

Second, Khumayni's Islam has had more than an influence on the outbreak of the war. Ever since Iraq launched its 'all-out war' (*Harb al-Shameleh*) against Iran on 22 September 1980, the Islamic ideology has been a major instrument of military mobilization for the conduct of the war. The decimated and demoralized Iranian armed forces were called on to defend Islam against 'Shah Husayn', or Yazid. Islam has also been a ferocious motivating force for the Muslim masses which form the backbone of the regular and especially the irregular forces. Soldiers of Revolutionary Guards (*Pasdaran*) and the Mobilization Force (*Basij*) are known to be among the youngest and most devoted disciples of Khumayni. Some *Basij* recruits threw their bodies on minefields to clear the way for the forward march of Iranian forces against the Iraqi troops. After the first successful Iranian thrust in the Shush–Dezful area in March 1982, Khumayni told both these revolutionary, and the regular, forces:

Our Revolutionary Guards Corps and the Mobilization Force had just been formed from the people and had just been armed with rifles, not having had proper military education and not having proper warfare machinery at their disposal, and with all the signs of weakness apparent in them. Only their faith in God, love of martyrdom for Islam and a spirit of self-sacrifice assisted them in this unequal war ... If the army and other armed forces did not enjoy the spiritual divine assistance, how otherwise could this extraordinary affair (miraculous victory) be explained?[27]

Third, Iran's hardline negotiating stance during the war has been consistently rationalized in terms of Islam as expounded by Khumayni instead of the Charter of the United Nations. In insisting on the withdrawal of Iraqi troops from Iranian territory as the prerequisite for peace negotiations, Iranian leaders invoke Qur'anic precepts. For example, Khumayni admonishes the representatives of the Organization of the

Islamic Conference who are trying to obtain a ceasefire between the belligerent countries:

As for the other Islamic countries that also claim to adhere to it [Qur'an], whose peoples accept the Qur'an, they should gather here. They should send their representatives. We shall then open the Qur'an, the Al-Jujurat verse, and read only one paragraph of this verse. They ought to come and comply with this verse. This verse tells how two Muslim tribes engaged in war should be treated. It says that if one tribe invades the other then all others are obliged to defend the latter in war, until they obey God. Once they obey God, then make peace with them.[28]

Fourth, and paradoxically, Islamic ideology has been invoked both in rationalizing Iran's defence against, and its invasion of, Iraq. Since in Khumayni's ideology there is a universal Islamic society, in which international frontiers are presumably of secondary importance, once an 'aggression against Islam' is committed, its defence cannot be stopped at the boundaries of the territorial state. After Iran's first major and successful counter-offensive in March 1982 Khumayni seemed to promise that Iran would not carry the war into Iraq, but it did despite the fact that Khumayni had declared:

Today Iran is still bound by what it said at the outset: we have no intention of fighting against any country, Islamic or non-Islamic. We desire peace and amity among all; to date we have engaged only in self-defence which is a divine duty and human right enjoined upon all. We have never had an intention of committing aggression against other countries.[29]

Gulf security

Another major issue area where the influence of Islamic ideology has been at work is the security of the Persian Gulf region. Raymond Aron observes that a small power restricts its ambitions to physical survival and the preservation of its legal independence, while a great power acts to achieve an ill-defined purpose which he calls 'the maintenance or creation of a favourable international environment'. This author has added that a medium power acts to create and maintain a favourable regional environment while aspiring to global political stature, a proposition which has been demonstrated in the case of pre-revolutionary Iran.[30] Has the revolution destroyed its validity? Not really, except that Iran, like all revolutionary regimes, big and small, acts to make both regional and global environment hospitable to its ideology as well as favourable to its position of power. The Shah's regime acted to make the Persian Gulf region safe for his regime and the Pahlavi dynasty by alliance with the West, particularly the United States. The revolutionary regime acts to make the region safe for its Islamic ideology and its own survival by militantly espousing a policy of non-alignment.

This policy is rationalized in terms of Islamic self-reliance as expounded by Khumayni. His Islam is perceived as a threat not only by Iraq, but also by all other Gulf states. As seen in the case of Iraq, it is perceived as a challenge to the secular Ba'thist ideology and regime, but in the other Gulf states it is perceived as a menace to their security and stability partly because in Khumayni's Islam there is no room for monarchical systems. Furthermore, Iran's militant non-alignment policy runs counter to the close ties that exist between conservative Gulf states and the United States. Saudi Arabia is regarded as the arch-agent of the 'Great Satan' whose Gulf policy is condemned in every respect, including massive arms sales, military facilities in Oman, American operation of AWACS aircraft in Saudi Arabia, the Western naval presence near the Strait of Hormuz, the Rapid Deployment Force, and so on.

As seen, Khumayni advocates the export of the 'Islamic Revolution' as a means of promoting the idea of establishing the rule of God on earth everywhere. 'If we remain in an enclosed environment we shall definitely face defeat,' he says. And no environment is closer to his Islamic revolutionary abode than the Gulf region. As we have also seen, he instructs his followers that the way to export his revolution is not by the use of the 'sword', but by propaganda and other non-military means. Nevertheless, this has proved unsettling to all conservative Gulf states where Khumayni's 'peaceful' means are perceived as threatening their internal stability and external security.

The best example of Khumayni's interpretation of Islam being used for making the Gulf region favourable to his revolution is the dispute between him and King Khalid of Saudi Arabia over the behaviour of Iranian pilgrims to Mecca. The incident broke out amidst growing recriminations between Saudi Arabia and Iran. The facts of the case are difficult to ascertain. Suffice it to say that Iranian pilgrims engaged in political demonstrations against the United States and Israel while carrying portraits of Khumayni. The embittered relations between Riyadh and Tehran finally prompted King Khalid to write to Ayatollah Khumayni on 10 October 1981 to the effect that some of the Iranian pilgrims indulged 'in activities in your name which not only were contrary to your aims but were also contrary to the aims of pilgrimage and the honour of holy places'. These pilgrims, the king continued, shouted slogans and demonstrated in the holy precincts; actions which 'disturbed and disgusted other pilgrims to the holy house of God and no doubt this action will damage Iran's credibility and prestige'.[31]

In his long, stern reply of the same date, Khumayni took exception to the king's view. He argued dogmatically that the purpose of pilgrimage was not religious worship alone. He contended that pilgrimage under all prophets, especially the prophet of Islam, had been 'completely linked to politics', the separation of which was the idea of the superpowers. He charged that the king had received a 'distorted version and false reports' of the incident, and admonished the king that if his government made use of 'the religiopolitical' ceremony of *hajj*, 'it would have no need of America, AWACS planes ... We know that America has put these planes at the disposal of Saudi Arabia so that America can make use of them in its own interests and in the interests of Israel.'[32]

Saudi–Iranian tensions reached a new peak about a month after this exchange between the two Gulf leaders. Iran was accused of having armed and trained a large group of Shi'i Muslims to carry out a 'plot' in Bahrain. Most members of the group were primarily from Bahrain and few were from Saudi Arabia. No Iranian national was involved. The group, 74-strong, apparently belonged to the 'Islamic Front for the Liberation of Bahrain' with its headquarters in Tehran. Significantly, about 35 per cent of the group consisted of students, and about 17 per cent were unemployed persons.[33] One wonders how effective Khumayni's export of the 'Islamic Revolution' could ever be without such adverse indigenous human conditions within the Gulf states themselves.

The crisis precipitated feverish security arrangements among the Gulf Arab states on various bilateral levels. Furthermore, the emphasis of the members of the newly-established Gulf Cooperation Council (GCC) shifted from economic matters to security concerns. The tension between Riyadh and Tehran was intensified. The Saudis signed a security co-operation agreement with Bahrain during a visit there by the Saudi Interior Minister Prince Nayif. He asserted that the Iranians had said at the beginning of their revolution that they would not act as the Gulf's policeman; they have now become, he said, 'the Gulf's terrorists'.[34]

Afghanistan settlement

With respect to no other foreign policy issue discussed so far has the influence of Khumayni's Islam been so clearly visible as in the case of Afghanistan. The Soviet invasion has been consistently condemned by Iranian revolutionary leaders; the Marxist puppet regime is viewed with utter contempt; the Afghan *Mujaheddin* are hailed; and nearly a million Afghan refugees are sheltered in Iran. To be sure, as with respect to the other issues already discussed, the Iranian policy toward Afghanistan is shaped by geographic proximity, historical experience, cultural and religious affinity as well as Khumayni's ideological stance. But the Iranian position in the case of Afghanistan is the best example of how far the Iranian revolutionary regime is inclined to go on pushing to create a favourable Islamic environment around Iran. In effect, Iran wants to replace the Marxist regime in Kabul with an Islamic government that is significantly modelled after the Iranian one.

The best evidence for this is the Iranian proposal for the solution of the crisis in Afghanistan. On 10 November 1981, the Iranian Deputy Foreign Minister, Ahmad 'Azizi, unveiled an 'Islamic solution', admitting clearly that it was 'based on the revolutionary experience' of Iran. As a backdrop to announcing the Iranian plan, he denounced numerous plans issued by various international organizations and by governments. 'In the opinion of the Government of the Islamic Republic of Iran,' he asserted, 'most of these plans have been designed to allow European and US forces to intervene in the region.' Instead, Iran proposed a plan, guided by two principles. These were: (1) unconditional Soviet withdrawal from Afghanistan; and (2) recognition of the right of the Afghan people to decide 'their political fate'.[35]

The five-point plan, however, amounted in effect to a scheme for the establishment of an Islamic state and government. Although the plan envisaged nationwide elections of the members of a constituent assembly that would draw up a constitution and define the type of government Afghanistan wanted, an Islamic council composed of 30 Muslim clergy was given such vast legislative and executive powers during the transition period that, for all practical purposes, it would be able to determine the outcome of the elections. An assembly and a government would emerge which would definitely be dominated by the clerics, or at least by their close associates. The Iranian experience is indeed pertinent. The Iranian Revolutionary Council insured during Iran's transition period that the clerics and their associates would rule. Why could not the same be repeated in Afghanistan? The plan proposed a 'peace-keeping force', consisting of Iran, Pakistan and another Muslim country. This force would replace the Soviet troops during a transition period, until Afghanistan, like Iran, was transformed into a theocratic Muslim state.

General observations

To sum up, the fluidity, complexity and confusion of the state of the Iranian revolution make it impossible to end this study with any customary set of conclusions. There are none. But a number of tentative propositions may be derived from the foregoing discussions.

In the first place, the prolonged revolutionary instability and lack of domestic cohesion over the past three years have at every stage been reflected in Iran's foreign policy. As a result, no stable foreign policy has emerged, although since the settlement of the hostage crisis and the ousting of Bani-Sadr, the regime's domestic capacity for activity in the external environment seems to have increased relative to the two earlier stages of the revolution.

Secondly, domestic political instability partly reflects the proliferation of ideologies of both secular and religious varieties, but at present Ayatollah Khumayni's interpretation of Islam prevails on both the domestic and international levels. The challenge of other ideologies, both secular and religious, is silenced more by resort to coercion than efforts at accommodation.

Thirdly, Khumayni's world view rejects the very conception of the contemporary international system as it is constituted today. As such, contrary to the characterization of most observers, Khumayni's ideology is neither pan-Shi'i nor pan-Islamic; it aims at the establishment of what could be termed 'Islamic world order'. Toward that ultimate end, it advocates the export of the Islamic Revolution to other countries everywhere by pacific means, especially by the example of Islamic behaviour and propaganda, and decries in theory both political subversion and armed aggression as instruments of an Islamic foreign policy.

Fourthly, because of the vagueness of the ideological precepts and the lack of political cohesion, as well as the determination of revolutionary leaders to make a clean break with the foreign policy of the late Shah and his father Reza Shah, two problems in particular destabilize Iran's foreign policy: (1) the official–unofficial division in the foreign-policy-making process; and (2) the decimation of both skilled diplomats and the organizational structure of the Ministry of Foreign Affairs. The taking of American hostages was the single most far-reaching foreign policy decision in revolutionary Iran. It, however, was taken unofficially and implemented by crowds in the streets of Tehran, and only then endorsed officially *ex post facto*.

A fifth point is that Khumayni's interpretation of Islam influences Iran's revolutionary foreign policy in a variety of ways. It motivates his own foreign policy pronouncements, decisions, commitments and strategies as well as those of his disciples who may believe in his line as dogmatically as he does. It also performs other functions, including communicating, rationalizing and justifying foreign policy behaviour. Above all, it is used to mobilize domestic support for the conduct of diplomacy, and the prosecution of war. Once a war is claimed to be waged in the defence of Islam, the usual distinction made between a defensive war and an invasion on the basis of the concept of the territorial state is cast to the winds.

The sixth proposition is that the overriding goal of Iranian revolutionary foreign policy is proclaimed to be absolute independence from the West and East. That means self-reliance and freedom from the domination of either power bloc not only politically, but also economically, culturally, intellectually, and psychologically. Toward this goal Iran is said to pursue a two-pronged policy: (1) a self-reliant non-alignment policy; and (2) a pro-Third World policy that accords first priority to Muslim countries and second priority to other Third World states.

Movement in these directions is evidenced by Iran's rejection of normal relations with the United States, but America is not the West. West European countries and Japan are still the principal trade partners of Iran. Relations with the Soviet Union are still strained, largely over ideological and political differences, but otherwise they are what Iranian leaders themselves characterize as good and friendly. Compared to the Shah's days, when considerable economic ties with Moscow also existed, current economic, commercial, and technical relations between Tehran and Moscow are more extensive. Adding this to the rigidly expanding trade and economic relations with East European countries, and to the influence of the communist Tudeh Party in Iran, some Western circles are alarmed at the perceived 'Iranian tilt' toward the East. However, it is too early to judge.

Movement in the direction of expansion of relations with the Third World states is also discernible as evidenced by emerging new ties not only with such Muslim states as Syria, Turkey, and Pakistan, which have revived the old notion of a common market among them, but also with such diverse Third World nations as North Korea, Argentina, Brazil, Nicaragua, India and others. Oil is still the principal commodity in the Iranian economy. It is being used in an ever-increasing number of barter deals with diverse foreign countries. The revolutionary regime has sold Iranian oil to the Soviet Union for the first time in the history of the relations between the two countries.

Finally, whether any of these foreign policy goals, means, and courses of action are durable, one cannot tell. Beyond Khumayni, the future of the 'Islamic Revolution' is unpredictable, and so is the future of Iran's foreign policy. But what is relatively ponderable is the deep and controlling influence of the political culture on Iran's foreign policy regardless of who rules the country and what is the dominant ideological stance. That is a different subject, which needs separate treatment. It could nevertheless be argued that there is one major aspect of the political culture that the 'Islamic Republic of Iran' has not so far been able to escape; namely the ancient habit of Iranian leaders to set unrealizable goals and to use inappropriate means in both domestic politics and foreign policy.

Notes

1. This conception of the 'twin revolution' has been used by the author elsewhere to suggest that every Middle Eastern revolution has had this external–internal characteristic as evidenced, for example, by the Egyptian revolution, which, according to Gamal 'Abd al-Nasir, was launched against 'foreign and internal despotism'. This characteristic is historically as applicable to Iran's own experience as it is to its 1978–9 revolution. Both the constitutional revolution of 1905–11, and the nationalist uprising of 1951–3 aimed simultaneously at independence from foreign control and freedom from domestic tyranny. For details, see R. K. Ramazani, *Beyond the Arab–Israeli Settlement: New Directions for US Policy in the Middle East* (Cambridge, Mass., Institute for Foreign Policy Analysis, 1977), pp. 36–40. See also R. K. Ramazani, 'Iran's Revolution: Patterns, Problems, and Prospects', *International Affairs*, 45 (1980), 443–57.
2. For a detailed analysis of the cumulative effects of US–Iran relations during the entire period of the Shah's regime on the Iranian revolution, see R. K. Ramazani, *The United States and Iran: The Patterns of Influence* (New York, Praeger, 1982). See also, R. K. Ramazani, 'Who Lost America? The Case of Iran', *The Middle East Journal*, 36 (1982), 5–21.
3. Unfortunately, the text of this important document is not available in English. For its text and related materials in Persian, see *Komitch Baray-e Defa'a Az Hoquq-e Bashar va Pishraft-e An dar Iran*, No. 16, 10 Dey 1357, pp. 99–100.
4. This was one of the earliest and most bitter attacks on the United States by Khumayni after his return to Iran from exile. For its full text see *Ettela'at*, 20 May 1979. For numerous other statements against the United States, see subsequent issues of this same source during the years 1979–82.
5. See, for example, *Ettela'at*, 7 March 1981.
6. With the approval of Khumayni, Saddeq Tabataba'i, a relative of the Ayatollah, was authorized to meet secretly with an American counterpart in West Germany. The details of this development are discussed by Pierre Salinger, *America Held Hostage: The Secret Negotiations* (New York, Doubleday, 1981). Salinger's account is reliable. This author has checked the information with Warren Christopher, who was President Carter's principal negotiator, and who has helpfully provided the author with a copy of his *Diplomacy: The Neglected Imperative* (n.p., n.d.).
7. See *The Christian Science Monitor*, 12 May 1982.
8. See the section authored by Yann Richard in Nikki R. Keddie, *Roots of Revolution:*

An Interpretive History of Modern Iran (New Haven, Yale University, 1981) especially pp. 205–6.

9. See Haj Ruhollah Mussavi Khomeini, *Kashf-e Assrar* (Tehran, n.p., 1944).
10. *Ibid.*, especially p. 267.
11. For the text see Foreign Broadcast Information Service (hereafter cited as FBIS), *Daily Report, South Asia*, 4 November 1981, Vol. VIII, No. 213.
12. *Ibid.*, 29 October 1981, Vol. VIII, No. 209.
13. *Tehran Journal*, 7 October 1981.
14. *Ibid.*, 25 October 1981.
15. *Ibid.*, 4 November 1981.
16. For the text see FBIS, *Daily Report, Middle East and Africa*, 24 March 1980, Vol. V, No. 058, Supplement 070.
17. FBIS, *Daily Report, South Asia*, 9 March 1982, Vol. VIII, No. 046.
18. See *Sourush*, March 1981, pp. 4–5.
19. FBIS, *Daily Report, South Asia*, 11 March 1982, Vol. VIII, No. 048.
20. *Tehran Journal*, 7 October 1981.
21. FBIS, *Daily Report, South Asia*, 8 July 1981, Vol. VIII, No. 130, Annex No. 015.
22. See his interview in *The Middle East*, April 1982, pp. 16–17.
23. These points are based on the author's *Iran's Foreign Policy, 1941–1973: A Study of Foreign Policy in Modernizing Nations* (Charlottesville, University Press of Virginia, 1975); *The United States and Iran: The Patterns of Influence* (New York, Praeger, 1982); and other works.
24. See FBIS, *Daily Report, South Asia*, 8 July 1981, Vol. VIII, No. 130, Annex No. 015.
25. See *The Middle East Economic Digest* (MEED), 30 April, 1982, p. 8.
26. *Baghdad Observer*, 16 October 1979, pp. 4–5.
27. FBIS, *Daily Report, South Asia*, 19 April 1982, Vol. VIII, No. 075.
28. *Ibid.*, 16 March 1982, Vol. VIII, No. 051.
29. *Ibid.*, 1 April 1982, Vol. VIII, No. 063.
30. See Rouhollah K. Ramazani, 'Emerging Patterns of Regional Relations in Iranian Foreign Policy', *Orbis*, 18 (1975), 1043–69.
31. FBIS, *Daily Report, South Asia*, 13 October 1981, Vol. VIII, No. 197.
32. *Ibid.*
33. These percentages are the author's calculations which are based on the information contained in *Ash-Sharq Al Awsat*, 16 March 1982.
34. FBIS, *Daily Report, The Middle East and Africa*, 21 December 1981, Vol. V, No. 244.
35. FBIS, *Daily Report, South Asia*, 12 November 1981, Vol. VIII, No. 218.

3 Islamic Values and National Interest: The Foreign Policy of Saudi Arabia

JAMES P. PISCATORI

Kings Faysal, Khalid, and Fahd have consistently argued that the first principle of Saudi foreign policy is Islamic solidarity and that the second is Arab unity. Toward that end the Saudis have expended large sums of money and even greater amounts of rhetoric to establish themselves as the natural leaders of Islam and Arabism. At least to the extent that Islam may be said to have acquired a patron currently, the Saudis have seemingly achieved some measure of success; the acquisition of a vast treasury has clearly given new meaning to Saudi activism in Islamic affairs in the past decade. However, Islam has been a longstanding feature of Saudi foreign policy – not necessarily in the sense of 'the promotion of the interests of Islam and the Islamic countries',[1] but certainly in promoting the interests of the Saudi regime in the Middle East. Many Saudi leaders are of course committed to advancing the causes of Islam throughout the world, but they must be seen to be pre-eminently committed to advancing their own stability and influence in the region.

'Abd al-'Aziz's foreign policy

The British Political Agent at Kuwait, Captain W. H. I. Shakespear, perceptively, if somewhat too respectfully, noted in 1915 that 'Abd al-'Aziz was animated, first, by 'intense patriotism for his country' and then by 'a profound veneration for his religion' as well as by 'a single-minded desire to do his best for his people by obtaining for them lasting peace and security'.[2] The record of 'Abd al-'Aziz's diplomatic activity bears out this primacy accorded to national – that is, dynastic – interest. From the first heady days of victory in Najd (roughly in the centre of Saudi Arabia), he had two overriding goals – the consolidation of his own authority and what he thought of as the recapture of territory that had in fact been under his ancestors' control intermittently in the eighteenth and nineteenth centuries.

Achieving the latter goal became so important to achieving the former that 'Abd al-'Aziz was willing to run the risk of upsetting his religiously conservative supporters, for he hoped to displace the Muslim Ottomans by turning for help to the non-Muslim British. In 1913 he vainly tried to secure British agreement to forestall an Ottoman counter-attack by sea if he were successful in occupying al-Hasa, the area along the Gulf coast. When the British refused to be drawn, he went ahead with his attack partly to convince them that he was an *emir* (ruler) whom they must reckon with.[3] He thought that it was essential to get British recognition in order to convince his followers that he was as important as the Trucial Coast *shaykhs* who enjoyed His Majesty's Government's protection. When the British were still not forthcoming, 'Abd al-'Aziz concluded a treaty with the Ottomans in 1914 in which he promised a political obedience that he clearly did not intend to give.

But the arrangement bought him time, during which the prospect of general war induced the British to reconsider their attitude toward him. Refusing to commit himself to aid the British cause in the event of war, 'Abd al-'Aziz forced the British hand and succeeded in 1915 in getting their recognition of him as an independent ruler. Now he was on a par with his chief rival, Sharif Husayn of Mecca, against whom he would invoke Article 2 of the Anglo-Saudi Treaty and whom he would brand, according to its terms, an aggressive 'foreign power'. As Philby noted in December 1917, 'Abd al-'Aziz was 'activated by consuming jealousy of the Sharif and genuine apprehension in respect of the latter's unveiled pretension to be considered the overlord, if not the actual ruler, of all Arab countries by virtue of his position as *de facto* supreme spiritual head of Sunni Islam'.[4]

The final straw came in 1924 when the *sharif* proclaimed himself Caliph. This, however, merely confirmed 'Abd al-'Aziz's suspicion of Hashimite political intentions and led to the decisive Saudi assault on the Hijaz (the area along the Red Sea Coast which includes Mecca and Medina) in 1925. Up to his final triumph over the Hashimites, 'Abd al-'Aziz regularly denounced the Turks and the Hashimites for their distortions of true Islam as a way of currying the favour of his domestic audience. But Islam played no role[5] in a foreign policy which was designed to secure the backing of British power for his political and territorial ambitions.

Having achieved his territorial goals, 'Abd al-'Aziz went to work on maintaining his kingdom's independence. There were four manifestations of this objective. First was his eagerness to have the European powers recognize his country and government, mainly at first in order to impress the Hashimite rulers of neighbouring Trans-Jordan and Iraq who might be tempted to avenge the *sharif*'s losses. To this end he was happy in February 1926 to receive the recognition of the Soviet Union, the first state to accord it. A far greater prize, however, was the Anglo-Saudi Treaty of Jidda in 1927, which, unlike the 1915 treaty, acknowledged 'the complete and absolute independence' of 'Abd al-'Aziz's dominions.

A second manifestation was his convening of the Muslim World Conference in Mecca in 1926. Ostensibly he wanted the Islamic states to guarantee the neutrality and inviolability of the Hijaz, but his main purpose must be seen as trying to secure Islamic international approbation of his control of the formerly Hashimite territory. The conference proved to be singularly unsuccessful since few delegations attended and since those that did disagreed with Wahhabi practices.

A third manifestation was his concern – although not a dominant one – that Arab leaders treat him as an equal. He was convinced that, in addition to the Hashimites, the Egyptians too were unwilling to accord him this status; consequently, the relationship with Egypt was troubled. There were no diplomatic relations between 1926 and 1936 after the puritanical Saudis had objected to the ostentatious way by which the Egyptians customarily delivered the *kiswa*, the covering of the Ka'ba, to Mecca. Even when relations were restored, 'Abd al-'Aziz looked warily upon the new King Faruq, whom he suspected, like King Fu'ad before him, of wanting to become Caliph. As in the earlier case of the *sharif*, the objection was primarily political: the revival of the caliphate would pose a direct challenge to the security of his political base.[6]

A fourth manifestation of 'Abd al-'Aziz's search for political independence was the desire to broaden his diplomatic contacts among the great powers. Although he unquestionably relied on Britain for support and aid, he also realized that it was good to have as many friends as possible. Three factors accounted for this realization. First, he was increasingly in economic trouble. Since the British had ended their subsidy in 1925, he was chiefly dependent on income from the annual Pilgrimage (*hajj*). However, the world depression was having the effect of severely curtailing the number of pilgrims. Second, Italy was posing a threat to the stability of the immediate region; in 1927 it concluded a treaty with neighbouring Yemen and later it invaded nearby Ethiopia. Third, 'Abd al-'Aziz was ambivalent toward the British. On the one hand, he needed their support to maintain his position in relation to the other British protected Arabs and to stave off any possible Italian advances at his expense, but, on the other, he was neither sure that they would in fact come to his help nor entirely willing to be seen to be a British client. The latter sentiment grew particularly pronounced after the 1936 Arab uprising in Palestine when he felt that he had to join the chorus of Arab nationalist denunciations of British policy if he were to placate his own people and, more importantly, to convince the other Arabs of his political worth.

These factors led him to develop relations with the Soviet Union, the United States, and Nazi Germany. Although there had been formal ties with the Soviets since 1926, there was an upgrading of relations in the early 1930s as both sides sought to improve their financial positions. The Soviets wanted to sell petroleum products to the Saudis, and the Saudis wanted to receive more Soviet Muslim pilgrims. In this regard, Prince Faysal paid a successful visit to Moscow in 1932 during which he met Stalin and Molotov. 'Abd al-'Aziz also thought that a possible way out of his difficulties was to grant a concession to the Americans for the exploration and production of oil. Consequently, Charles Crane negotiated Saudi Arabia's entry into the petroleum market, which led to the Arabian–American Oil Company (ARAMCO) concession of 1932 and the discovery of oil in 1935. The Americans had the triple advantage of technical expertise, political unoffensiveness, and potential world power. From 1931 to 1939, as well, the Saudis tried to develop contacts with Hitler's Germany. The primary purpose was to induce the Germans to rein in their allies, the Italians; this became critical to 'Abd al-'Aziz after April 1938 when the Anglo-Italian Agreement appeared to him to establish a kind of joint protectorate over his kingdom.[7] He was also hedging his bets against the day when Britain might be defeated and when he might strengthen his hand in the British-dominated region.

In the period from the conquest of the Hijaz in 1926 to the outbreak of World War II, then, 'Abd al-'Aziz was principally engaged in consolidating his control over his land and people and maintaining his independence. As Islam had not served as an ideology determining his foreign policy in the earlier period, it also did not prevent his consorting with the infidel Americans and with the godless Soviets in this period. Even the break in diplomatic contacts between Saudi Arabia and the Soviet Union in September 1938 had nothing to do with ideology. The Soviets had declared that withdrawing their legations from Saudi Arabia and the Yemen was meant to show their displeasure at the conclusion of the Anglo-Italian Treaty, but it was more probably due first to the fact that the legation had very little work to do in Jidda, and secondly to the Soviet policy at that time of reducing its representation abroad, which had already led to the closure of consulates in Turkey, Persia, and Afghanistan.[8] At any rate, the initiative was taken by the Soviets and had nothing to do with Saudi antipathy to communism. This period shows, then, that 'Abd al-'Aziz followed a policy based on the cold calculation of interests, and this led him to conclude that he had more in common with some non-Muslim states than with many Muslim ones. The one time that he actively sought the approval of Muslims throughout the world, in the Mecca conference of 1926, he was disappointed. He was better at impressing 'outsiders', particularly those from whom he was soliciting countenance, by invoking his status, however self-proclaimed, as guardian of the holy places, to make it seem that his influence reached beyond his own frontiers.

Two main issues dominated the wartime and post-war periods – Arab unity and Palestine. Regarding the former, there is no evidence that 'Abd al-'Aziz acted for any reason other than being, as the *Palestine Post* described him, 'a supporter of political realism'.[9] Although he encouraged individual movements like that of the Syrian nationalists, he was distinctly cool to any plans that aimed to recongregate the newly independent peoples into a larger unity. In particular, he opposed the Greater Syrian Plan, which King 'Abdullah of Trans-Jordan proposed, and the Fertile Crescent Plan, which Nuri al-Sa'id, the Iraqi king's chief minister, advanced. He naturally saw these as Hashimite – and perhaps British-backed – designs on his independence, and he made no attempt to hide his acute hostility to the formation of either a general Arab union or a particular union of countries to the north of his borders. Indeed, it is clear that he was little influenced by the pro-unity propaganda of both the Arab nationalists and the Muslim Brothers, who apparently found support among some of his non-Saudi-born advisers, notably Fu'ad Bey Hamza. Rather than being convinced that there was an ethnic and religious imperative to get together, 'Abd al-'Aziz believed political decline would flow from such projected cohesion and feared financial loss from a customs union that would control the Pilgrimage.[10] In opposing the move for a strong Arab League in 1945, he even found at least one Islamic loophole:

The attempt to unify educational and constitutional methods in Arab countries is to be praised. However, the Saudi Arabian Kingdom, whose territory includes certain holy places, thereby claims a special status and cannot sanction any educational or constitutional program that is not consistent with the tenets and traditions of Islam.[11]

Later expression of pro-unionist sentiment needs to be weighed against this determined refusal to be drawn into any scheme of meaningful integration. For example, in 1949 the Saudis momentarily argued that all Arab states should be unified in matters of mutual defence and security in order to protect themselves against Israel and the Soviet Union. Yet it is clear that the Saudi government had no intention of pursuing the matter, for its real concern was not Israel or the Soviet Union but its neighbours. So concerned was it that it prevailed upon the Americans to urge the British government to be ever vigilant in restraining its local allies.[12] This Saudi fear of encirclement was not entirely unjustified as long as people like Jordan's Prince Talal made views like this known: 'While it is unlikely that [the] Hashimite House, particularly King Abdullah, would ever attempt any armed action ... it is clear that [the] Moslem world would not continue to sanction [the] Wahabis as guardian of [the] Holy Places in [the] Hedjaz.'[13]

If specifically political interests understandably governed the Saudi reaction to the first issue of Arab unity, political and Islamic considerations affected the response to the second issue, Palestine. It is impossible to separate the motivations. 'Abd al-'Aziz could not ignore the risk to his position at home and abroad if he failed to be more vocal about a matter which so exercised Arab and Islamic sentiment. But he is also known to have shared with some Muslims a hostile view of the Jews, based in part on a misinterpretation of Islamic history, and to have believed that because the resurrection of all Muslims will take place in Palestine, that land must remain in the hands of Arab Muslims.[14] To take it upon himself to pressure the West into resisting the Zionist demands was thus, in his view, the politically wise and only religiously proper thing to do.

It was obvious to him that he would derive greater political benefit from being seen, by Westerners and fellow Arabs, not as following but as leading Arab Muslim opinion. Hence, although in the late 1930s he had contented himself with asking ARAMCO to make quiet representations on his behalf to the State Department, he now forcefully presented his case to the Americans in person – to Roosevelt at Great Bitter Lake – and in many strongly worded letters.[15] In this sense, his anger at President Truman for disregarding Roosevelt's promise to consult the Saudi monarch before any major change of policy on Palestine may have been due to the slight as well as to the change of policy itself.

Faysal's foreign policy

Apart from the Palestine question, there seems to be little evidence that Islamic values played a central role in the formulation of the foreign policy of the first Saudi king, and even in aiding its implementation. But the Islamic dimension became more pronounced under his successors, not necessarily because they were more devout but because different considerations presented themselves. The death of 'Abd al-'Aziz in 1953 roughly coincided with one of the most significant events in the modern Arab world – the launching of the Egyptian revolution. The accession of King Sa'ud at this time was unfortunate, for it brought an incompetent to the throne precisely at the time that the charismatic 'Abd al-Nasir was making Egypt the premier Arab state.

'Abd al-Nasir quickly became 'the voice of the Arabs', and with that voice passionately denouncing the twin evils of imperialism and reactionary rule, pro-Western, monarchical Saudi Arabia clearly found itself on the defensive. This defensiveness was manifested in the cooling of the relationship with the United States and in a relative *rapprochement* with Egypt. In 1954 the Saudi government made public its objection to the fact that the United States was giving more technical aid to Israel than to the kingdom. In March 1956 it signed an agreement with the Egyptian and Pakistani governments for the establishment of the short-lived and vaguely defined 'Islamic Congress', and in June 1956 the government refused to extend the Dhahran Air Base lease for more than a month at a time. This posturing must have seemed appropriate to the Saudi elite when 'Abd al-Nasir enhanced his heroic image at Suez later that year and confirmed his popularity by a triumphal visit to Riyadh itself.

But there was no mistaking the basic problem for the Saudis: no matter how much they tried to distance themselves from the Americans, in the end they could see no advantage as a conservative state in doing what the radical states had done and accept a Soviet offer of weapons and the realignment which that implied (although there were some hints throughout 1955 and 1956 that they might do just that). As the United States correspondingly looked to Saudi Arabia to be an anti-communist pillar in the region, the Saudis became even more identified with the imperialists. The Iraq revolution of 1958 polarized the region further, and it was in this environment of needing to find friends where they could that the Saudis did what had been unthinkable under 'Abd al-'Aziz – conclude a joint agreement with the Jordanians to coordinate their foreign and military policies.

But the Yemeni civil war, which erupted a month later in September 1962, put the very survival of the Saudi regime in question. Thousands of Egyptian troops were at the country's southern borders and Egyptian aircraft were occasionally strafing Saudi villages. In time, an outright invasion grew increasingly unlikely as the Egyptians became mired in Yemeni tribal complexities and as the United States pledged itself to protect the kingdom. But the internal danger was always more trouble-some; Nasirism was taking its toll. There were open criticisms from highly placed people, and defections of several airforce pilots as well as princes who in Cairene exile worked to 'liberate' Saudi Arabia of their own family's 'feudal' control.

The real battle was over ideas, but Faysal, who now held all executive power, did not find it useful to counter-attack by appealing to Islam in either domestic or international politics. Domestic politics, in which Islam was the main ingredient of the regime's legitimacy, was badly in need of reform; and Arab nationalism was clearly the international ideological wave of the moment. But there was some usefulness in advancing an indirect Islamic initiative which at least could make it seem that the Saudis were still defenders of Islam and far from being thoroughly immoral as their critics were charging. Consequently, during the 1962 *hajj*, delegates from 43 countries agreed to establish a Muslim World League (Rabitat al-'Alam al-Islami), which would 'combat the serious plots by which the enemies of Islam are trying to draw Muslims away from their religion and to destroy their unity and brotherhood'.[16] From this beginning, the League continuously func-tioned in effect as a non-governmental Saudi spokesman.

By late 1965, however, Faysal felt able to launch a more direct initia-tive and called for an alliance of all Muslims. In doing this, it is clear that Faysal had in mind a major attack on the ascendancy of the radical Arab states, especially Egypt. He felt that it was necessary to do so generally because of their continuing attacks on the Saudi regime itself and specifically because of his disillusionment with Egypt in the wake of the Jidda Agreement of August 1965; for although 'Abd al-Nasir had virtually pleaded for a way out of the Yemen conflict, he soon accepted the offer of Soviet aid and prepared to launch another offensive in 1966. Moreover, Faysal believed that it was now possible to challenge the leftists for several reasons. One was that he was finally and indisputably in control, having formally displaced Sa'ud on the throne and having restored much political and economic stability to the country. Another was that the dissident princes who had gone to Cairo were back disil-lusioned and repentant in Riyadh. Yet another reason was that Nasirism suddenly seemed vulnerable because of the failure of the Egyptians to win a clear victory in the Yemen or to transplant their revolution successfully anywhere else.

Although Faysal argued that there could be no conflict between Islamic and Arab cooperation, there is no doubt that he saw an Islamic *entente* as the counterweight to the leftist states in the Arab cold war. The way to avoid political and ideological encirclement was to go on the political and ideological offensive. But little success was in fact to be derived since, although the more conservative states like Iran, Jordan, Pakistan, and Malaysia supported the Saudi initiative, the more radical states like Algeria, Syria, Iraq, and Indonesia vigorously opposed it. Predictably, the Egyptians led the denunciations accusing the Saudis of proposing a neo-imperialist scheme to reintroduce the Baghdad Pact and of leading a reactionary, anti-Arab nationalist movement.[17]

The next call for Islamic cooperation proved to be more successful because two key developments made the atmosphere more receptive. The first was the defeat of Egypt and Syria in the 1967 Arab–Israeli war. The Saudi *bêtes noires* found themselves in need of Saudi financial aid, and although they did not abandon their ideological hostility, their threats became less menacing and less effective now. Furthermore, the defeat generally prompted the Arabs to traumatic self-examination, which produced a questioning of the validity of Nasirism and Ba'thism and a renewed appreciation of Islam for the political and social guidance that it can give. The second development was the burning of the al-Aqsa Mosque in Jerusalem; because everyone believed that Israel was responsible, it brought all Muslims – and most Arab states – together in common outrage. Twenty-five states assembled at the resulting Rabat summit of September 1969.

The Organization of the Islamic Conference (OIC), which came into existence in 1972, provided a permanent institution through which the Saudis could express their views and emphasize their special role in the Islamic world, thereby strengthening their position among the Arabs. It was a happy development for Faysal since it gave him a means to develop his commitment to improving the lot of Muslims while also advancing the political interests of his country. This latter task was made easier by the change in political climate in the region after 'Abd al-Nasir's death in Egypt, Asad's rise to power in Syria, and Numayri's triumph over the communists in Sudan; all the changes heralded a new relative moderation in important states.[18] But like his father before him with regard to Arab unity, Faysal showed no interest in turning the OIC into an authority above his own; rather, he was careful to speak of it as an inter-governmental organization and to see to it that its charter was respectful of existing national sovereignties. His call was not for Islamic unity but for Islamic solidarity (*tadamun*),[19] and he actively encouraged the development of institutions as diverse as the Islamic Development Bank and the International Islamic News Agency to enhance the prospects of this solidarity. The proliferation of such institutions, of course, testified not only to his zeal but also to the extent of his influence.

Faysal also became increasingly influential in the Arab–Israeli conflict; in fact, unlike his predecessors he came to play a major role. This too, however, was because of both the strength of personal beliefs and the calculation of interest. Prior to the 1967 war he had been financially cool toward the various Palestinian organizations and specifically the Palestine Liberation Organization (PLO) because they were in league with the radical states and had even threatened the Saudi monarchy itself. But his attitude changed after the 1967 war, partly because of his deeply held belief that Jerusalem must be liberated from Israeli occupation and partly because of the new, more favourable configuration of Arab politics. His financial support of the PLO since then, though not being unlimited, was at least constant. He backed the Palestinian resistance for its participation in what he emotionally yet vaguely thought of as a *jihad*, but only up to a point; he knew that if it became too strong, it would pose a challenge to his own throne. The 'Black September' of 1970 in Jordan must have confirmed his wariness.

Generally by the time of the 1973 war, however, several factors combined to make the Saudis relatively more militant. One was the steady increase in their economic strength and another was the growing warmth between the Egyptians and the Saudis on the one hand, and the Syrians and the Saudis on the other. For both these reasons Faysal proved remarkably successful at transferring the Arab–Israeli conflict from the exclusively Arab plane to the broadly Islamic one. Egypt, Syria,[20] Libya, and most other Arab states accepted this redefinition, and Faysal tried to encourage it among the African states as well, some of which he visited in November 1972. This approach fulfilled his sense not only of what was right but of what was shrewd: stressing the Islamic dimension of the issue was an effective way of certifying his commitment to the *Arab* cause, thereby helping to legitimate his regime in the eyes of his own people and the other Arabs – a constant necessity for a dynastic ruler even in favourable times – while simultaneously advancing his claim to Arab leadership. His support of the 1973 oil embargo must be seen in this light. In this period, then, Islam proved useful in the implementation of foreign policy – it made it acceptable and gave it coherent form – but Islam was also involved, to a lesser extent, in the formulation of policy.

Contemporary foreign policy

If Islam's role in Saudi foreign policy under Faysal was both the natural result of relative Saudi strength and a contributor to that strength, under his successors it may be conditioned by new circumstances pointing to a potential comparative weakness of the Saudi position. It is, however, important to note first that the more active Saudi style which has come about finds its origin in the war and oil-price rises of 1973–4. In a very short time Saudi Arabia was catapulted from being a hesitant and sometimes marginal player to being an assertive and always central player. Yet this rapid rise means that it was slow to evolve a coherent strategy. This problem was immensely complicated by two important series of events, which account for the change of circumstances in the post-Faysal period – developments in the Arab–Israeli problem and the Iranian revolution.

Regarding the first, the Egyptian peace treaty with Israel in 1978 was both startling and unwelcome; the Saudis had not been consulted despite their closeness to Sadat and the Americans, and they feared, quite rightly, the radicalization of Arab politics by way of response. The chain of events known as the 'Camp David' process put the Saudis on the spot; their past association with the Egyptians and the Americans tainted them and they could not be seen to be approving, yet they were hesitant about too closely identifying themselves with the 'rejectionists' like Qadhafi. But, as seen before in Saudi diplomatic history, the Saudis opted to secure their domestic and regional base. In this case it meant supporting the Baghdad summits of 1978 and cutting off support for Egypt – a decision which disappointed the Americans and angered Sadat but which brought them approving nods from the Arabs. In effect the Saudis were only moving to the centre of the Arab political spectrum in order to reduce the distance between them and everyone else.

A further impetus to activism in regional politics came from the second series of events – the overthrow of the Shah and his replacement by an assertive Islamic leadership. The example of a dynasty being destroyed was alarming, as was the appeal of an Islamic ideology that railed against monarchy and concentrated wealth. The Saudis felt themselves on the defensive at the same time as they were outraged by Israeli actions. A good way of responding was to threaten a *jihad*, as Fahd did in August 1980 when the Israelis proclaimed Jerusalem their eternal capital. The Saudis were certainly motivated by their own sense of outrage, but they were also fearful of criticism from both the Arab states and revolutionary Iran.

But while 'Camp David' made them somewhat wary of too close an alignment with the United States, they had also to consider the dangers of the opposite – too great a distance. The Soviet invasion of Afghanistan raised the possibility of increased Soviet involvement in the Gulf region, and the Soviet access to facilities in South Yemen and Ethiopia suggested the image of an encircled kingdom. More alarming, however, was the outbreak of the Iran–Iraq war in September 1980, for this endangered the security of the oil lanes while it stimulated fearsome thoughts of militant Iranians on the Arab side of the Gulf. As a result, even though they feel the Americans are not sufficiently sympathetic to their basic concerns, the Saudis have seen the prudence of staying relatively close to the Americans – buying more and more advanced weapons and calling on their help in local problems, such as the Yemeni war of 1979. But even in this latter instance the Saudis showed the ambiguity of their attitude toward the United States: they wanted American aid to go to the North Yemenis, but not too much aid since that would upset the strategic balance with their neighbour and, more importantly, leave the Saudis open to the general charge that they were facilitating American imperialism.

Although Saudi Arabia sometimes sides with the more radical Arab states, it is clear that it is naturally a conservative state. The threat from Iran has only enhanced this predisposition: the Saudis have encouraged the Gulf Cooperation Council to move quickly to improve the security of its six members; and they are working closely in a kind of conservative *entente* with others such as the Jordanians, Moroccans, Iraqis, and Pakistanis. The military relationship with the Pakistanis is proving to be particularly useful since it allows the Saudis to get needed expertise without going to the infidel Americans or to other Arabs who could interact easily with the local population; the Pakistanis have the advantage of being Muslim and non-Arabic-speaking.[21] Fahd's peace plan, which failed to be approved at the Fez summit of September 1982, also indicates how the Saudis want above all to preserve the viability of a conservative order. In pointing to a solution of this conflict, this plan would, in their opinion, also help to avert the further radicalization of the region.

The turbulence of the early eighties affected the Saudi use of Islam in foreign policy in two ways. First, increasing Arab discord tended to reduce the common ground that obtained in the immediate aftermath of the 1973 war. Although the war in Lebanon temporarily brought the Arabs together, the underlying pattern remained one of polarization. In this contentious environment, appeals to Islamic solidarity seemed weak; the political differences were too great to be smoothed over by the emotional invocation of Islam. There has also been a polarization of Muslims, which presently is increasingly working in favour of Saudi Arabia's Islamic competitors. Khumayni's influence is broad, and even the less appealing Qadhafi scores a point when he accuses the Saudis of defiling the holy places by letting American military planes fly in their airspace.[22] The *hajj*, which has long served to give focus to Saudi Arabia's privileged position in the Islamic world, is also suddenly proving to be worrisome. Confrontations with Khumayni's supporters in the Pilgrimages of the past few years can hardly have enhanced the Saudis' reputation as an effective guardian of peace in the holy land; what is more, the Saudis cannot deny access to these Muslims without calling into question the validity of their guardianship itself. Given these constraints, the Saudi authorities must look with great anxiety on the 80,000 Iranian pilgrims who regularly descend on Saudi Arabia.

Second, the turmoil in the area has accentuated the Saudis' ambivalence toward the superpowers and called into question the relevance of Islam to formulating the Saudi position. There has been a widespread assumption that commitment to Islam has predisposed the Saudis, if not toward the United States, then certainly against the Soviet Union. But, as was indicated above, in the time of King 'Abd al-'Aziz national interest, not ideology, governed. It is likely that in the time of King Faysal personal conviction more than ideological dogma itself governed the anti–communist emphasis. There is no doubt that he passionately loathed and consistently connected international communism and Zionism. At the same time it is likely that, given the Soviet Union's backing of his Arab competitors, he saw no hard reason to be sympathetic toward it.

This suggests that Islam will not play a predetermined role in shaping future policy toward the Soviet Union and that other considerations will prevail. Yet, as has been suggested, these considerations are complex. United States' policies in the area make it increasingly difficult, even dangerous, for Saudi Arabia to be seen in the company of the Western superpower; however, the US has global influence and sophisticated weapons. On the other hand, the Soviet Union has invaded Afghanistan, which the Saudis deplore for violating both Islamic rights and regional stability; yet, it has been supportive of the Arab cause and is active in Arab countries whose policies the Saudis wish to moderate. The record shows that a re-evaluation of sorts is going on with regard to the Soviet Union. Prince Sa'ud, the foreign minister, has said that it makes no sense to pretend that great states like the Soviet Union do not exist.[23] Although he said this just prior to the Soviet invasion of Afghanistan, he apparently made no effort to rescind or revise his comments for their publication shortly after the invasion.[24] It is likely, however, that the Saudis are thus playing 'the Soviet card' in order to signal to the West that they should not be taken for granted, and to their fellow Arabs that they are not entirely dependent on the United States. Whether they eventually resume regular diplomatic contacts with the Soviet Union or not, it is clear that considerations of *realpolitik*, not of ideology, are uppermost in their minds.

But while political realism seems to govern Saudi foreign policy calculations, it would be wrong to suggest that Islam plays no role. On the contrary, precisely because most of the Saudi leadership believes that it has an obligation to work for Islam ('the greater *jihad*'), it has invested vast sums of money in Islamic institutions and individual countries with Muslim communities. There are four kinds of recipients. First, there is the formal Islamic institution, which receives regular membership dues from the Saudis in addition to often more significant voluntary contributions. The formula for determining membership dues in the OIC network is not public, but one indicator of the formal contribution is the Saudi payment of 10 per cent ($1 million) of the budget of the General Secretariat of the OIC; it is, of course, the single largest payment. But however much of the budget the Saudis provide to the various organizations, it is clear that their voluntary contributions are weighty: in 1981, for instance, they contributed $35 million above their regular dues to various parts of the OIC.[25] As an example of one such donation, they gave $800,000 toward the construction in Karachi of the new headquarters of the Islamic Chamber of Commerce, Industry and Commodity Exchange, an affiliated organ of the OIC.[26] Perhaps the most significant institutional commitment, however, is Saudi Arabia's pledge to the Islamic Development Bank – 27.8 per cent of the total subscription of $577.43 million (506.37 million Islamic dinars),[27] again the single largest subscription by far.

A second type of recipient is the government of an OIC member state. The Saudi government sometimes makes outright grants and sometimes loans. In mid-1981 the Saudis reported that they had provided Lebanon with $24.7 million in aid, and given loans to Tunisia that totalled $16.7 million, but in both instances the time frame is not

clear. Included in this category are emergency aid donations, such as
$5 million to Somalia for flood relief in 1981 and $10 million to The
Gambia for food and medical supplies after an unsuccessful coup against
President Dawda Jawara. Table 1, however, suggests that the overwhelming majority of aid is to Arab governments, even though Pakistan
has emerged as the single largest recipient.

A third kind of recipient of Saudi largesse is the individual association
or project in Islamic countries. For example, the Saudi government gave
$35 million toward the establishment of the new Islamic University in
Islamabad. A major instrument is the Saudi Fund for Development,

Table 1. *Saudi aid to OIC countries (million US$).*

Recipients	1975	% of total	1976	% of total
Arab countries				
Bahrain	1.7	0.1	100.0	5.0
Egypt	948.9	53.9	496.8	24.9
Jordan	49.3	2.8	165.0	8.3
Morocco	25.0	1.4	—	—
Oman	100.0	5.7	—	—
Sudan	95.3	5.4	163.5	8.2
Syria	242.2	13.8	189.8	9.5
Tunisia	19.5	1.1	—	—
Yemen AR	94.8	5.4	121.8	6.1
Yemen PDR	—	—	100.0	5.0
Non-Arab countries				
Afghanistan	18.3	1.0	7.8	0.4
Cameroon	17.4	1.0	—	—
Chad	1.7	0.1	0.1	.01
Comoro Islands	—	—	2.1	0.1
Gabon	10.4	0.6	—	—
Guinea	—	—	0.2	.01
Indonesia	—	—	6.9	0.4
Mali	16.0	0.9	—	—
Mauritania	—	—	94.1	4.7
Niger	13.2	0.7	2.1	0.1
Pakistan	74.8	4.2	514.8	25.8
Senegal	—	—	5.0	0.3
Somalia	17.2	1.0	22.8	1.1
Turkey	10.0	0.6	—	—
Uganda	5.3	0.3	0.1	.01
Total	1,761		1,992.9	
Total Arab countries	1,576.7	89.5	1,336.9	67.1
Total non-Arab countries	184.3	10.5	656	32.9

Source: Adapted from *Arabia and the Gulf,* 24 July 1978.

which provides soft-term loans. From 1974 to 1979 it allocated about $3,833 million (13,414 million Saudi riyals) for the financing of 173 projects in 55 countries, presumably most of them Islamic.[28]

A fourth kind of recipient is the individual association or project in a non-Islamic country. Saudi money has largely built the new mosques in major European cities. A more specific example is the Saudi donation in 1980 of $100,000 to the Federation of Islamic Associations in the United States and Canada for the construction of its new headquarters in Detroit.

In addition to these governmental disbursements, there are the more limited funds spent by Saudi-based non-governmental institutions, principally the Muslim World League. Its budget comes mainly from the Saudi government, and its head is Shaykh Muhammad 'Ali al-Harakan, a former minister of justice and pillar of the establishment. The League is mostly concerned with supporting *da'wa* (missionary) activities but will also from time to time make donations for relief from natural disasters. To give an example of its main work, from 1975 to 1981 it spent $2.6 million in several African countries on training *imams* (prayer leaders), publishing and distributing Qur'ans, building a mosque, establishing several medical centres, and creating an Institute for the Memorization of the Holy Qur'an.[29] Related to the League is the Supreme World Council for Mosques located in Mecca and headed by Shaykh 'Ali Mukhtar. It had budgeted about $29 million for the maintenance of mosques throughout the world, half of which was to be spent in South-east Asia.[30]

It is difficult to find an aggregate figure for all of Saudi Arabia's aid to Muslims or even a percentage of its GNP spent on them, though Table 1 gives a rough picture of aid for two years, 1975 and 1976. The Saudi press has given indications of the dimensions, but their reliability can be doubted. Dr Mahsun Jalal, Chairman of the International Development Fund of OPEC, reported that Saudi Arabia gave $20,000 million or 6 per cent of its GNP to developing countries as a whole from 1976 to 1980 and that of the annual average of $4,000 million, $1,500 million was in grants and $2,500 million in loans.[31] Prince Talal is also reported as saying that Saudi Arabia regularly allocates 5 per cent of its revenue for aid to the developing world, but independent observers record a decline in percentage. In 1975 the total Saudi overseas development aid was 6.22 per cent of Saudi GNP; in 1976, 5.73 per cent; in 1979, 3.01 per cent; and in 1980, 2.60 per cent.[32] It is unclear how much of this goes to the Islamic countries, but it is at least clear, first, that the amount is very substantial indeed although the amount to the non-Arab Muslim states is very small compared to that given to the Arab Muslim states; and, second, that Saudi Arabia provides far more than any of the other Islamic states.

Asking what Saudi Arabia gets out of all this munificence is like asking what any Western state gets out of its foreign aid. Similarly, the answer must be as ambiguous. There is no question that the aid props up regimes like Pakistan's with which the Saudi government has a good working relationship. Although it is impossible to quantify influence or leverage, surely the Muslim recipients of significant amounts of aid are attentive, though not necessarily submissive, to the Saudis. The Saudis were able to induce the Somalis to turn away from the Soviet Union, but the aid to Egypt did not deter President Sadat from his visit to Jerusalem, nor did the aid to Syria make President Asad echo Saudi positions.[33] Yet there are times when well-timed Saudi aid or threatened reductions in aid can produce results. For example, many observers believe that President Marcos has made concessions to the Muslims of the southern Philippines out of fear of losing vital Saudi assistance. The belief that this is so clearly enhances Saudi prestige. Yet there may be other times when the Saudis are working against their broader interests. For example, they are supporters of Islamic groups in Indonesia which are hostile to the present basically pro-Western regime in Jakarta. However, the most probable benefit which generally results from the giving of aid is to the Saudi rulers who, in being seen to be such inspired alms-givers, may add to their legitimacy at home and their standing abroad.

Conclusion

Despite all the aid that Saudi Arabia gives to other Islamic states, it is not economically well-integrated with them. Table 2 gives some idea of the small amount of Saudi trade with OIC members. In effect, only 6 per cent of Saudi Arabia's exports and only 5 per cent of its imports were with OIC states in 1980 and the vast majority of that was with its natural trading partners, the Arab states. The reasons why Islam has been important in Saudi foreign policy, then, must lie elsewhere. There are perhaps three factors which explain it.

First, because most Saudis view their commitment to Islam as natural and unshakeable, Islam becomes the people's ideology, imposing from below constraints on the leaders above. Thus for the rulers to emphasize the need for international Islamic cooperation is to do the minimum that is expected of them. Second, because few individuals have dominated decision-making, their strongly-held views make a difference. Faysal's and Khalid's devotion served to magnify Islam's relevance to

Table 2. *Direction of Saudi Arabia's trade.*

A. (million US $)	Exports		Imports	
	1978	1980	1978	1980
OIC countries	1,805	6,429	1,550	1,592
Arab countries	1,262	4,048	1,354	1,151
Algeria	1	2	—	2
Bahrain	805	2,218	102	92
Iraq	—	13	3	6
Jordan	104	408	53	91
Kuwait	3	28	620	136
Lebanon	132	352	363	362
Libya	—	2	1	1
Morocco	38	267	8	29
Oman	15	17	1	27
Qatar	3	31	9	100
Sudan	7	330	42	158
Syria	53	14	40	78
Tunisia	43	2	1	2
UAE	6	54	103	52
Yemen AR	19	237	4	13
Yemen PDR	33	73	4	2
Non-Arab countries	543	2,381	196	441
Bangladesh	4	84	—	2
Djibouti	3	—	11	1
Guinea	—	—	1	—
Indonesia	90	1,025	1	14
Iran	1	20	15	24
Malaysia	214	671	37	69
Pakistan	201	511	74	158
Somalia	1	15	38	110
Turkey	29	55	19	63
Non-OIC countries	34,763	94,179	20,510	29,457
Total	36,568	100,608	22,060	31,049
B. (percentage)				
% of OIC trade with Arabs	70	63	87	72
% of OIC trade with non-Arabs	30	37	13	28
% of total trade with OIC	5	6	7	5

Source: Adapted from *Journal of Economic Cooperation Among Islamic Countries*, No. 10 (January 1982), p. 89.

the definition of the national interest. Third, because the regime is conservative and pro-Western, Arab nationalists and leftists have put it on the defensive. Emphasizing Islam as either superior or complementary to Arabism[34] has been the saving retort.

Explaining why Islam is important, however, does not answer when it is relevant to foreign policy. The third point suggests that the regime might find appeals to Islam relevant when its position is weak internationally, but even that generalization would be misleading. Islam played virtually no part in the early days when ʿAbd al-ʿAziz was trying to establish the kingdom's place in Arab politics, and today when revolutionary Iran is challenging the Saudi position, relying on Islam may prove ineffective. The only constant that seems to emerge from Saudi diplomatic history is that Islam becomes relevant and a pronounced factor when Saudi leaders think that it will enhance the Saudi position in Arab politics. It seems most likely to do so in fact when conditions are fairly favourable – such as when there is a decline in the leftists' influence and appeal, a relative moderation of Arab politics, and an absence of competing Islamic ideologies. In unfavourable conditions Islam is likely to be more relevant to domestic politics, as a way the rulers utilize to convince their own people of their legitimacy.

In general, the Saudi case leads us to question, first, whether there is such a thing as an Islamic foreign policy, and second, whether Islam plays as much of a role in Saudi foreign policy as is customarily thought. If by an 'Islamic foreign policy' one means that a set of values uniformly determines what policy will be, then there is no such thing. It would be too much to expect of any ideology to be such an absolute determinant. But there is another sense of the term – Islamic values have some importance in foreign policy but the importance varies according to the issues and the decision-makers. It is in this relative sense that Saudi Arabia may be said to have an Islamic policy. But it must be added that this does not mean that the Islamic dimension is as strong as the Saudis say it is. There are times when Islamic values enter into the formulation of policies because decision-makers believe that they are important, as in the case of Palestine, but even in these instances Islam is not the only factor that counts. In the sense that Islam coincides with, and does not contradict, other pragmatic considerations, it reinforces narrow self-interests; as a reinforcer, Islam adds a reason for devising a policy and does not merely justify other reasons. But by far Islam has been more important in the implementation of Saudi policies – that is, in legitimating them by expressing them in terms attractive to their own audiences abroad. In this, it is clear that Islam does play a role

in Saudi foreign policy, but in the final analysis the overriding purpose
of that policy is to preserve the Saudi regime and Saudi independence.

Notes

1. Sir John Wilton, 'On the World Scene Saudis Promote the Interests of Islam', .
    The Times, Special Supplement on Saudi Arabia, 30 June 1982.
2. Confidential letter No. S-13, Shakespear to Cox, 4 January 1915, India Office
    Records, R/15/5/25.
3. See Jacob Goldberg, 'The 1913 Saudi Occupation of Hasa Reconsidered', *Middle
    Eastern Studies*, 18 (1982), 21–9.
4. Iraq (British Administration), Office of the Civil Commissioner, *Report on Najd
    Mission, 1917–1918* (Baghdad, Government Press, 1918), p. 26.
5. When such expressions are used in this chapter, it is by way of a shorthand.
    'Islam' is what the Saudis say it is and its 'role' is the way they use it.
6. An American official, writing in 1931, gave some idea of why the Saudis would
    be concerned. 'The obstacle to [the] initiation of relations really lies with HM
    King Fuad who is bent on asserting his primacy among Moslem rulers and who
    cherishes a resentment towards Ibn Saud for that ruler's independence and failure
    to show any indication of accepting the role to which King Fuad aspires.' Con-
    fidential Despatch No. 67, Jardine (Cairo) to Secretary of State, 18 February 1931,
    US National Archives (hereafter, NA), 890F.404/3.
7. D. C. Watt, 'The Foreign Policy of Ibn Saud, 1936–39', *Royal Central Asian
    Journal*, 50 (1963), 156.
8. I am grateful to J. P. Bannerman for bringing these points about the relation-
    ship with the Soviet Union to my attention. I am also grateful to Dr Joseph
    Kostiner for his valuable comments generally on the draft of this chapter.
9. *Palestine Post*, 17 October 1935, as transmitted in report of Brent (Jerusalem)
    to Secretary of State, 15 November 1935, NA, 890F.001 IBN SAUD/19.
10. See Secret Airgram No. 53, Childs (Jidda) to Secretary of State, 10 March 1944,
    NA, 890B.00/3-1047; and Secret Airgram No. 544, Tuck (Cairo) to Secretary
    of State, 6 October 1944, NA, 890B.00/1-2245.
11. Letter No. 17/9/1/278, Shaykh Yusif Yassin (Saudi Deputy Foreign Minister)
    to Ahmad Maher Pasha (Egyptian Prime Minister and Head of Preliminary Com-
    mittee to Pan Arab Conference of 1945), 19 Muharram 1364 (3 January 1945),
    Enclosure No. 2 to Despatch No. 570 from Cairo legation to Secretary of State,
    17 February 1945, NA, 890B.00/2-1745.
12. Secret telegram No. 660, Childs to Secretary of State, 14 November 1949, NA,
    890B.00/11-1449; and Secret Despatch No. 245, Childs to Secretary of State,
    6 December 1949, NA, 890B.00/12-649.
13. Secret Despatch No. 79, Stabler (Amman) to Secretary of State, 28 July 1949,
    NA, 890B.00/7-2849.
14. He believed that 'Jews had been hostile to Arabs from [the] time of Prophet
    Mohamed to [the] present.' Reported in Strictly Confidential Telegram No. 723,
    Kirk (Jidda) to Secretary of State, 17 April 1943, NA, 890F.00/81. And he is
    reported as saying, 'Whether we die in the Hijaz or Najd, we shall be raised in
    Palestine'. See *al-Misri* (Cairo), 21 January 1946.
15. For example, in a letter to Truman he wrote that '[the Jews'] ambitions [*atma'hum*]
    are not limited to Palestine alone but include the neighbouring Arab countries
    and even places in our sacred country'. 'Abd al-'Aziz to Truman, 20 Dhu'l-Qi'da
    1356 (15 October 1946), NA, 867N.01/10-1546.

16. Quoted in al-Jazairi, 'Saudi Arabia: A Diplomatic History, 1924–64' (unpublished Ph.D. thesis, University of Utah, 1971), p. 80.

17. See 'Abd al-Nasir's comments reproduced in *al-Tadamun al-islami*, No. 3 (Beirut, Dar al-Abhath li-Nashr, 1966), for example p. 53.

18. 'Abdullah M. Sindi, 'King Faisal and Pan Islamism', in Willard A. Beling (ed.), *King Faisal and the Modernisation of Saudi Arabia* (London, Croom Helm, 1980), p. 192.

19. See any number of his speeches in *Khutab al-malik Faysal ibn 'Abd al-'Aziz fi wufud al-hujjaj al-muslimin, 1384–1390* (Beirut, Dar al-Kitab al-Jadid, n.d.).

20. As an indicator of the evolution of Syrian attitudes, Syria participated for the first time in an Islamic foreign ministers' conference in Jidda in 1972.

21. Shirin Tahir-Kheli and William O. Staudenmaier, 'The Saudi–Pakistan Military Relationship: Implications for US Policy', *Orbis*, 26 (1982), 162.

22. *The Jordan Times*, 23 May 1982. That the Saudis feel bruised by such accusations can be gauged by the extensiveness of the media attacks on Qadhafi recently. As one example, see *al-Madina*, 12 Sha'ban 1402 (4 June 1982).

23. *Neues Deutschland*, 11 January 1980; see also *al-Hawadith*, 3 March 1979.

24. Dev Murarka, 'Saudi Arabia and the Soviet Union: A Shadowy Relationship', unpublished paper delivered at the Symposium on State, Economy and Power in Saudi Arabia, University of Exeter, 4–7 July 1980, pp. 6–7.

25. Interview with Secretariat officials, OIC, Jidda, 14–21 May 1982.

26. This figure, like the ones to follow (unless otherwise qualified), has been found in the Saudi media.

27. Islamic Development Bank, *Sixth Annual Report, 1401 A. H. (1980–81)* (Jidda, 1982), p. 101.

28. The Saudi Fund for Development, *Annual Report, VI (May 1979–May 1980)* (Riyadh, 1980), p. 7. For the period March 1975 to July 1976, 52 per cent of Fund loans went to Asia, 45 per cent to Africa and 3 per cent to other continents. The largest loans went to India, Bangladesh, Indonesia, and Malaysia. See André Simmons, *Arab Foreign Aid* (London and Toronto, Associated University Presses, 1981), p. 63.

29. *The Muslim World League Journal*, 9, No. 6 (Jumad al-Thaniya 1402 or April 1982), p. 25.

30. *Ibid.*, p. 19.

31. *Al-Jazira*, 25 Rajab 1401 (29 May 1981). By way of a very rough comparison, $1,722.1 million was disbursed in aid in 1978 and approximately $2,121 million (7,000 million Saudi riyals) was budgeted for foreign aid in 1979–80. For the first figure, see United Nations Conference on Trade and Development, *Handbook of International Trade and Development Statistics, Supplement 1980* (New York, 1980), p. 321; for the second, see Saudi Ministry of Finance and National Economy, Central Department of Statistics, *Statistical Yearbook*, 16 (Riyadh, 1400 or 1980), p. 444.

32. UN Conference on Trade and Development, *Financial Solidarity for Development; Effects and Institutions of the Members of the OPEC, 1973–1976 Review* (New York, 1979), p. 62; Organization for Economic Cooperation and Development, *Development Cooperation, 1981 Review* (Paris, November 1981), p. 110.

33. From 1973–6, 'over 80 per cent of [Saudi aid] was granted to the countries directly engaged in confrontation with Israel, namely Jordan, Egypt, and Syria'. Simmons, *Arab Foreign Aid*, p. 60.

34. In the confrontational era with 'Abd al-Nasir the Saudis tended to emphasize the superiority of Islam to Arabism, but in the 1970s they mostly spoke of Islamic solidarity as a 'complement' (*makamal*) to Arab solidarity. For example, see interview with King Khalid in *al-Mussawar*, 16 Rajab 1395 (25 July 1975).

4 Libyan Loneliness in Facing the World: The Challenge of Islam?

B. SCARCIA AMORETTI

To raise the question of the influence of Islam in Libyan policy, and particularly in foreign policy, poses two levels of problem: the first is concerned primarily with Islam's role in motivating political attitudes and decisions; and the second is related to the effectiveness of Islam in the implementation of policies.

Western public opinion, perceiving Islam as an important factor in Libyan policy, accepts an image of the Libyan regime marked by fanaticism and contradictions. On the other hand, when the role of Islam is denied, Libya is still presented as a dangerous country where religion is manipulated merely to justify extreme radicalism and cynical interests.[1] Both approaches take as a point of departure a preconceived notion of Islam, which is not based on a rigorous analysis of Libyan political trends, which in turn makes the identification of values and ideals, and whether these are Islamic, nationalist or society-based, a questionable exercise.

This analysis aims at a more pragmatic approach, even if it is concerned not so much with the foreign policy of the Jamahiriya as with the ideological journey which underlines such a policy. Naturally, one must take into account the fact that Islam, like any other ideological factor, lends reason, pretext and language to certain political operations, but it only determines them to a limited extent. Nevertheless, a dynamic interaction does occur: the invocation of religion as an ideology does affect individual and social patterns, and these patterns in turn emphasize and give credence to the principles of religion. That such interaction is much more evident in the Islamic world in relation to the specificity of Islam, which is often considered as a total life system (*al-nizam al-shamil*), integrating state and church (*din wa dawla*), does not substantially modify the terms of the problem.

The recurrence of certain themes in the ideology through which the

Libyan regime endeavours to explain its foreign policy is more than evident in the Libyan press which represents more or less the official point of view.[2] While Qadhafi is obviously the compulsory reference point, nevertheless it would be a little excessive to consider him the only one in charge of all Libya's ideological elaboration. Even though one considers Qadhafi, his speeches and the Green Book as the primary source for any research on the influence of Islam on Libya's foreign policy, the analysis should extend to the currents which the Libyan press has made and is making about the Third International Theory.

Formally, there is no contradiction between what Qadhafi declares and what the press states. But many points, especially in relation to Islam, are emphasized, underlined, elaborated so as to suggest some explanatory guidelines to Qadhafi's theories which are not always immediately clear. The resultant impression which emerges is richer, more articulate, and not simply as one-dimensional as it would appear from a mere reading of the Green Book. On the other hand – and this is something that has to be emphasized, if only for methodological purposes – this is the accepted method of inquiry when working with Islamic theorizations. In fact, political, as well as theological and philosophical, divergencies in Islam have always been expressed through a codified mechanism, namely that of exegesis. Starting from the same presuppositions, verifying itself on the same texts, using the same language, exegesis allows the expressions of theoretical differences, the proposal for modifications in cultural and political models, and the support for innovations in relation to tradition. It is still largely used and it is absolutely necessary to take it into account if one wishes to decodify the political and ideological range of Islam. But at the same time, it is also true that the process of acculturation undergone by all Muslim intellectuals and theoreticians, Qadhafi included, has naturally created a gap in relation to their own peculiar forms and categories of expression.

When questions about international politics are dealt with in Libya, the first point which stands out is the demonization of the West and above all of the USA, while the Soviet Union, as a state, is considered 'a friendly country ... from which to take weapons and not ideas'.[3] Therefore the anti-communism which is a major theme in domestic propaganda does not seem to play any direct role in international choices. Anti-communism intervenes only on an ideological level, when Islam is defined as a medium and necessarily successful path 'between atheistic communism and materialistic capitalism', both of which have failed.[4] The idea is not exclusive to Libyan theorization. But in Libyan attitudes there seems to be something more explicit, in which overcoming the

actual bipolarism dominating the international scene is presented as a
necessary religious duty, in the sense that 'Islam is meant to protect
all the world',[5] and as such constitutes 'the crowning element in the
human effort for achieving social justice'.[6]

In terms of Libyan images of the West, some cases are usually emphasized to highlight Libyan attitudinal antipathy to Western policies. The
emphasis on such cases is rarely matched by accurate information or
by thorough analysis. Therefore, from the analysis point of view, it is
considered simply as information on, or evidence of, the role that Libya
intends to play internationally. Thus, setting aside for the time being
the Palestinian question, whose importance in the elaboration of Libyan
ideology is so fundamental that it must be dealt with separately, the
cases referred to are, broadly speaking, divided into two categories. The
first includes the activities of liberation movements in countries from
El Salvador to Granada. These movements, however, are not all considered on the same plane. The ones that seem to be considered by
the Libyans as the most important are those which represent a precise
demand for national self-determination (Polisario, Eritrea), which itself
is translated into concrete political proposals (autonomy, independence,
sovereign state, change of regime, etc.). Yet this is not what the Libyan
press focusses its attention on. What makes these movements more
worthy of attention is the fact that the majority of their militants profess
Islam. Their fight against 'imperialism' and their other demands are
of special significance because Islam constitutes more than a secondary
component in their political programme.

The case of the Muslim rebellion in the Philippines is illuminating
in its definition of Libyan aims. Libya sees itself as an important factor
in the 'struggle between Islamic minorities and dominant powers (e.g.
Philippines)'. What is meant by this is not only the justification for
Libya's help to the Muslim revolutionaries, but also the role played
by Qadhafi in the negotiations between the government of the Philippines and its Muslim minority.[7] Consequently, in the ideological prism
of Qadhafi and his collaborators, the struggle for national liberation
becomes fundamental when it aims at a rejection of Western values and
at an affirmation of the revolutionary potential in Islam.

Complementary to the first category of cases mentioned so far is the
second which includes the countries in which Libya is interested because
of their geographical proximity. The obvious candidates are the neighbouring Arab states of Egypt and Tunisia, and some African states which
are vital for Libya, such as Chad and Sudan. Apart from the strategic
significance of these states to Libya, there are furthermore ideological

motivations that govern Libyan attitudes to these states. These motivations are manifested usually in the form of appeals to Arab brotherhood, but when Arabism becomes problematic, as in the cases of Sudan and Chad particularly, it is in the name of the common adherence to Islam that Libyan claims and interferences are legitimized.

In fact Islam is a constant which appears regularly in the field of foreign policy. It was under the banner of 'Islamic solidarity' that Qadhafi's Libya adopted a pan-Arab policy. In one of his first speeches after the revolution (14 October 1969), Qadhafi expressed in religious terms his reaction to the Arab defeat of June 1967. Mentioning the fire at al-Aqsa Mosque he said that the Arab people were shaken, as the mosque represented the weight of Islam, and the birthplace of the Islamic call directed to all the world. Very similar are the conclusions of the communiqué delivered by the Permanent Secretary of the Congress of the Arab People (December 1980) about the Iran–Iraq war:

The outbreak of this war has no acceptable motivation and it is in full contradiction with our national interests . . . The military forces of the two countries, the economies of the two peoples, their petrol resources are destroyed in a mad and tremendous way. The Arab nation has lost a part of the potential which was necessary to the struggle for its liberation, its progress, and its welfare. Moreover the Arab nation has lost one of its most important allies, the Islamic revolution of Iran . . .[8]

Libya's emphasis on Islam could be explained by a reference to the Qur'anic phrase: '. . . If they ask your help for religion's affairs it is your duty to help them . . .' (Qur'an, VIII, 72). Or it could be explained in terms of historical continuity and implementation of Senussi expansionism which itself was based on Islamic claims. Yet neither explanation is relevant to contemporary Libyan foreign policy. For Libya, through the Third International Theory, universalism is directly connected with militancy, and the ecumenical perspective of Islam, in the Libyan version, assumes a militant dimension.

The vigorous pursuit of a militant universalistic Islam was naturally based on, and in a sense extended from, Libya's domestic political and social experience. The major domestic experiment was the effort to liquidate all the residual left-overs of colonialism; a liquidation which became concrete with the sanctioning, on 2 March 1977, of the Jamahiriya. This event was described by a representative of the regime as '. . . the birth of the world's first *jamahiriya* and the opening of a new era in mankind's history, the era of the masses'.[9] From the very beginning, then, the Jamahiriya was not conceived only as an experiment in national realization. For in itself the export of Islam does not contain anything exceptional considering that universalism belongs to all the theories which claim to be revolutionary. However, since Qadhafi seems to admit to placing himself in the path of Islam ('These achievements are not to be taken as standard. They are a blessing from God which He endowed upon us'),[10] the establishment of the Jamahiriya takes on another implication. It is no longer a matter of mere exporting of a theory as much as the activation of a mechanism which would involve the largest possible number of institutions, individuals, nations, peoples, for the purpose of putting such a theory into practice.

Similar considerations are to be found in the ideological prescriptions of the Islamic Republic of Iran. The aspirations of universality as well as militancy are nourished by Iran's ideologists:

The ideal society of Islam is called the *umma*. Taking the place of all the similar concepts which in different languages and cultures designated a human agglomeration or a society such as 'society', 'nation', 'race', 'people', 'tribe', 'clan', etc., is the single word *umma*, a word imbued with progressive spirit and implying a dynamic, committed and ideological social vision ... Islam by choosing the word *umma* has made intellectual responsibility and shared movements toward a common goal the basis of its social philosophy.[11]

Not only that. At the time when in Libya it is being stated that 'a popular revolution such as the Libyan experience must take place', it is interesting to make a comparison with the Iranian ideologists in relation to the meaning of the terms *popular* and *people*:

The word 'people' has a profound meaning and distinct significance in Islam. It is only the people as a whole who are the representative of God and His 'family'. The Qur'an begins in the name of God and ends in the name of the people ... The word does not denote a mere collection of individuals. On the contrary, it has a sense of 'society' as opposed to 'individuals' ...[12]

It is certainly not claimed here that there is direct interdependence between the Libyan and Iranian ideologists. But it should nevertheless be underlined that while one postulates the necessity of revolution (the Iranian) and the other claims to realize it (Qadhafi), the ideal points of reference are very similar and in both cases Islam is needed to express the universality of their messages. Thus, despite the undoubted peculiarities of the Libyan situation and the acknowledgement of the exceptional personality of the Libyan leader, Libya is not a case on its own.

A further important factor underlying the proposal of universality in the Third International Theory is the role that Libya and its leader see for themselves in the Arab world. It is well known that Arab unity as expounded by 'Abd al-Nasir was part of the heritage which nourished the revolution of the Libyan officers from the very beginning. And indeed, the Nasirist inspiration has never been denied either by the regime or by Qadhafi himself. On the contrary, Qadhafi has effected a recovery of Nasirism in Islamic terms, especially in the context of the debate on the nature of the new Libyan republic. This attitude is as ideological as it is tactical. The document which announced officially on 17 April 1971 the federation between Libya, Egypt and Syria contained a clear reference to Islam when it stated that the federation would adopt the *shari'a* as the principal source for its law-making. And indeed Libya's stress on Islam became more pronounced when Sadat himself began to make use of Islamic propaganda in order to contest 'Abd al-Nasir's policies, especially in the field of international affairs. In this, Qadhafi, who has consistently claimed to be the true interpreter of the classical theory of pan-Arabism, insisted that the Arab dimension of Nasirism is linked to the relation between Islam and Arabism – a formula espoused by many Arab nationalist intellectuals who contend that it is practically impossible to isolate Arabism from Islam, given the pre-eminence which the Arab element has traditionally had in Islamic civilization. The Libyans see their revolution as operating within the same aims: 'it expelled colonial powers, liberated and reconstructed the land as well as the people'. And this was because it upheld Arabism and Islam. Since 'the Libyan people waged their most violent battles in the name of the Arab and Islamic heritage', for the purpose 'of Arab and Islamic ideals, it is not to be wondered at that Libya has become a fortress for the defence of Islam and Arab nationalism'.[13]

Qadhafi's notion of the ultimate goal of Arab nationalism, namely Arab unity, is different from the interpretation held by other Arab leaderships, and was demonstrated by his attitude towards the Arab summit held in Fez in September 1982, in which he accused the other Arab countries not only of pursuing a failed policy but also of committing treason against the Arab cause.[14] To Qadhafi, Arab unity is an essential condition for the qualitative improvement of the nationalist and anti-imperialist revolutionary struggle. However, if the possibility of the achievement of Arab unity is retarded by 'reactionary' moves, such as the Camp David accords, then Arab unity becomes an end and not a means to advance the revolutionary process enunciated in Qadhafi's theory. Thus, the various forms of federation which, in many ways, Libya has solicited and continues to solicit with neighbouring countries, and within the 'Arab motherland' (*al-watan al-'arabi*) are not always directly related to the objective of Arab unity. They have tactical connotations, that constitute in many instances a response to needs. One must wonder, therefore, to what extent a theoretical or ideological analysis is involved when the Libyans address themselves to the question of relations with Egypt; when they engineer a mini-invasion of Tunisia; when they try to destabilize Sudan, or when they endeavour to establish a military presence in Chad.

Even the shift from a pre-eminently Arab orientation in the early and mid-1970s to an African orientation in the late 1970s did not show a real change of course either on an ideological level or on the political plane. It was undoubtedly a tactical adjustment necessitated by the difficult isolation which was imposed on Libya by the Arab countries. Moreover, the Libyans needed to ensure the supply of some raw materials and to keep tabs on situations which could become dangerous for Libyan national security.

The Libyans' increasing emphasis on the African perspective, rather than on the concept and practice of pan-Arabism, can also be explained by the existence of domestic resistance to the regime for the latter's insistence on Arab solidarity. Therefore, the regime's answer to internal resistance consisted in widening the horizons within which Libya intended to work. This was done by broadening the axes of Libya's political initiative outside the Arab world. This shift has been explained by the Libyan leadership in Islamic terminology: 'faithfulness is due not only to the principles of Arabism and Arab solidarity',[15] but also to Islam and to the Islamic world in its globalism. The result is that, especially after 1977–8, Libya's motto of Arab unity does not seem to include a concrete political project, functional to its realization. Arab unity continues to play a role in Libyan propaganda, but politically it has become something more elusive, more theoretical and more abstract. Simultaneously, African concerns have gained in importance, and in this the Islamic factor, not having to compete with pan-Arabism, became ideologically more coherent.

It would be a mistake, nevertheless, to interpret Qadhafi's designs simply in a pan-Islamic sense. His ambitions are, in many ways, much larger, even though the Islamic world, especially in its African dimension, seems to be replacing the Arab 'motherland' as the primary target for Libya's ideological, political and economic intervention. The goals of the Third International Theory reach beyond what traditionally and historically has been called pan-Islamism.[16] In fact, Libyan ideology does not necessarily relate to the tradition of the great Arab and Islamic movements of the beginning of the century. It concentrates on *humanism* and *naturalism* as essential factors in the development of human society.

Formally its dependence on Islam, ideal as it may be, is not expressed; similarly, the sources to which Qadhafi refers are not made explicit. The demonstration that Libyan ideology is compatible with Islam, better still, that it derives from Islam, has been the domain of the official exegesis. Such a demonstration, therefore, has internal rather than international aims. It is used to gather around the regime popular consensus; it is used to mobilize the masses, to enlist the participation in political activity of even those who are factually excluded from the political process. However, in the foreign policy field, the emphasis on humanism, which is much more readily understood universally than Islam itself, helps Islam to be projected on the global plane as the highest historical achievement of humanity and the essential matrix of all the history of humanity.[17]

Rather than an abstract discussion about the root of Qadhafi's Islam, be it Qur'anic (i.e. the rejection of the other three roots of the *shari'a* which, with the Qur'an, form the bases of the law which the believer is obliged to observe in so far as principles and behaviour are concerned), or be it instead a particular version of the various modernisms which, for more than a century, have marked the phases of 'Islamic renaissance' following the colonial impact on the Muslim peoples, it is worth our while to stop and discuss the specific use that Qadhafi makes of his sources of inspiration. It is certainly not new that Qadhafi has been influenced both by Rousseau and by Ibn Khaldun. In both he finds a vision of history that he can define as *naturalistic*, which would allow him to place man with his social aspirations at the centre of the historical process. One can, with some approximation, claim that his is a Rousseauian reading of Ibn Khaldun. The evolutionary stages which Ibn Khaldun posits suggest to Qadhafi a language that still largely corresponds to the structuring of the actual Libyan society: family, tribe and people. If this evolution is a part of the divine project for humanity, it can also be expressed, analysed and viewed in natural, i.e. human, terms. Islam is therefore at the basis of Qadhafi's ideological concepts, but it does not interfere in their formulation.

There is, of course, another step that must be considered: it concerns the revolutionary potential of Islam. The following observations of a progressive Egyptian Muslim who is not likely to be among Qadhafi's sympathizers are the best comments on this question. In fact his position is particularly suitable for explaining in what sense a Muslim believer can find in Islam a revolutionary incentive. It is very true that, generally speaking,

People in the Third World are still religious. They still have a religious spirit. Religion is still a source of energy. In such a case where masses are illiterate in its majority, an ideology and social science analysis may be a little bit difficult for them to understand and may take a long time. While a religious revolutionary interpretation is nearer to their heart and channels this source of latent energy in the revolution, the masses can move in the name of God. Nothing in this is similar to ancient religion's war. The masses in their simplicity and sincerity know very well their enemies. Religion in its simplicity as a revolutionary motivation is the nearest revolutionary education for the masses . . .[18]

But it is even more true that Islam can be considered particularly fit to be a revolutionary movement, because

A religion without priesthood and a sacerdotal body has more chances to be a revolutionary religion. All humans will be priests. There is one World, one action, one life. God spoke for the benefit of Man. Revolution came to give Man a system for his life and for his relation with others. The only world is this world where Man exists. The spiritual is the temporal and the temporal is the spiritual. The sacred is the profane and the profane is sacred . . .[19]

The principles of universalism, of humanism, of adherence to nature are very evident. It is equally evident that, if we start from such premises, the most serious contradictions are to be found where these similar principles are used for different purposes. Certainly it is not Khumayni's Iran that can be seen as a competitor since, to a certain extent, it has strengthened the Libyan position in the Islamic world, by demonstrating that utopia can have a chance to achieve a concrete realization. On the contrary, the most dangerous enemy is, therefore, Saudi Arabia, which represents the opposite pole to Libyan policy. Both regimes start from the assumption that Islam has to be rebuilt in its primary purity, both boast Islam's universalism, but they arrive at very different conclusions, apart from the implicit affirmation of the hegemonic role that they suppose themselves to play when they propose their concepts. The terms 'progressive' and 'reactionary' are inadequate for the definition of such concepts, and consequently explain very little in a concrete way. It is more useful to analyse the divergent concepts of Islam by looking at the activities and behaviour of both regimes (Libya and Saudi Arabia) in specific situations.

Nothing is more emblematic than the Palestinian question. The Palestinian question sums up all the elements that have been considered up to now. First of all, from the perspective of Arabism, the Palestinian people have been depicted as the victims of one of the most cynical colonial operations of history, and since the Palestinians are considered to belong to the Arab nation, therefore it follows that all the Arab world has undergone such violence. Moreover, in Arab perceptions, inserting in the Arab 'homeland' an alien presence, useful to the West, in order to maintain the West's grasp on the whole area, is seen simply as the persistence of a colonial presence and as a continuous challenge against the Arab world with the purpose of denying its identity, its cultural and historical specificity. These words are not casual. In fact these definitions are nothing more than the paraphrasing of what Arab nationalism has been stating for many years.

Apart from this essentially nationalistic interpretation of the Palestinian problem there is another interpretation. Here, it is Islam, rather than Arabism, which is taken as the important element of analysis. The presence of Israel's Zionism has not only violated and offended Arabism; Islam also, as a whole, has been hurt. To hand over Jerusalem means to give up a necessary defence of Islam's integrity, not only in political terms, but also, and above all, ideally and culturally. This is the Saudi thesis. Through it Saudi Arabia obtains an acknowledgement of its role as the guarantor of Islam, as the pillar of orthodoxy, as the unquestionable authority in matters of religious purity; all things that Saudi Arabia would not easily obtain simply through her prerogative as the guardian of the holy places, which in itself is undermined by her restricted Wahhabi beliefs. It is thus Palestine that opens for Saudi Arabia the possibility of assuming the leadership in the Islamic world and representing it externally. This is probably why so many Palestinian organizations deal with Saudi Arabia, even though this could damage their credibility among their militants.

Libya's attitude is very different. While Islam intervenes in the motivation of almost all Libya's positions in foreign policy, in relation to the Palestine question Islam is not a fundamental factor. The nationalistic and Arab aspects of the problem clearly prevail over the Islamic. This fact is very explicit, especially after the Camp David agreements:

The question does not deal any more with the problem of independence or of non-independence; it is now a matter of being or not being at all ... The Arab existence today is threatened in all the Arab motherland by American bases and by American protection which make up a strategic umbrella for zionist advancement ...[20]

To a certain extent, we can assume that, in relation to the Palestinian question, the normal ideological *démarche* which brings Arabism inside Islam seems to be overturned as the omnicomprehensive element of all historical processes. One of Qadhafi's most important collaborators expresses himself thus with regard to Sadat's policy towards Israel:

The Arab nation has a history marked by courage. It has struggled through many battles in the name of humanity. I challenge any nation to demonstrate that it has given to humanity even a small part of what the Arab nation has presented. We have strategic means, as well as human and economic means. Behind us we have the Islamic nation. When I visited Turkey, I was welcomed by forty-five thousand Turkish students whom I met, calling for '*jihad! jihad!*' They presented me a demand. They asked why, since every year one million Muslims go on a pilgrimage to Mecca, the learned men of Islam don't take the decision of cancelling the pilgrimage and make all these people go to Palestine. This would be the real pilgrimage which would complete the visit to the holy places of Islam ... We have behind us seven hundred million Muslims. We have behind us the socialist forces. But, first of all, we have our own means ... We are the nation of the peace. We greet each other in the name of peace (*Salam 'alaykum*) ...[21]

Here there is a kind of radicalism which does not always coincide with the wishes of the Palestinians and, in a certain way, excludes the consideration of any political design aimed at the achievement of the recognition of the Palestinians' rights. There is no evolution in the Libyan attitude, whatever the facts may be, as it has recently been shown. This is to say that revolutionary coherence, the Nasirist heritage, the recovery of identity are considered in relation to the level of radicalism expressed on the Palestinian question.[22] All this is linked with the other aspects of Libyan foreign policy through the different meanings that the term anti-imperialism can acquire. Solidarity in the struggle for Palestine is obviously the most unambiguous action of anti-imperialism. But it is not only a matter of defeating the major enemy, the USA, and the most faithful executor of their policy, Israel. The question is rather that of considering the West as a unitarian block which historically has always upheld the USA on this point. Colonialism, in Libyan perceptions and calculations, not only exists but it is also latent in Western civilization as such. This is in any case embodied in the universalistic and Islamic presuppositions of the Libyan concepts analysed above. Within this context, the problem of colonialism and imperialism in their actual manifestation (Israel) and the possibility of their continuous rebirth can have only a global solution: a solution which may be effective for everybody and in which everyone is involved.

It is because of this that Libya's foreign policy towards Africa has been seen as a systematic attempt at opposition to Israel's influence in the area. In this way, Libya's activity in Africa is given an acceptable motivation.[23] So Libyan help to Uganda, or to Gabon, especially after the conversion to Islam of its president, could be an example of the pre-eminence of the Palestinian cause in Qadhafi's strategy.[24] But, while admitting that 'our policy has good results: Israel is practically away from Africa', Qadhafi has said also that 'it would be absurd to speak for Africa in terms of marketing'. And he added: 'we have always told the Africans that we too are Africans. If it is understandable that the states which have no relations with Israel and which support the Arab cause get more chances to be sustained by us ... we don't think that this is a way which leads us to Palestine. Even though we could eliminate all Israeli embassies in Africa, where they actually exist, even if all the world would refuse to recognize Israel, still Israel would continue to exist.'[25]

Once again it is probably the connection between the utopia of universalistic Islamic aspirations and practical exigencies that best elucidates Libyan attitudes. An interesting case is that of Libya's policy towards Christian, yet progressive, Ethiopia. Here, Libya needs to create a network of ties with so-called progressive countries in order to contain the pressures put on it by its neighbours, particularly Egypt. Similarly, it could be argued that the main cause for Libya taking the side of the Polisario front rests in its necessary opposition to Morocco's aspiration for leadership of the African Muslims and its craving for influence, along with friendly Algeria, in the Sahara region.[26] Within the context of this sensitivity to Libyan 'interests', Libya has often, for example, shown preference to African states with a Christian population *vis-à-vis* Muslim African states, if these countries happened to be the object of competition for influence between Libya and conservative rich Islamic countries, particularly Saudi Arabia, Kuwait and the other Gulf emirates.[27] This kind of 'Islamic pragmatism' on the part of Libyan foreign policy towards Africa was pursued more vigorously after the failure of various Libyan-inspired federations within the Arab world. With their attention turned towards Africa, the Libyan leaders now speak of special relations with African states, which might signify an intention to create an 'Islamic Federation' in the sub-Sahara region under Libya's political hegemony.[28] The term 'Islamic', in this context, however, has no specific significance, being possibly used as an alternative to 'Arabic'.

In order to ascertain the Islamic factor in Libya's policy in this area of the world, it is more significant to take into account Libya's cultural activities than its economic or diplomatic agreements, and this both on a multilateral and on a bilateral level of relations. Libya's regime has committed itself to the export of Islamic culture: Qur'anic schools have been created; mosques have been built; teachers of Arabic and of Islamic history have been recruited; institutes of Islamic studies are planned. Mauritania, Nigeria, Mali, and many other African states have accepted this kind of cultural expansionism. And Libya, unlike, say, Saudi Arabia, has usually accompanied this kind of activity with intense propaganda, and it is this vigorous public relations exercise that gives rise to the suspicion that Libya's cultural activities in Africa are meant to achieve more than mere 'solidarity' with the respective countries.[29]

Whether Libya's foreign policy, through an examination of the way it is implemented, could be called one of *realpolitik*, or one of precise adherence to Islamic ideology, is not of great importance. What is evident is that Libya pursues a policy which can be called in certain respects 'Islamic', but that this Islamic element is simply one pillar, which, along with Arabism, Africanism, and a pragmatic assessment of Libya's political and strategic interests, motivates and constrains the conduct of Libya's foreign policy.

Notes

1. F. Tana, 'Il sogno dell'unità araba e le mire espansionistiche: il caso della Libia. La politica estera', *Politica Internazionale*, 6 (1981), 68–76.
2. The papers that were consulted were: the weekly *al-Zahaf al-Akhdar* (Italian, English, and Arabic version), 1980–81; *al-Fajr al-Jadid*, 1981; *al-Talib*, 1980–82; a certain number of issues of *al-Thaqafa al-Jadida*, and also of *al-Jamahiriya*, 1980–2.
3. M. Bianco, *Kadhafi, messager du désert* (Paris, Stock, 1974), pp. 253ff, and M. Vignolo, *Gheddafi: Islam, petrolio e utopia* (Milan, Rizzoli, 1982), p. 117.
4. J. Wright, *Libya: A Modern History* (London, Croom Helm, 1982), p. 183.
5. Bianco, *Kadhafi*, p. 260.
6. M. Qadhafi, *The Battle of Destiny* (London, Kalahari Publications, 1976), pp. 18–19.
7. M. el-Shahat, *Libya Begins the Era of the Jamahiriyat* (Rome, 1978) pp. 38 and 22.
8. R. Otayek, 'La Libye révolutionnaire au sud du Sahara', *Maghreb-Machrek*, 94 (1981), 7.
9. El-Shahat, *Libya Begins*, p. 11.
10. Qadhafi's speech at the final sitting of the People's General Congress in its second session, November 1976.
11. 'Ali Shari'ati, 'The Ideal Society: the Umma', *On the Sociology of Islam* (Berkeley, 1979), p. 119.
12. *Idem*, 'The Dialectic of Sociology', *On the Sociology of Islam*, p. 117.
13. For this question, the best reference is el-Shahat, *Libya Begins*, particularly pp. 123, 8off.
14. *Le Monde*, 12–13 September 1982.
15. R. H. Dekmejian, 'The Anatomy of Islamic Revival: Legitimacy Crisis, Ethnic Conflict, Search for Islamic Alternatives', *Middle East Journal* (Spring 1978), 1–12; F. Ajami, 'The End of Pan-Arabism', *Foreign Affairs* (Winter 1978–9), 355–73; AA.VV. *La Libye nouvelle: rupture et continuité* (Aix-en-Provence, CRESM, 1975), pp. 110–11.
16. H. Bleuchot and T. Monastiri, 'L'Évolution des institutions politiques 1969–1978', *Annuaire de l'Afrique du Nord*, 16 (1977), 141–87; H. Bleuchot, 'La Politique africaine de la Libye 1969–1978', *Annuaire de l'Afrique du Nord*, 17 (1978), 59–85; F. Constantin and C. Coulon, 'Espace islamique et espace politique', *Annuaire*

de l'Afrique du Nord, 17 (1978), 172–211; the special issue on 'Libye: 1978–1981', *Maghreb-Machrek*, 93 (1981), 5–55.

17. B. Scarcia Amoretti, 'Presupposti ideologici e culturali dell'antimperialismo nell'ideologia libica contemporanea', paper presented to the international meeting *Libia: storia e rivoluzione*, 27–29 January 1981, Rome, Istituto per l'Africa (in press).

18. H. Hanafi, *Religious Dialogue and Revolution* (Cairo, 1977), p. 204.

19. *Ibid.*, p. 208.

20. Qadhafi's speech at a Solidarity Celebration with the Palestinian People, 14 May 1981.

21. Procès légal et national du rénégat Sadate, Tripoli, 5–8 December 1977: discours de 'Abda al-Salam Jallud.

22. Examen et réfutation des deux accords de Camp David émanant des réunions de la 7ème session du Secrétariat du Congrès du Peuple Arabe.

23. Otayek, 'La Libye révolutionnaire', pp. 5–35 (this reference is intended for all that concerns Libya's African policy).

24. Vignolo, *Gheddafi*, pp. 96ff.

25. Bianco, *Kadhafi*, pp. 261–2.

26. Wright, *Libya*, pp. 208ff.

27. Vignolo, *Gheddafi*, pp. 168–171.

28. M. V. Stevovic, 'Le Tchad et autour du Tchad', *Revue de Politique Internationale*, 743 (1981), 25–8; C. Crocker, 'A Libyan Interference in Chad', *State Department Bulletin*, 1981.

29. J. Kraus, 'Islamic Affinities and International Politics in Sub-Saharan Africa', *Current History*, 78, no. 456 (1980), 154–8, 182–4; L. S. Anderson, 'Religion and Politics in Libya', *Journal of Arab Affairs*, 1 (1981), 53–77.

　　In Search of an Identity:
　　　　Islam and Pakistan's Foreign Policy

SHIRIN TAHIR-KHELI

> One lesson I have learnt from the history of Muslims. At
> critical moments in their history, it is Islam that has saved the
> Muslims and not vice-a-versa.　　　　　　　　　　　　　*Iqbal*

This view is certainly corroborated by Pakistan's history since 1971. After nearly a quarter century of frustration, Islamic renaissance has finally touched 'official' Pakistan. This chapter examines a particular facet of this contact: that is, has Islam motivated any aspects of Pakistani foreign policy? If so, what has been the impact of Pakistani foreign policy on the Islamic world? And, finally, how has the Islamic world impinged on Pakistan?

The background

External relations have always been of major importance to Pakistan. The trauma of partition and the unfortunate history of subsequent Indo-Pakistani relations ensured almost an obsession with threats to national security. In search of ways to supplement military capability, the Pakistani elite looked toward the only major source of assistance available at the time – the United States. Even as Pakistan entered into alliance relationships with the West, it regularly expressed a desire to cultivate its Islamic ties, reminding the Muslim world that Pakistan was the only modern state created exclusively in the name of Islam.

These exhortations were more than mere lip service, but they were less than a definite commitment to the evolution of a purely Islamic state. Given the feeling that the first requirement was 'security above all else', in the perception of the elite the Muslim world looked weak and incapable in the 1950s of supplying the wherewithal required for Pakistani defence. Thus, Suhrawardy's comment as prime minister in 1956 that Pakistani cultivation of ties with Islamic countries was difficult because 'zero plus zero still equals zero' has to be taken in the perspective of overall defence needs.

The development of the Western connection did not simply occur by default. Deliberate options were pursued by the Pakistani elite, which was primarily Western in its orientation. Years of exposure to the West was a direct consequence of the British Raj, and the resultant Western socialization of the elite led it to look to the West. Throughout the formative years, Pakistan's political, military, and bureaucratic elite, who constituted the policy-making group, moved the nation in directions that were contrary to the fundamental Islamic ideology that was officially espoused by the state. A two-tier system evolved: a mass culture which was steeped in ethnic and religious traditions; and an elite culture which mimicked the West, at least in its outer trappings.

The exclusively Western orientation of Pakistani foreign policy in the 1950–62 period was promoted to the people as a necessity occasioned not only by threats from Hindu India, but as a means of securing Pakistan from 'the Godless communists'. Thus was Pakistan's identification with anti-Soviet and (to a lesser degree) anti-Chinese alliances projected. This identification was not simply a figment of the elites' imagination. Given their pro-Western proclivities, Pakistani leaders shared prevailing Western antipathy toward communism. During these years, Islam was routinely used by the elite to justify a foreign policy chosen for other reasons.

Disenchantment with the West, particularly the US, set in firmly after the latter's shipment of arms to India in 1962. Ayub Khan, who had been particularly instrumental in forging ties with the US, was deeply stung by the extent of the American support for India following the Sino-Indian clash. At that time, finally, the elite admitted the *raison d'être* of the alliance relationship. In the first real public debate on foreign policy, Foreign Minister Bogra, who had served as prime minister in 1954 when Pakistan signed the defence agreement with the US, said:

When we entered into these pacts ... we did so purely for defensive purposes ... We were in desperate need of arms and equipment and while we are interested in the defence of our region, we were no less interested in boosting the morale of our people. Now with a change in military strategy, the military importance of these pacts has necessarily diminished ... Friends that let us down will no longer be considered our friends.[1]

The balance brought into Pakistani foreign policy after 1962 led to the normalization of relations with the Peoples Republic of China (PRC) and the Soviet Union.[2] Close relations with Islamic countries remained a desired but distant goal. US–Pakistani relations dipped to a low after the imposition of the American arms embargo following the Indo-Pakistani war of 1965. Not until after the election of Richard Nixon to the US presidency and the subsequent Pakistani role in arranging Kissinger's secret trip to Beijing did Islamabad refocus on the American connection.

The rise of Bengali nationalism and its culmination in the Indo-Pakistan war of 1971 was taken by many outside Pakistan to mean that the experiment in Muslim nationalism, epitomized in the idea of Pakistan and the subsequent partitioning of India, had failed. To observers who felt that Jinnah's 'two nation' theory was based on a false premise, the disintegration of Pakistan of 1947 was eminent proof of the fact that twentieth-century nationalism needed more than religion to glue together a nation.

Quite unexpectedly, the loss of East Pakistan did not result in Pakistan embracing a secular philosophy. Rather, a process of closer and ever more deliberate identification with Islam began to take place. This development was in part a consequence of internal Pakistani dynamics. A major impetus, however, came from external events over which Pakistan had little or no control.

Shift in focus

The 'loss' of East Pakistan was traumatic enough an event, but the manner in which the eastern wing separated was of major consequence to the policy-makers of Pakistan. The adverse reaction in the Western world to the army's crackdown on East Pakistan left the image of a Pakistan in shambles. In 1972 began a painful process of international rehabilitation. In the face of isolation from the rest of the 'civilized' world, the Pakistani psyche turned inward.

The mind of [the] Pakistani intellectual has often been agitated by a consideration of the question of our national identity ... But since the traumatic events of 1971 this self-questioning has assumed the proportions of a compelling necessity ... What are the links that bind the people of Pakistan? What is the soul and personality of Pakistan? What is our national identity and our peculiar oneness which makes us a nation apart from other nations?[3]

Zulfikar Ali Bhutto, the new leader of a beaten and truncated Pakistan, understood the new reality of a changed position. It was obvious that Pakistan's interest in South-east Asian affairs had vanished with the formation of Bangladesh. Furthermore, India's powerful position after

1971 substantially raised the costs of any future conflict. While Pakistan could not ignore the Indian 'threat', it had to look elsewhere for a new focus with which to revitalize the country's foreign policy. As summed up by Bhutto:

The severance of our eastern wing by force has significantly altered our geographic focus. This will naturally affect our geo-political perspective ... at the moment, as we stand, it is within the ambit of South and Western Asia. It is here that our primary concern must henceforth lie.[4]

The change in focus to South-west Asia meshed neatly with the resurgence of Islam in the wake of the reassessment of national identity. The rediscovery of Islamic roots offered the Pakistani elite a chance of moving nearer a public that had always remained closer to Islam than had the leadership. Furthermore, the move offered a way out of public outcry against the débâcle of 1971.

Pakistani foreign policy in 1972 emphasized the country's links to the Islamic world. The political leadership and the Foreign Office actively sought an identification of the Pakistani position on the non-recognition of Bangladesh (because of the use of Indian military force and the incarceration of 90,000 Pakistani prisoners of war in India) with that of other Islamic countries. Regular consultations, particularly with the conservative Arab regimes, became part of a new pattern of diplomacy. Disappointment with Western alliances was accompanied with a great deal of frustration at the inability of the P R C to move forcefully in support of Pakistan in the 1971 war.

Much of the distress with past directions of Pakistani foreign policy was the consequence of the fact that, because of its perceptions of particular vulnerability, the Pakistani elite felt the need for dependency beyond the realm of ordinary alliance. Instead, what was desired was a linkage which would 'transcend immediate self-interest because it [was] based not upon a calculation of gain and loss, but a commitment involving deeper moral obligations between the two parties'.[5] Thus, after 1971, the Islamic world offered Pakistan a chance to seek out the 'deeper moral obligations'.

The Islamic connection

The development of a new and vigorous Islamic consciousness after 1973 took place in all countries with substantial Muslim populations, albeit to varying degrees. For Pakistan, Islam offered new opportunities as much as it satisfied old desires.[6] There were a number of ways in which the formulation and execution of Pakistani foreign policy was touched by Islamic resurgence.

In the first place, Islam reinforced the national interest. If the first and most fundamental Pakistani concern remained survival as a nation state, the renewed interest in Islam worldwide made the national commitment toward Islamic values sound insurance. Henceforth, any attack on Pakistan became not simply a clash of rival states, but rather an attack threatening the destruction of the Islamic state, thus drawing in other Islamic powers. Secondly, Islam bestowed an instant ideology on Pakistan. It helped rationalize years of vacillating foreign policy orientations by finding a suitable niche for Pakistan in the world's competing ideologies.

Thirdly, Pakistani foreign policy capitalized on the economic assets of the oil-rich Muslim states by linking these countries to the rest of the Third World, of which Pakistan was a part; a process which 'would complement their individual resources and give them collective strength'.[7] Thus, Pakistan could be useful in adding to the overall strength of the Muslim bloc in return for assistance to shore up its economic and diplomatic position. The Pakistani leadership successfully sold this argument and hammered away at the opportunities which had been opened up because the 'Muslim countries are now so placed as to be able to play a most constructive and rewarding role for cooperation among themselves and with other countries of the Third World'.[8]

Pakistan did not have to compete with India within the Islamic bloc, whereas in the Third World movement, India remained a formidable force, one which Pakistani foreign policy endeavoured to displace. Thus, by clever public relations tactics, Pakistan set out to destroy the myth of Indian non-alignment by citing the Indo-Soviet treaty of 1971 as proof of what Pakistan considered to be near total alignment of India with the Soviet Union. In this venture, Islamabad was greatly assisted by the PRC which had itself worked hard to gain access to the Third World movement, and whose goals in decrying the Indo-Soviet axis paralleled those of Pakistan.

As Pakistani diplomats worked to reduce India's prestige in the Third World movement, they embarked simultaneously on an active campaign to focus the movement's attention on its connections with the Islamic world. Islam's declared principles of concern for the less fortunate, absence of caste system, condemnation of racial bias, and its outward-looking philosophy to engage in a 'struggle for a more equitable world order',[9] were cited. Thus, Pakistani diplomats constantly tried to project their country as a champion of Islamic and Third World causes, and saw Pakistan's political and economic destiny linked to this bloc.[10]

Throughout the 1970s Pakistan achieved considerable success in these endeavours, whereby it used the Islamic links to help gain access to the Third World movement, and the latter to further cement Pakistan's ties to the Islamic world. These ties, along with the Third World connections, were extremely beneficial to Pakistan. For example, they enabled Islamabad successfully to resist Washington's pressure on limiting Pakistan's nuclear programme. It also made it enormously more difficult for the French to renege on their contractual agreement to supply a nuclear reprocessing plant. The French came under heavy US pressure to cancel the deal, but given France's very considerable dependence on Middle East oil and its lucrative commercial interests in the Arab world, the existence of the Pakistani connection with these nations checkmated US pressure for a number of years.

Fourthly, Pakistani diplomacy brought the earlier experience with Pakistan's 'bilateral tri-lateralism', namely good relations bilaterally with each of the the three superpowers, to bear on the cultivation of friendly ties with three important Muslim countries: Saudi Arabia, Iran and Libya. As Islamabad paid homage to Saudi Arabia for being the centre of the Islamic world, and King Faysal as the Keeper of the Faith, the Shah was cultivated as an enlightened monarch and an old friend of Pakistan, while Libya's Colonel Qadhafi was welcomed with a great deal of pomp and ceremony.

Finally, an Islamic summit, the second ever, was called for February 1974 in Lahore, Pakistan, and attended by 37 countries. The meeting was sponsored jointly by Pakistan and Saudi Arabia. Though its immediate goal was the liberation of Jerusalem and Arab lands held by Israel, the agenda was more broadly based and encompassed the role of the Muslim states in global perspective. The Islamic Conference institutionalized Pakistan's role as a key Muslim state. The fact that a Pakistani leader was elected Chairman of the Conference reflected the new-found identity which enabled Islamabad to play a more dynamic role in Islamic affairs than warranted by virtue of its size and economic resources.

The economic dimension

The economic costs of political agitation in 1971 were high. In May, Pakistan was forced to request an extraordinary moratorium on its aid repayments. Then came the war which cost some $200 million in lost military equipment. To make up for these losses, Pakistan spent $115 million on military purchases in 1972, and defence expenditures rose to the highest percentage of the annual GNP–i.e. 6.7 per cent.[11] Pakistan desperately needed to increase its exports in order to underwrite economic reconstruction and military improvement.

In a variety of ways, the Islamic countries of the Persian Gulf and Arabian Peninsula were particularly helpful after 1971. First, they quickly replaced Bangladesh as a market for Pakistani exports. Secondly, after the oil-price increase of 1973, the oil-rich states began to underwrite the cost of economic programmes in Pakistan as they augmented the more traditional sources of assistance. While, in general, the aid was erratic and personal in nature, certain countries such as Saudi Arabia, UAE and Iran did give project assistance, enter into joint ventures (e.g. in fertilizers, polyester, textiles and cement) and make substantial personal donations to offset dwindling foreign exchange reserves and, occasionally, to help defray oil-price increases.[12] Thirdly, Libya and countries of the Gulf and Arabian Peninsula became markets for skilled, semi-skilled and unskilled Pakistani labour. In the mid and late seventies, around 1.2 million Pakistanis in the Gulf and Middle East returned more than $2 billion in annual remittances to Pakistan. This critical sum met the foreign exchange requirements of the country and also helped the government by creating pockets of 'prosperity' in areas which otherwise might have been ripe for political discontent. Fourthly, the Gulf countries became important outlets for Pakistani entrepreneurs whose unhappiness with the early nationalization policies of the Bhutto regime first led them into overseas investment.

Pakistan also actively attempted to create institutional channels for development aid from the Muslim bloc. The establishment of the Islamic Development Bank, whose main function is to participate in providing equity capital in enterprises in Muslim countries, is one such example. In addition, a number of joint-venture financial institutions provide foreign exchange loans or equity for large industrial projects, e.g. the Pak-Kuwait Investment Company, Pak-Libya Holding Company and Pak-Saudi Investment Company.

Islamic revival and impact on foreign policy

The vision of 'socialist' Bhutto playing a role in Islamic forums clashed with the absence of any real programmes to transform Pakistani society into an Islamic state. While the Pakistan People's Party (PPP) had coined the catchy label of 'Islamic socialism' as a means of getting around this dilemma, it was no secret that such PPP stalwarts as Mubashir Hasan, J. A. Rahim and Khurshid Hasan Meer wished to move the country in directions which had little to do with Islam. In 1974, when Pakistan's relations with the Islamic countries were on a firm footing, Bhutto decided to sacrifice the left in his party. While the ostensible reason given was the unhappiness of conservative Arab leaders, such as King Faysal, with the socialist wing of the PPP, Bhutto, at the time, was also trying to get the Americans to lift the arms embargo, and here too the left was a liability. In addition, Bhutto resented the implications that he owed his 1971 victory to the efforts of the aforementioned individuals in organizing the PPP and managing the election programme.

Recognizing that the shift in national focus from the West and the East, manifested respectively by the US and PRC, to the Islamic bloc had greatly aided the credibility and prestige of the right-wing political parties (since they had always espoused what Bhutto discovered only in 1971, i.e. that Pakistan's future lay in its Islamic connection) Bhutto moved to steal the march on his opposition. The 1977 election manifesto, written primarily by Yusef Buch,[13] focussed on Islamic egalitarianism and some highly publicized changes were promised, for example changing the weekly holiday to Friday instead of Sunday. When election returns resulted in a massive anti-Bhutto movement led by the right, the beleaguered prime minister sought to correct his image by prohibiting the use of alcohol and banning nightclubs and gambling, which led one Pakistani leader to remark; 'Now he's lost middle and upper class support!'

Bhutto kept his fences with the Islamic bloc carefully mended. He even accepted Saudi mediation in attempting the resolution of his difficulties with the opposition. It was indeed ironic that Bhutto, who carefully cultivated an image of a Muslim leader and had used his connections with Saudi Arabia and Iran in pressing the Pakistani case for arms in Washington, never managed to identify himself within Pakistan as anything except a 'Muslim of convenience'. His departure, therefore, was followed by even more serious attempts at Islamicization.

Apart from differences in personality and style, there were substantial differences in the Zia regime's emphasis on Islam. Soon after his takeover, Zia admitted that Pakistan was 'created in the name of Islam' and would 'survive only if it sticks to Islam'.[14] The prevailing feeling was that in its pursuit of an Islamic system, the country must develop political, economic and social institutions which reflected the *shari'a*. A genuine shift in these directions was expected to help resolve Pakistan's difficulties by strengthening the system from within and ensuring closeness with the rest of the Islamic world, which, as stated by General Zia in an interview with this author,[15] constituted 'a firm pillar' of Pakistani foreign policy.

Impact of the Iranian revolution

The fall of the Shah had important consequences for Pakistan, not only because of the Iranian monarch's role in guaranteeing Pakistan's economic and military security but also because a militantly Shiʻi regime in Tehran could create mischief within Pakistan. Officially, remarkably little was made by Islamabad of the change in Iran as the government continued to stress the historical ties and good relations traditionally existing between Pakistan and Iran. The Pakistani foreign minister journeyed to Iran and received several audiences with the Ayatollah. Pakistan and Iran jointly announced their withdrawal from CENTO in March 1979, an act which symbolized for Iran a deep displeasure with the 'Great Satan', and for Pakistan a clear recognition that for all practical purposes the alliance was dead anyway.

However, no amount of studied diplomatic niceties could cover the difficulty for Pakistan. Both the Islamic right and the Mujaheddin left in Iran identified Pakistan with the Shah. Consequently, a great deal of verbal abuse was hurled at the country. Khumayni called upon the people of all neighbouring countries to rise up and overthrow their 'tyrannical' regimes and on occasion the Zia government was specifically mentioned by Tehran radio. Protests from Islamabad elicited the response that no one was clearly in charge in Tehran and the government could thus not accept responsibility. The potential for trouble was amply demonstrated when Pakistani crowds, reacting to broadcasts from Tehran citing American CIA collusion in the capture of the Grand Mosque in Mecca in November 1979, burned down the US embassy in Islamabad. Rumour, fed by mischief-making from both the Pakistani left and the right, created an explosive situation for the Zia regime within the country and in the United States.

President Zia has generally been helped domestically by the fact that his own proposals for fulfilling the Islamic aspirations of Pakistan preceded Khumayni's revolution. Yet, the split caused by the divisions between Khumaynism and the conservative Arab regimes, with whom predominantly Sunni Pakistan identifies more closely, means walking a fine line and offending neither side by endeavouring to focus on the larger issues in Islam that cut across secular lines. However, Khumayni's influence with the substantial Shiʻi population in Pakistan carries the potential of creating difficulties for Pakistani proposals to incorporate Islamic principles into the political, economic and social life of the country. For example, when the government proposed the imposition of a mandatory Zakat tax in 1980, the Shi'is rebelled. Perhaps fed by a new sense of identity with others across the Iranian border, large-scale Shi'i agitation began in Islamabad in July 1980. The capital was carefully chosen not only to magnify Shi'i defiance of the government by demonstrating in a city with controlled access, but also to ensure that the difficulties faced by the regime were recognized by the diplomatic community residing in Islamabad. The tactic worked; the government relented and the Shi'i community was exempted from governmental measures.

Potential for further trouble in Pakistani–Iranian relations appeared in 1980 when a report from Moscow claimed that the aircraft used in the abortive US rescue mission to get out American hostages took off from Pakistan. Vehement denials by the government and the later identification of Oman as the take-off point finally defused the crisis, and Pakistan rode out the storm through continued moderation in its policy toward Iran.

The Soviet invasion of Afghanistan

The dovetailing of Pakistani security concerns with those of the Islamic countries and the US occurred in December 1979 as the 80,000 Soviet troops moved into Afghanistan.[16] While the rationale for Soviet actions is not to be dwelt on here, it is important to note that Moscow's attempts to move decisively in support of the communist regime in Kabul exacerbated Pakistan's security concerns just as it alarmed the conservative Arab regimes and the United States. The common vision was one of regional security crumbling as a result of attacks by the Khumaynist right in Iran and Soviet-supported communist left in Afghanistan, not to mention direct Soviet involvement. In this way, external fears helped internationalize the crisis.

Pakistan thus became a front-line state against further Soviet encroachment. There was little the country could actually do alone diplomatically or militarily to ensure that no such action by the Soviet Union took place. However, by aligning itself closely with the Islamic Conference and once again identifying the Pakistani predicament with the fate of Muslims everywhere, Pakistan could raise the stakes for Moscow. This line of reasoning proved successful. Not only was the Soviet invasion soundly condemned by a vote of 104 to 18 (with 30 abstentions) at the United Nations in January 1980, it was also dealt with firmly by the Islamic bloc. Meeting in Islamabad in January 1980, the Conference voted unanimously to condemn the invasion, withhold recognition from the Babrak Karmal regime until all Soviet troops were withdrawn, sever diplomatic relations, and urge all Muslim states to support Islamic countries neighbouring Afghanistan.[17] Thus, the Soviet invasion of Afghanistan brought Pakistan closer to the Islamic Conference and institutionalized General Zia's role as spokesman for the group, as was evident when he came to address the United Nations General Assembly in September 1980. In his capacity as spokesman of the Islamic Conference, Zia also made several, generally unsuccessful, attempts at ending the Iran–Iraq war.

The military strategic dimension

Increased Pakistani military cooperation with key Muslim countries is a corollary of enhanced identification with the Islamic bloc. While Pakistani military advisers have been serving in Jordan, Saudi Arabia, and the Gulf since 1965, the rapid increase in their numbers and their role has taken place since oil wealth made these countries more vulnerable. Also, the desire for enhanced security resulted in huge expenditures on defence unmatched by an adequately trained manpower base. This development coincided with Pakistan's search for expanded interaction with the Islamic bloc. Furthermore developing a military dimension was, for Bhutto (under whom the cooperation accelerated), also a way of ingratiating himself with the Pakistani military establishment. In addition, cooperation with Islamic nations helped develop a second strategic front, thus shifting the focus of the Pakistan military away from India to the West.

Over the years, the number of Pakistani advisers serving in the Middle East has grown. The Pakistani government predicates its advisory and manning programme overseas on non-involvement in Arab affairs, but there has been at least one instance where this policy has run into difficulty.[18] The fall of the Shah and the Soviet invasion of Afghanistan have led to closer collaboration with key Islamic countries. The evolving military relationship with Saudi Arabia is a case in point. The notion of joint interests between the two countries was discussed during the visit of Crown Prince Fahd's visit to Pakistan in December 1980. The Prince openly declared that Saudi Arabia envisions its security tied to that of Pakistan and that 'Any interference in the internal affairs of Pakistan would be considered interference or injury to the Kingdom of Saudi Arabia'.[19] Saudi leaders remain well aware that their own perceptions of increased vulnerability, coupled with a sense of threat, mesh with Pakistan's insecurity in the face of the Soviet move into Afghanistan which for the first time in Pakistan's history opens up the possibility of a two-front war. Pakistan has the necessary trained manpower, but its general military preparedness is adversely affected by obsolete arms and an empty treasury. As a scholar of South Asian strategic affairs notes: 'The South Asian security system is an insecurity system, and the trade-offs for each regional government involve minimizing insecurity, not maximizing security.'[20] Developing a military relationship with Pakistan offers Saudi Arabia an intermediate option between relying on its own limited manpower and the full force of a US response.

The presence of common sources of threat moved the Saudi–Pakistani military relationship forward, propelled by positive perceptions of each other. In particular, the Saudis (especially King Fahd) sought to bring Pakistani soldiers into Saudi Arabia despite Saudi sensitivity to the presence of foreign workers amidst their own populace. Yet, clearly, at a first choice, the Saudis would definitely prefer to be self-reliant. But given the fact that they face tremendous shortages in trained manpower, they have no option but to rely on external sources. While the Saudis have enough funds to pay for Western manpower for training far beyond present usage, Western and particularly American trainers or advisers (since much of the Saudi equipment is from the US) are a political liability. Saudi rulers must walk a tightrope between their need for US support and military sales,[21] and their fear of creating the impression within the country and the region that the Saudi ruling family is indeed propped up by the 'Great Satan', to use a favourite phrase of Iran's Ayatollah Khumayni.

Thus, given their inability to be self-reliant or to bring in a direct US presence, the Saudi leadership looks for more palatable alternatives.[22] From this perspective, for a variety of reasons, Pakistan appears as the most viable option providing for the augmentation of Saudi capability. First, it has a large military establishment which has been tested in wars. The discipline and organization of the Pakistani military makes it one of the few effective fighting forces in the area. Second, the Pakistanis are Muslims. It is no secret that Saudi Arabia is considered to be a special place by all Muslims. This feeling is especially strong in Pakistan where Muslim nationalism is totally meshed with religion as the *raison d'être* of the state. The commitment to Saudi stability then is part and parcel of Pakistan's concern for religion. While outsiders may ponder the difference between Pakistan's commitment to Saudi Arabia and concern for the Saudi ruling family, there is little indication thus far that a distinction is drawn in Pakistan itself between the two. The present Iranian instability which has engendered real fears of the break-up of Iran or its absorption into the Soviet orbit convinces the Pakistanis that any change in the status quo in Saudi Arabia could have similar repercussions there with a possibility of denial of future access to Islam's holiest places. Third, while Pakistanis are indeed Muslims, they are not Arabs. As such, they do not speak Arabic, even though they read the Qur'an in Arabic, and they are unable to interact with the Arab work force employed in Saudi Arabia. Nor are the Pakistanis able to communicate with the Saudi population. Thus, unlike soldiers brought in from other Arab countries, the Pakistanis are basically isolated from local elements, dissident or otherwise. This fact, coupled with their separation in military cantonments, keeps them from becoming involved in local politics.

From the perspective of the Pakistani officers and soldiers, a tour of duty in Saudi Arabia is a lucrative proposition. Because the remunerative rewards of their service are considerably higher than any that is available at home, the incentive to go to Saudi Arabia is strong. In addition, the Pakistanis are quite aware that continued service depends on their non-involvement in Saudi affairs. The above should not be identified with the notion that the Pakistanis are merely 'mercenaries' because it is the religious links that form the real basis of the relationship and thus far outweigh even the rather substantial economic rewards available. The Saudi–Pakistani military relationship provides and opportunity to enlist Saudi assistance for Pakistani modernization, and also to train on the more advanced American weapons that are available in Saudi Arabia but not in Pakistan.

Finally, the military relationship with Saudi Arabia offers Pakistan a more dynamic role beyond the borders of South Asia and the traditional preoccupation with India. It is in this spirit that the Pakistani military serve as 'the soldiers of Islam', a role that evokes much pride in Islamabad. This is psychologically important for a country that was allowed relatively late entry into the inner sanctums of the Islamic movement.

Islam and Pakistani foreign policy: an assessment

Pakistani leaders have deliberately been aggressive in their use of Islam as a major factor in the nation's foreign policy after 1971. Islam is the symbol of the nation's return to its original mission; the personification of the states' justification. Careful use of Islam can indeed mobilize not only the population of Pakistan, but also the Islamic world within which the Pakistani role is increasingly dynamic. Hence, recent regimes in Islamabad have laid great emphasis on maintaining strong ties with Muslim countries, and recognized that self-interest dictates that Pakistan should ensure that their relations are not jeopardized.

However, the emphasis on Pakistan's relations with the Islamic bloc and an officially propagated Islamic revival within the country is not free of cost. Domestically, the elite cannot indefinitely use Islam as a mobilizing and legitimizing force without at some point facing the consequences of raised expectations. A polity which largely practises Islamic values may begin to demand harsher compliance from its leaders. In other words, Pakistan may not be able to sustain the varying strands of culture as it has in the past. Additionally, the higher standard of education, which is a consequence of its Western colonial history and not of its Islamic roots, and which so far has enabled Pakistan to play a leading role in the Islamic world, may not survive attempts to create a uniformly egalitarian system. Measured against a purely Islamic yardstick, Pakistan cannot aspire to the leadership it seeks.

Secondly, persistent emphasis on Islam within the country and in its foreign policy cannot logically continue without affecting the Kashmir issue because it involves the rights of a Muslim populace to self-determination. If Kashmir is made an Islamic issue, Pakistan cannot really hope to have sustained improved relations with India.

Thirdly, the leading role that Pakistan played within the Islamic Congress in condemning the Soviet invasion of Afghanistan means that Pakistan cannot reach a separate understanding with Moscow on the Afghan issue. The Islamic bloc, which helped raise the diplomatic costs of the invasion for Moscow in 1980, may constrain Pakistani search for fresh options if the burden of three million Afghan refugees becomes a heavy one. Despite the fact that Pakistan is the most directly affected nation, its policy on the Afghan issue is forced to operate in tandem with the rest of the Islamic world.

Fourthly, after 1971, the emergence of South-west Asia as an arena for involvement offered psychological and material rewards for Pakistan. It provided a much welcomed opportunity to sidestep the quarrels of South Asia where Pakistan remained vulnerable because India continued to dominate. Since 1979, the fall of the Shah, the Soviet invasion of Afghanistan, the Iran–Iraq war, and the Israeli invasion of Lebanon to which the Islamic bloc could not fashion any coordinated response have all become poignant reminders of the smouldering problems which beset the area. In the changing security picture confronting the countries to its west, Pakistan may learn the hard way that its entanglements can be costly, particularly as Israeli leaders begin to point out that Pakistan cannot escape Israeli wrath for its Middle East involvement.

Finally, thus far Pakistan has managed to stay largely free of involvement in the partisan tendencies that often exist in the Islamic world. As the polarization continues between the vision of Ayatollah Khumayni's Islam and that of the conservative kingdoms befriended by Pakistan, Islamabad will have to demonstrate a more sophisticated, multi-dimensional approach to the use of Islam in the conduct of its foreign policy. Failure to do so may indeed affect Pakistan's ability to deal with instability spilling over from the Muslim countries that sit astride its borders.

Notes

1. National Assembly of Pakistan, *Debates, Official Report* (Karachi, Government Printing Office, 11 November 1962), p. 10.
2. To multiply its options, Pakistan entered into discussions with both the Soviet Union and the PRC. It signed a $30 million agreement with the USSR for assistance in oil exploration in Pakistan in 1960 and began discussions toward a border agreement with China in 1961. Herbert Feldman, *Revolution in Pakistan: A Study of the Martial Law Administration* (London, Oxford University Press, 1967), p. 191.
3. Waheed-uz Zaman, 'Editor's Note', *The Quest for Identity* (Islamabad, University of Islamabad Press, 1974), p. 1.
4. *Dawn*, Karachi, 6 April 1972.
5. Stephen P. Cohen, 'The Strategic Imagery of Elites', in James M. Roherty (ed.), *Defense Policy Formation* (Durham, Carolina Academic Press, 1980), p. 159.
6. Pakistan leaders had consistently voiced pro-Islamic sentiments. See, for example, Keith Callard, *Pakistan: A Political Study* (London, Allen and Unwin, 1957), pp. 18, 314; S. M. Burke, *Pakistan's Foreign Policy: An Historical Analysis* (London, Oxford University Press, 1973), p. 65.
7. Zulfikar Ali Bhutto, *The Third World: New Directions* (London, Quartet Books, 1977), p. 86.
8. *Ibid.*, p. 86.
9. *Ibid.*, p. 100.
10. Even though only 13.7 per cent of Pakistan's total exports are to the Islamic countries, 55 per cent of Pakistan's overall exports are to the Third World nations. IMF/IBRD figures, cited in *Dawn*, 17 May 1980.
11. Arms Control and Disarmament Agency (ACDA), *World Military Expenditures and Arms Transfers, 1969–1978.*
12. Interviews, Islamabad, 1980. Also, *Pakistan Economist*, 16–22 January 1982, pp. 19–20.
13. Not known in Pakistan for living the life of a true believer.
14. *Pakistan Times*, 7 July 1977.
15. Islamabad, 8 July 1980.
16. For a discussion of Soviet involvement in Afghanistan and its implications for Pakistan, see Shirin Tahir-Kheli, 'Soviet Fortunes on the Southern Tier:

Afghanistan, Iran and Pakistan', *Naval War College Review* (November–December 1981), 3–13.

17. Department of State, 'Soviet Invasion of Afghanistan', Special Report, No. 70 (April 1980), p. 3.

18. In 1979 Qadhafi wished to involve Pakistani pilots serving in Libya more closely, threatening to retaliate for non-compliance with expulsion of all Pakistanis from Libya. The crisis was averted after intense high level consultation and Qadhafi demurred. The government of Pakistan was quite aware of the economic and political consequences of the expulsion and dislocation of 80,000 well-paid Pakistanis.

19. *New York Times*, 11 December 1980.

20. Stephen P. Cohen, 'Security Issues in South Asia', *Asian Survey*, 15 (1975), 214.

21. Saudi purchases of US military hardware between 1973 and 1980 totalled $34 billion. In the period between 1950 and 1972 such purchases amounted to only $1.2 billion. Planned 1982 arms purchases amount to $27.5 billion. *The Military Balance: 1981–1982* (London, The International Institute for Strategic Studies, 1981).

22. These arguments are fully developed in Shirin Tahir-Kheli and William O. Staudenmaier, 'The Saudi–Pakistani Military Relationship and Its Implications for US Strategy in Southwest Asia', *Orbis*, 26 (1982), 155–71.

6 The Limits of Instrumentalism: Islam in Egypt's Foreign Policy

ALI E. HILLAL DESSOUKI

The relationship between Islam and foreign policy has hardly been investigated or analysed. For a while Islam was seen as a factor of decreasing significance in the formulation and implementation of the foreign policy of Islamic countries. Three factors have accounted for this conclusion. There was first the widely held belief that the crucial influences defining the national interests, and therefore the foreign policy orientations, of Islamic states were of a strategic, economic and political nature. Second, during the 1950s and 1960s efforts to reinstitute Islam as a force in inter-Arab or inter-Islamic relations achieved limited success. For instance 'Abd al-Nasir's Islamic Circle in his *Philosophy of the Revolution* (1954) was abandoned and replaced by the policy of nonalignment. Also, Saudi Arabia's efforts in 1959 and 1964 to create a kind of pan-Islamic organization was met by 'Abd al-Nasir's fierce opposition. It was only in 1969, after the defeat of 1967 and the burning of al-Aqsa Mosque in Jerusalem, that the first Islamic summit meeting was held. Third, Islamic states were divided along 'secular' ideological lines. Some were closer to Western powers, others to the Soviet Union and a third group struggled to maintain a non-aligned posture.

Thus, it was not surprising that most of the speakers in a conference on Islam and International Relations held at Duke University in 1963 'maintained that Islam is actually of quite limited significance in shaping the attitudes and behavior of muslim states in international relations today ... few were prepared to dismiss its relevance altogether'.[1] Fayez A. Sayegh, a contributor to the conference on the issue of Islam and Neutralism, concluded that 'Islam has had little, if any, noticeable influence upon reasoning, planning, decision-making, or expression of muslim policy makers, neutralist or counter neutralist alike.'[2]

In the 1970s Islam reasserted itself as a force in the political life of most Muslim societies. By the early eighties, there was hardly a

84

Muslim community that had not experienced some sort of Islamic resurgence.[3] Domestically, Islamic organizations demanding the implementation of *shari'a* mushroomed. Externally, a number of international Islamic organizations were established, such as the Islamic World League which was established in 1966 with headquarters in Saudi Arabia; the Conference of the Islamic World, which was instituted in 1967 with headquarters in Jordan; and the Organization of the Islamic Conference which was established in 1969 with headquarters in Saudi Arabia. Furthermore, the Islamic revolution in Iran, its defiance of the West, and its ability to score major successes in its war with Iraq under the banner of Islam, provided added impetus for bringing Islam into the foreground. Indeed, in April 1982, many Islamic states observed a 24-hour anti-Israel strike that had been called by King Khalid of Saudi Arabia in protest against the attack on the Dome of the Rock, a sacred site in Islam.

Most studies on the contemporary Islamic resurgence have concentrated on the internal dimension of the phenomenon. Fewer writings have investigated its external implications, such as the spill-over of Islamic resurgence activities to inter-state relations and the transnational consequences of such activities. Our research problem, therefore, is to determine what is the impact of such a resurgence in the hands of regimes or dissident groups on the foreign policy of a particular country or on inter-state relations in a particular region.

In this context, the experience of modern Muslim states shows that there is no specific foreign policy orientation that can be identified as Islamic. States which proclaim Islam as the organizing concept in their social life, such as Saudi Arabia, Pakistan and Iran, follow different, indeed contradictory, foreign policies. Central to this argument is the multiplicity of perceptions and practices of 'Islamic' foreign policies. Islam's role, as a capability or constraint, is conditioned by other factors such as the sources of legitimation in the system, competing ideologies and strength of opposition groups (particularly the Islamic one), the role of religion in society, and the types of foreign policy objectives adopted by the ruling elite.

The main argument of this paper is that Islam has primarily been a capability and a resource to Egypt's foreign policy. Both 'Abd al-Nasir and Sadat used Islam as an instrument. Islam was more of a rationale or vindication for policy choices, rather than a motivation or a constraint. In Egypt, official Islam was 'nationalized' by the state, and consequently religious institutions and symbols have been used to justify support, and to discredit political adversaries. It is further argued that with the resurgence of Islamic groups in the 1970s, Egyptian rulers resorted to more Islamic symbolism as a means of coopting and appeasing them.[4]

Islam and foreign policy under 'Abd al-Nasir

Nasir's main Islamic opposition came from the Muslim Brothers Association which, until the advent of the Iranian revolution, constituted the most influential religo-political movement in the Arab world. The Association was subject to the repression of the pre-revolutionary regime in the late 1940s. Its leader was assassinated in a way implicating the government and the organization was disbanded in 1949, to be reinstituted in 1951. Its major clashes, however, took place with 'Abd al-Nasir, leading to the confrontations of 1954 and 1965. In both cases thousands of its members were arrested and several of its leaders executed.

In an analysis of 'Islam and the Foreign Policy of Egypt' under 'Abd al-Nasir, P. J. Vatikiotis argues that 'there is a significant and fundamental relationship between Egyptian policy and Islam, especially in the complex area of ideology – in the formulation and reformulation of social and political goals and values for modern Egypt, and in the Nasser regime's conception of Arab nationalism and the unity of the Arab countries'.[5] While this assertion is primarily correct at the level of orientation, the complex and varied relations between Islam and foreign policy under 'Abd al-Nasir are better understood if we distinguish between three phases. The first (1952–6) witnessed the active reliance on Islam in Egypt's policy towards Africa and the Arab world. In the second (1956–67), Islam was overshadowed by other concepts such as Arab nationalism or non-alignment. In this period, 'Abd al-Nasir rejected notions of pan-Islamic solidarity as being pro-imperialist. The third phase (1967–70) witnessed Nasir's compromise with Saudi Arabia over Yemen and the gathering of the first Islamic summit meeting in Rabat in 1969. Let us look briefly at the main features and landmarks of each phase.

In the first phase, 'Abd al-Nasir advocated the idea of a pan-Islamic organization. In 1954, he wrote about his feeling during the Pilgrimage: 'as I stood before the Qa'ba ... I fully recognized the need for a radical change of our conception of the pilgrimage ... the pilgrimage should have a potential political power'. Nasir thought of it as a 'World Islamic Parliament, which should include heads of all the Islamic states, leaders of opinion, scientists, eminent industrialists and prominent businessmen'. They would gather to draw up 'the broad lines of the policies to be adopted by their respective countries and lay down the principles ensuring their close cooperation until they have again gathered together in the following session'.[6] 'Abd al-Nasir spoke of an 'Islamic Circle' for Egypt's foreign policy, which came third after Arab and African ones. He envisioned this circle to include 'those hundreds of millions of Muslims, all welded into a homogenous whole by the same faith' and whose cooperation would 'ensure for them and their brethren in Islam unlimited power'.[7]

In 1953–5 Islam was a major theme in Egypt's foreign policy. Addressing the Arab–Islamic conference of liberation organizations held in Cairo in August 1953, 'Abd al-Nasir emphasized that the Arab and Islamic worlds were facing one enemy: imperialism. In December 1953, Egypt participated in the First East African Islamic Conference held in Nairobi. In August 1954, 'Abd al-Nasir, King Sa'ud and Ghulam Muhammad, the prime minister of Pakistan, established the Islamic Congress with headquarters in Cairo. Anwar al-Sadat was appointed as secretary-general and the Congress was directly affiliated to the presidency. According to Sadat in his autobiography, the objective of the Congress was to work for closer links between Arab and Muslim countries as well as for certain foreign policy objectives of Egypt such as 'frustrating the Baghdad Pact'.[8] The Congress awarded scholarships to students from Islamic countries to study in Egypt. In January 1956 the minister of endowments travelled to Senegal and Liberia to show Egypt's concern for the welfare of Muslims there. By 1956, 'Abd al-Nasir started to grow impatient with his Islamic policy and the hope for an effective pan-Islamic organization started to fade away. The conflict over the Baghdad Pact and the convening of the Bandung Conference were crucial factors in the development of his thought. From these two experiences he recognized that Arab and Islamic states are divided along 'political' lines, as he later related, and discovered the importance of the emerging Afro-Asian movement and the notion of positive neutrality in world affairs.

In the second phase, while the hope for an Islamic front diminished, Egypt continued to use Islam as an instrument of foreign policy. Law number 103 of the year 1961 which reorganized al-Azhar was justified in part by the need for graduates who combined training in modern science with a religious background. Article 2 of the law states that 'al-Azhar carries the burden of Islamic mission to all nations'. An Islamic research council and a department of Islamic education and missions were established.

In March 1964, al-Azhar sponsored the first Afro-Asian Islamic

Conference. Delegates from 44 countries attended and the conference was addressed by Egypt's Vice-President Husain al-Shaf'i. The second conference was held in May 1965 and it discussed among other things the religious aspects of the struggle against imperialism. In 1963–4, al-Azhar had students from 32 African states. The budget for scholarships for foreign students to attend al-Azhar increased from £E 15,000 in 1952 to £E 375,000 in 1963. By 1964, al-Azhar had more than two hundred *'ulama* all over the world. Also in 1964, al-Azhar established a daily 13-hour radio programme, 'The Voice of Islam', for reciting the Qur'an. A year later, the programme expanded its services throughout Africa and included broadcasts in many indigenous languages.[9] In 1967, there were Islamic cultural centres in Morocco, Libya, Ghana, Liberia, Nigeria, Tanzania, Somalia, Mauritania, and Sierra Leone.

The other institution that was instrumental in implementing Egypt's Islamic policy was the Supreme Council for Islamic Affairs, established in 1960 and headed by an ex-officer, Mohammed Tawfiq 'Oweida. The Council published scores of books and pamphlets in different languages as well as a monthly journal *Minbar al-Islam* (The Forum of Islam), invited prominent personalities from Islamic countries, and worked closely with Muslim students studying in Egypt.

In this phase, Islam was identified with 'Abd al-Nasir's revolutionary and anti-imperialist policy. He attacked the reactionary regimes of Saudi Arabia and Jordan which he saw as deviating from the true Islam. According to him true Islam, the religion of justice and equality, was promoted by Egypt which presented the Arab world with a model of regenerated Islam.[10] Mohamed Fayek, director of the African Affairs Office in the presidency under 'Abd al-Nasir and the person most responsible for Egypt's African policy in the 1950s and 1960s, reported that Egypt's Islamic efforts in Africa were extensive. Egypt sent teachers, opened schools, offered medical aid, donated books and thousands of copies of the Qur'an and established mosques and Islamic centres.[11] Egypt maintained relations with almost all Islamic groups including Sufi orders and supported their cultural and educational activities. For instance, it has close relations with the Tiganiya order; its leader, Shaykh Ibrahim Anyas, was invited many times to Egypt, and 'Abd al-Nasir made a point of receiving him at home. 'Abd al-Nasir was aware of the non-participation of some of these orders in the anti-colonial struggle in their countries, and his support to them was based on their role in 'preserving Islam and spreading Arab and Islamic culture in Africa'.[12]

In the aftermath of the crushing defeat of 1967 the religious theme became more visible in 'Abd al-Nasir's speeches. He asserted that Egyptians were very devout people, and that it was religion that made their unity. He added that defeat was predestined and that faith was the only road to victory. Even so, although 'Abd al-Nasir could no longer oppose the convening of the Islamic summit conference in Rabat in 1969, he nevertheless registered his displeasure by failing to show up, sending Sadat instead.

To sum up, 'Abd al-Nasir used Islam to further his political objectives. He did not hesitate, however, to support non-Muslims against Muslims in international conflicts such as the Indo-Pakistani conflict or the Cyprus problem. Furthermore, 'Abd al-Nasir supported the revolution against a Muslim Sultan in Zanzibar in 1964 and refused to support secessionist tendencies among Kenyan Muslims.[13] Finally, the influence of Islam was more evident in regional, Arab and African, rather than global, policies.

Islam and foreign policy under Sadat

Lacking in charisma and legitimacy, President Sadat resorted more frequently to religious symbolism so that his speeches teemed with Islamic allusions. One of his early actions was to release and rehabilitate the imprisoned members of the Muslim Brothers. He encouraged Islamic groups on campuses as a countervailing force to the active leftist and Nasirist opposition. Initiating a new practice, Sadat delivered a speech on the occasion of *Mawlid al-Nabi* (the birthday of the Prophet) in 1971.[14] The war of 1973 started on the 10th of the holy month of Ramadan and its code name was Badr. The battle was joined in 'Allah's will' as the 'sacred duty' of 'the soldiers of God' who achieved 'victory by his will'. Afterwards, Sadat's frequent references to 'the miracle of October, the miracle of the crossing and the miracle of the Israeli collapse, were reflections of the metaphysical concept of a military power imbued with faith'.[15]

For the first time, the principles of *shari'a* were written into the constitution of 1971 as a major source of legislation (part I, article 3), and in 1980 it became the major one. Parliamentary committees were established to codify the *shari'a* and to issue new Islamic codes. Laws controlling the sale of alcohol were issued and Muslims were no longer allowed to drink in public places. Sadat was usually introduced to the public as 'the believing president'. He used to perform the Friday prayers in front of a crowd of photographers and cameras, used Qur'anic and religious images frequently in his speeches, described himself once as 'a Muslim leader of a Muslim country', and justified his actions as 'his duty as a Muslim leader'.

An obvious case to illustrate Sadat's efforts for religious legitimization was his visit to Jerusalem. Addressing the People's Assembly in November 1977, he referred to the determination to achieve national goals because 'almighty God commands us to fight in order to preserve the sacred rights of the nation'.[16] The official announcement of the visit issued on 17 November mentioned that the president accepted the invitation to visit Jerusalem in the name of peace and to perform the feast prayers in al-Aqsa Mosque.[17] His speech in the Kenesset had definite religious overtones, and he used the symbolism overlaying the timing of his visit which coincided with the Islamic feast *al-adha* and Abraham's sacrifice. His words bordered on projecting the image of a quasi-prophet. He told his audience that he had asked God to 'inspire' him with strength and that God dictated his destiny to shoulder the responsibility of peace. 'I did not come here except to deliver a message,' he said, and then to bear witness that he did, he repeated Zakaria's call for peace and rightness.[18] Two years later, when the Camp David accords were criticized, Dar al-Ifta'a of al-Azhar issued a *fatwa* (a religious legal opinion) to the effect that the treaty did not contradict Islamic principles.[19] Introducing his idea of a canal from the Nile to Jerusalem, Sadat said 'in the name of Egypt and its great al-Azhar and in the name of defending peace, the Nile water will become the new Zamzam well [a holy well in Mecca] for believers in the three mono-theistic religions'.[20]

Despite all his Islamic symbolism, Islam did not seem to be much of a constraint on Sadat's foreign policy behaviour. He was thus a resolute critic of the Islamic revolution in Iran. The Egyptian press reported the events of the revolution with great caution and selectivity and emphasized its Shi'i character. Sadat invited the deposed Shah to Egypt where he eventually died after a troubled residence in other countries. He refused to call the revolution 'Islamic'; in fact he thought that Khumayni gave Islam a bad name. 'What happens in Iran is a disgrace to Islam, to humanity, and to human dignity ...',[21] he said. It is a 'crime against Islam',[22] irrational,[23] and Khumayni is involved in 'petty revenge'.[24] Seemingly satisfied with the initial Iraqi victory over Iran, Sadat sold ammunition and weapons to an Iraqi regime that had con-demned Egypt over the Camp David accords. In another context, President Marcos's troubles with the Muslim community in the Philip-pines did not hinder the development of cordial relations between the two countries and the two 'First Ladies'.

Thus, Islam seems to have been subservient to other goals and objectives. Sadat's support for the Afghani struggle was a consequence of his anti-Sovietism. The establishment of the League of Arab and Islamic peoples in 1980 was a reaction to Egypt's isolation from Arab and Islamic councils in the aftermath of the Camp David accords. Sadat criticized governmental organizations such as the League of the Arab States and the Organization of the Islamic Conference as being unrepresentative of their peoples. The League of Islamic and Arab Peoples was intended to be a non-governmental organization to encourage and coordinate common Islamic and Arab endeavours. Nothing shows the ambiguity of its concept more than Sadat's inaugural speech on 9 November 1980, which coincided with the 2nd of Moharram of the Islamic year 1401. In this speech, Islam and Arabism appeared identical; Sadat spoke of 'the Islamic Arab Umma' and 'the Islamic Arab Unity', and article 4 of the League's charter referred to 'the Islamic and Arab peoples as one nation'. However, the League was born with very little chance of success and its activities remain hardly noticed by anybody.

The analysis of Sadat's view of the Islamic world and the role of Egypt in it supports our conclusion. Till the late 1970s, the Islamic world had a marginal place in his thought. It was only after Camp David and the ensuing Egyptian isolation that the Islamic Circle became increasingly important. His speeches in the early 1970s did not count much on Islamic support. The basic thrust was Arab and his conception of the conflict with Israel was primarily 'nationalist' and not 'religious'.[25] In his speech to the Islamic summit conference in Lahore in 1974, he hoped that Muslims' position toward the Arab–Israeli conflict would be no less than the African and the non-aligned one.[26]

Islamic states became more evident in his foreign policy in the mid-1970s with Egypt's growing relations with Iran and the West. By 1979–1980, Sadat had developed a view of the international role of the Islamic states. The point of departure in his view was the Islamic *umma* which shared similar problems and whose main enemy was Soviet communism. According to him, with the signing of the Camp David accords and the initiation of the process for comprehensive peace in the Middle East, the major threat to the Islamic world was manifested in Soviet ambitions and activities in the region. The Soviets threatened the heart of the Islamic world in the Gulf, and hence the importance to Sadat of the Afghanistan issue as a microcosm of the Islamic–Soviet conflict. On the other side, Sadat believed in the commonality of interests between the Islamic states and the West; oil in exchange for technology and the common interest against the Soviet threat.[27] Thus, the Islamic states had to coordinate with the US to defend themselves. In this regard Egypt would play a focal role by providing the US with military facilities[28] to 'defend all Arab and Islamic states as far as Indonesia'.[29] The crucial factor in understanding Sadat's Islamic policy, therefore, is his anti-Soviet orientation. The other factor is the growing political weight of Islamic groups in Egypt and Sadat's attempt to coopt and appease them.

The foreign policy orientation of Islamic dissent

As mentioned earlier, for a while the Muslim Brothers and other Islamic groups seemed to be in alliance with the regime and they effectively checked the influence of secular opposition groups in Egypt, particularly in the universities. By 1977, cooperation ran its course and *al-Da'wa*, the Brothers' journal, became a major forum for expressing dissent. Throughout the 1970s, a number of militant Islamic groups challenged the authority of the government and resorted to military action. These included Muhammed's Youth (Saleh Sariya's group which attacked the Military Technical College in April 1974); the Repentance and Holy Flight Group (originally arrested in July 1975 and again in 1977); and al-Jihad Group (which was originally recognized in 1978 and was responsible for the assassination of Sadat).

In September 1981, Sadat attacked the Muslim Brothers and other Islamic associations and accused them of collaborating with opposition groups in order to bring down his regime. The crackdown involved the arrest of some 1,536 persons, including some *imams* of mosques, the closing down of two Islamic journals and the seizure of the Brothers' funds and assets. All private mosques were to be administered by the Ministry of Endowments. Sadat's assassination a month later was a culmination of a confrontation process between the regime and the Islamic groups. In 1977, Sadat introduced a bill authorizing the death sentence or hard labour for those convicted of belonging to political organizations involved in military training. In 1980, he suspended all Islamic associations in the universities, accusing them of promoting religious fanaticism, extremism and communal unrest.

Sadat's courtship of the West was a basic cause of friction between Islamic opposition groups and the regime. His need to appear modern to a Western audience helped erode his base at home. Sadat's policies, it was argued by his critics, diminished Egypt's independence and increased its vulnerability; cut off from the Arab world, it stood exposed. Sadat's peace initiative with Israel also had great effect on the Islamic groups. They were naturally opposed to Camp David as they saw the historical clash between the Muslims and the Jews as longstanding and insoluble. Confronted with increasing Islamic-based criticism of his policies Sadat employed more Islamic symbolism. Ironically, the more he legitimized his policies in Islamic terms the more vulnerable he became to this kind of criticism.

Let us deal now with the world view of the Muslim Brothers as an example of the Islamic groups in Egypt. The analysis is based on the writings published in the monthly *al-Daʿwa* which the authorities banned in September 1981. In reading *al-Daʿwa*, one finds a perception of a polarized world divided along religious lines, Muslims against non-Muslims. The polarization is characterized by constant hostility and unceasing struggle. There exists a feeling of a worldwide conspiracy against Islam and the Muslims. The list of enemies includes almost everybody, the crusading Christian West, the atheist Red communists, the Jews and the infidel Buddhists.

In the case of the US, *al-Daʿwa* emphasizes the Americans' incessant support of Israel.[30] The West in general is hostile to Islam. While it is very much willing to educate Muslims in destructive western ideas such as secularism, it deliberately withholds its scientific knowledge and technology.[31] Christians, however, are still viewed by the Muslim Brothers as the People of the Book contrary to the totally atheist Red communists who are determined to liquidate Islam and the Muslims. All means of coercion are employed by the communists to weaken Muslim power. The primary example is that of the 50 million Muslims in 'Russia' who are subject to all kinds of oppression. Muslims of China, Bulgaria, Albania have undergone similar experiences.[32] Muslims in India are equally persecuted and face 'collective massacres' and liquidation.[33] The same situation prevails in Thailand, Burma and the Philippines.[34] The writers of *al-Daʿwa* believe that communists, crusaders, Jews and Buddhists have not only conspired against the Muslims living in their midst but have managed to creep into the Muslim and Arab worlds spreading corruption, evil and atheism everywhere, and establishing their agents from among Muslim rulers.

To face such a challenge to Islam, Muslims have no choice but to close ranks, strengthen Islamic solidarity and support all Islamic causes. The writers of *al-Daʿwa* consistently supported the Iranian revolution and attacked the Shah's residence in Egypt. Throughout 1981, almost every issue contained a feature on the struggle of Muslims in Syria against the Nusairi regime of Hafiz al-Asad; the Taghut who sold his soul to the devil and collaborated with the enemies of Islam.[35] *Al-Da'wa* defends Muslim rights in India, the Philippines, Uganda, Nigeria, Eritrea, Chad, and of course in Afghanistan. As to the last, *al-Da'wa* strongly believes that both the US and the Soviet Union conspired together to prevent the establishment of an Islamic state. The Soviet invasion helped American objectives in arousing the fears of the Gulf rulers, made them more vulnerable and in need of American arms and help.[36] Another constant concern of *al-Da'wa* is the issue of Palestine, Israel and Egyptian–Israeli relations. In this, *al-Da'wa* writers did not hesitate to use the harshest words to express their views. Again, in every issue one finds an essay or a report on the 'Jewish' crimes in Palestine, the importance of Jerusalem for the Muslims, the dangers of establishing economic and cultural relations with Israel and Israeli expansionist designs.

The Muslim Brothers' position is based on a number of propositions. The Jews have always believed in themselves as the 'chosen race' which is destined to dominate and domineer. Jews use all methods to achieve their goals and they have a history of violating treaties and breaking promises. Israel's main objective is the establishment of greater Israel and it views reconciliation or peace as the first step toward the realization of this goal.[37] Reconciliation with Israel provides it with an opportunity to penetrate and control the Arab countries economically and culturally. Cultural penetration was a favourite theme of *al-Da'wa* writers. One article suggested that Israel would encourage the spread of secular and anti-Arab ideas in Egypt.[38] Mumtaz Nassar warned against Israeli attempts to print issues of the Qur'an not including those verses which painted Jews in negative images.[39] Israel would use its influence to prevent teaching those verses in schools or reciting them on radio and television. Shaykh Salah Abu Ismail suggested that Israel would encourage the government to repress Islamic groups.[40] It would also export to Egypt films and television programmes whose objective was to spread moral looseness, corruption, prostitution, and gambling. He also warned against Israeli attempts to exploit communal differences in Egypt, to incite Copts, and to appear as a defender of their rights. *Al-Da'wa*'s other criticisms of the Camp David accords do not differ much from those forwarded by secular opposition. The treaties primarily satisfy Israeli conditions, constitute an infringement on Egyptian sovereignty, do not deal with the issue of Jerusalem, and fail to provide an adequate solution to the Palestinian question.[41]

In general, the Muslim Brothers' Association believes that Egypt should pursue an Islamic policy which is neither 'Eastern nor Western';

in other words a non-aligned policy. Furthermore, Egypt must enhance its relations with the Islamic world, which can be a major source of political and material support.

Conclusion

In the case of Egypt, it seems that both 'Abd al-Nasir and Sadat used Islam as an instrument of their foreign policies. The use of Islam depended on the issue involved and was more effective at the Arab and African regional levels. Both men were keen to maximize Islam's utility as a capability and minimize the constraints attached to it. In this regard, 'Abd al-Nasir's selective use was to a great extent success-ful.[42] The assassination of Sadat by members of al-Jihad Islamic group testifies to the limits and dangers of the instrumental use of Islam à la Sadat. As Eric Rouleau accurately wrote, Sadat 'believed he could confine the muslim activities to the role of auxiliaries, while making Islam one of the principal instruments of his power'.[43]

Notes

1. Harris Proctor (ed.), *Islam and International Relations* (New York, Praeger, 1965), p. vii.
2. Fayez A. Sayegh, 'Islam and Neutralism', in Proctor, *Islam*, pp. 61–2.
3. In general see the author's essay, 'The Islamic Resurgence: Sources, Dynamics and Implications', in Ali E. Hillal Dessouki (ed.), *Islamic Resurgence in the Arab World* (New York, Praeger, 1982), pp. 3–31.
4. On the political role of Islam in Egypt see the two contributions by Gabriel R. Warburg, 'Islam and Politics in Egypt: 1952–1980', *Middle Eastern Studies*, 18 (1982), 129–57 and Louis J. Cantori, 'Religion and Politics in Egypt', in Michael Curtis (ed.), *Religion and Politics in the Middle East* (Boulder, Westview, 1981), pp. 77–90.
5. Proctor, *Islam*, p. 123.
6. Gamal 'Abd al-Nasir, *The Philosophy of the Revolution*, translated by Dorothy Thompson (Cairo, Government Printer, n.d.), p. 69.
7. 'Abd al-Nasir, *The Philosophy*, p. 72.
8. Quoted in Warburg, 'Islam and Politics', p. 140.
9. The best source for the use of Islam in Egypt's African policy is Tareq Ismael, *The UAR in Africa: Egypt's Policy Under Nasser* (Evanston, Northwestern University Press, 1971), pp. 142–53.
10. P. J. Vatikiotis, 'Islam and the Foreign Policy of Egypt', in Proctor, *Islam*, pp. 122, 128.
11. Mohamed Fayek, *Nasser and the African Revolution* (in Arabic) (Beirut, Dar al-Wihda, 1980), p. 77.
12. Fayek, *Nasser*, p. 80.
13. Fayek, *Nasser*, p. 81.
14. Address on 6 May 1971.

15. Raphael Israeli, 'The Role of Islam in President Sadat's Thought', *The Jerusalem Journal of International Relations*, 4 (Winter 1980), 5.
16. Address on 9 November 1977.
17. Sadat frequently repeated this. See his interview with American television, 29 November 1977; his interview with Tunisian television, 2 December 1977; and his interview with the Kuwaiti newspaper *al-Siyasa*, 9 December 1977.
18. 20 November 1977. See an analysis of the speech in Norman Salem Babikian, 'The Sacred and the Profane: Sadat's Speech to the Kenesset', *The Middle East Journal*, 34 (1980), 13–24.
19. Text of *al-fatwa* in *al-Ahram*, 14 July 1979.
20. Quoted in Warburg, 'Islam and Politics', p. 144.
21. 25 December 1979.
22. 8 June 1980.
23. 29 January 1980.
24. 29 January 1980.
25. Message to the Islamic conference on 23 June 1974.
26. Address on 25 February 1974.
27. Interview with *The Washington Post*, 27 May 1980, and address at Alexandria University, 30 September 1980.
28. Address on 26 March 1980; interview with *Le Monde*, 13 September 1980.
29. Address on 2 October 1980.
30. *al-Daʿwa*, October 1977, pp. 50–1 and December 1979, p. 4.
31. *al-Daʿwa*, January 1977, pp. 4, 18–19.
32. *al-Daʿwa*, January 1977, pp. 19–20.
33. *al-Daʿwa*, January 1977 and April 1977, p. 20.
34. *al-Daʿwa*, January 1978, pp. 19–20 and May 1981, p. 54.
35. *al-Daʿwa*, August 1980, p. 13 and November 1980, p. 82.
36. *al-Daʿwa*, August 1980, p. 54.
37. *al-Daʿwa*, October 1978, p. 4.
38. *al-Daʿwa*, March 1980, p. 48.
39. *al-Daʿwa*, March 1979, p. 56.
40. *al-Daʿwa*, March 1980, p. 56.
41. *al-Daʿwa*, June 1977, pp. 22–3.
42. A. I. Dawisha, *Egypt in the Arab World* (London, Macmillan, 1976), p. 91.
43. Eric Rouleau, 'Who Killed Sadat', *Merip Reports* (February 1982), 4.

7 Explaining the Nearly Inexplicable: The Absence of Islam in Moroccan Foreign Policy

I. WILLIAM ZARTMAN

Contrary to current images and expectations, it is probably safe to state as a fact as well as an interpretation that Islam is unnecessary to both the conduct and the content of Moroccan foreign policy,[1] and that it appears only to some lesser extent among its symbols of presentation. Moroccan foreign policy can be understood and is practised through more universal terms and concepts, and Islam figures only secondarily among the referent values that give that policy meaning and legitimacy to its subjects and objects alike. Once this is demonstrated, the more interesting question addresses the reasons for the shyness of Islamic symbols and explanations. To an extent, evidence of the absence gives reasons for it as well, since it highlights what takes the place of religion as more important referents. But other levels of explanation are also required. One such level is found in the roles Morocco has assigned itself in foreign relations, although in establishing these roles interpretation is obliged to go beyond direct evidence, leaving the alternative explanation epistemologically weaker than the rejected one. Therefore, to help clinch the argument, other explanations must be found, including ones that address the inadequacy of Islamic symbols for Morocco's self-assigned roles and for Moroccan society.

In making this argument, a number of endless debates about evidence and arguments must be plugged, before attempting to tackle the substance of the subject. To begin with, some of the data for the debate will be found in official Moroccan statements, by foreign policy spokesmen and by the King. The challenge can always be made that such statements are not real, sincere, complete, or profound. One answer to the challenge is that these statements are all there is to work with, but a more assertive and important answer is that official statements do represent much, if not everything; they represent above all what people want to believe about themselves and what they want others to believe, and so are the very evidence that is required.

Another challenge, from a different quarter, concerns the meaning of 'Islam' (or any other religion) in regard to foreign policy. With a little interpretation nearly anything can be justified through reference to a particular religion, and so Islam, as revealed and interpreted, gives little guide to an unambiguous content of many aspects of human behaviour, above all foreign policy. One can become lost in a scholastic argument if one begins to debate the Islamic content of foreign policy, that is, whether those who claim a particular policy to be religious are themselves faithful to the true content of that religion. The best that can be done is to locate Islamic symbols and language, without trying to judge whether they are 'rightly' used. Again, one is left with the need to take the spokesmen at their word, even if they are contradicted by other spokesmen.

The analytical device employed in this paper is based on a cognitive approach to foreign policy analysis. This approach assumes that parties see foreign issues and events through the prism of established images. These views can be established through content analysis of foreign policy statements, since the word is often the act in foreign relations or stands as the basis for it. Images can be portrayed most rigorously as cognitive maps,[2] although the maps do not explain the origins of their components. Furthermore, cognitive maps are a quantitative device, whereas such precision is neither necessary, sufficient, nor even always accurate for an understanding of foreign policy. An additional element, which should be used as the second analytical device, is needed; namely an understanding of the structures and roles within which the state operates. This approach assumes that states through their spokesmen, reflecting the values of their society, assign themselves notions of appropriate roles and then seek to harmonize their specific behaviours in accordance with such role notions.[3] Since such roles occur within perceived power structures in international relations, the notion of 'role' ties together the concepts of 'image' and 'system' and the analytical approaches which they represent, to provide a coherent and specific foreign policy analysis. Finally, the act and event must also be taken into account and analysed, not as something which is distinct from the image or the perception, but as part of the whole picture.

The following analysis is based on all relevant statements of King Hassan II during 1970–1, 1978–9, and 1982, official statements made before Parliament during 1981 by Prime Minister Ma'ti Bou'abid and Foreign Minister Mhamid Boucetta, foreign policy statements of Prime Minister Ahmed Osman in 1972–9, and the 13 presentations on

Moroccan foreign policy made by the foreign ministers before the plenary sessions of the 25th to 37th General Assemblies of the United Nations from 1970 to 1982.[4] This is combined with an examination of the record of action – what Morocco did as well as what it said – since 1970.

The first conclusion of an examination of these policy statements and justifications is negative: Morocco does not have or claim to have an 'Islamic foreign policy'. There are several senses in which such a claim could have been made. Moroccan spokesmen could claim to have a foreign policy that is Muslim in its content, behaviour, and inspiration, in the same sense as Morocco follows Muslim family law. It could also have a policy with a special content directed toward Muslim states, meeting conditions and criteria specifically related to their, rather than Morocco's own, concerns and sensitivities, in the same sense as Morocco has a European policy. Or it could follow a policy of improving relations with other Muslim societies on the basis of the common belief in Islam or common membership in the Islamic world, in the sense that it has a Maghrebi policy. Strictly interpreted, Morocco's foreign policy has none of these characteristics.

The absence is all the more worthy of note since there are groups within Moroccan society which have called for such a policy from time to time. Under and around 'Allal al-Fassi, the Istiqlal party has called for greater Islamic solidarity in the past and for support of Turks against Greeks in Cyprus, Eritreans in Ethiopia, and other Muslims against non-Muslim authorities in Black Africa. When in office as foreign ministers, however, the party's presidents, Ahmed Balafrej in the late 1950s and early 1960s, and Mhamid Boucetta in the late 1970s and early 1980s, did not use the same language as the party's za'im, al-Fassi, nor carry out the same policies.[5] On occasion, the 'ulama called for similarly Islamic orientations for foreign policy. A typical statement by the congress of the 'ulama in early 1974 called on the Indian, Ethiopian, Filipino, Tanzanian, and Portuguese Angolan governments to cease the persecution of their Muslims which was 'guided by the desire of world Zionism and Christian fanaticism to see Islam disappear'.[6] Calls for an Islamic foreign policy are therefore in the air, at least from time to time, in Morocco. As in many other countries where religious organizations comment on politics and where religious and political discourse overlap in public discussion, such statements find little place in official pronouncements.

Following a slightly looser interpretation, however, some characteristics of an Islamic foreign policy are not entirely absent from Moroccan practice. While Moroccan foreign policy does not adhere to an explicitly Islamic model, nevertheless, in its dealings with fellow Muslim states, Morocco does use a Muslim political language in terms of religious referents and symbols, and does have a special policy plank aimed at gathering together Muslim states to take relevant action. The plank refers to the Islamic summit conference which was held on 22–25 September 1969 as a result of a skilfully pursued Moroccan initiative following the fire in al-Aqsa Mosque.[7] The conference resulted in a common stand among its 25 participants and the selection of Boucetta as its executive officer for the next decade. Although it would be hard to say that the Islamic summit has been the keystone of Moroccan foreign policy or has established or even reflected its basic orientation, the summit and its organization have been considered serious and important events in the conduct of Moroccan foreign policy.

Once again, ten years later, Morocco joined another initiative of the same sort during the tenth foreign ministers' meeting of the Organization of the Islamic Conference at Fez on 8–12 May 1979 when Saudi Arabia proposed the creation of a Higher Committee for the Liberation of al-Quds, to be presided over by King Hassan.[8] Once again the King gained prestige from his Islamic policy and his skill in conducting it, and Morocco has been active ever since in pursuing the business of the committee. It is, however, hard to say that the *démarche* has brought new ideas to the foreign policy issue, particularly new ideas related in any way to Islam, nor that it has had any serious effect on the outcome of the debate over the status of Jerusalem to date. On the other hand, both organizations have coordinated members' positions, increased public pressure, and raised international consciousness among members and non-members on issues of their concern.

In addition to the collective international interactions of which Morocco is a part, bilateral relations can also be used to gauge the role of Islam in Morocco's foreign policy. And here, the topic is immediately thrown into perspective. For if one examines Morocco's relations with all countries to ascertain the place of those which are Muslim, it is clear that through measuring the volume of trade and aid contracts, Morocco's closest relations outside its immediate area are with non-Islamic states: France, the United States, Ivory Coast, Zaïre, even the USSR. Morocco has other equally close relations with Muslim states and societies, namely Senegal, Egypt, Tunisia, and to a lesser extent Mauritania. However, these close relations are explained by the fact that these states are in the same region or are even neighbours of

Morocco. It therefore becomes hard to identify any role of Islam in the selection of Morocco's partners, especially when its two most active opponents are Algeria and Libya.

But that answer is too facile, for it begs for others the very question that is being investigated for Morocco: what is the role of Islam precisely in the foreign policy of a society that is Muslim? It would therefore be more insightful to examine Morocco's relations with other states covered in this book, giving them the possibility of ranking themselves according to the Islamic role in their own foreign policies. The leader is Iran under the fundamentalist Shi'i regime of Khumayni. However, the correlation with Moroccan foreign policy is quite negative, and for specifically religious reasons. To Morocco, 'Khumayni is a shi'i, a heretic in the eyes of the 900 million Muslims – his dogma is a heresy and can be condemned by all the Muslim universities from the Phillipines all the way to Thailand [sic].'⁹ It is interesting that the heresy of the Shi'a was condemned by King Hassan for the same reasons as he condemned partisan interference with the monarchical system: both involved intermediaries placed between sovereign (national or Eternal) and people. This position, expressed in 1979, has somewhat softened, to the point where the King has become more tolerant of the heretical government, but Morocco's relations with Iran, with which it has no diplomatic ties, have not improved.

Yet those relations once were much closer when Iran like Morocco was a monarchy. Indeed, the King's cousin, Ahmed 'Alawi, wrote a newspaper editorial in 1973 calling for a 'Holy Alliance' between Iran and the Arab countries, against Israel, justified by the view that 'Islam is more important than Arabism and that the Arabs need the international weight of Iran'.¹⁰ In the Moroccan official view, as the King expressed it, the value of Iran was perceived in *realpolitik* terms but related to Islam: a strong Iran, led by the Shah, was considered to be the best bulwark against the spread of Soviet influence into the Gulf to threaten the Muslim holy places, just as a weak regime under Khumayni was seen to be a possible stepping-stone from Russia to Saudi Arabia. Later, after the revolution, the Shah spent some time in Morocco in 1979 as guest of the King. If there had been a connection between Islam and Moroccan attitudes toward his regime, it was in regard to a third party, Saudi Arabia, and not in regard to the position of Islam in Iran itself, Ahmed 'Alawi notwithstanding. A second country that ranks high on the list of Islamic concerns in this book is Saudi Arabia. Here there is no change to affect relations and, as monarchy to monarchy, bilateral relations have been excellent. There is no doubt that the Islamic position of Saudi Arabia colours Moroccan views. As the King said with a flourish during a visit of King Faysal to Morocco,

There is nothing surprising in our joyous reception of your visit. Muslim Morocco turns its face five times a day toward the country where Islam was born, thousands of Moroccans make their pilgrimage every year to renew their faith and reaffirm their beliefs, and in Morocco reigns a family who, with its people, finds pride in belonging to the family of the Prophet whose sacred tomb, along with those of his apostles, is preciously guarded on the soil of your country.[11]

Yet, as will be discussed more fully below, the term 'Arab' was used as often as words referring to 'Islam' in the greeting to Faysal, a point that shows the importance of Islam with regard to the close relations with Saudi Arabia since in general Moroccan foreign policy discourse, 'Arab' terms of reference far exceed 'Islamic' terms of reference. Saudi Arabia is seen as a 'moderate Muslim Arab monarchy'. In Moroccan eyes, these are indeed four positively reinforcing terms.

Finally, two other states discussed in this collection deserve special mention because of their regard for Islam and their position in Moroccan bilateral relations. Libya has been a continuing source of extreme annoyance to Morocco ever since its military coup in 1969.[12] At that time, the coming to power of Mu'ammar Qadhafi was looked upon with disapproval because he overthrew a fellow monarch, to be followed two and three years later by attemps by the Moroccan military to do the same thing. Qadhafi not only congratulated the Moroccan officers, but began to emit a steady stream of anti-monarchical propaganda against Morocco until the short-lived truce of mid-1981. Libya was also the initial supporter of the Polisario Front in the Western Sahara in 1973 and has generally been the largest financial and material supporter ever since, although exceeded on occasion in the later 1970s by Algeria. Moreover, along with Algeria, Libya has been one of the major supporters of an anti-Moroccan orientation in Mauritania. Qadhafi has a personal dislike for Hassan, somewhat reciprocated, whom he regards as a feudal, pro-Western anomaly; Morocco and Libya have consistently been on opposing camps within the Arab community. In Moroccan–Libyan relations, therefore, Islam seems only a subsidiary to much broader and more dominant personal, tactical, and ideological considerations.

The opposite is true in many ways with regard to Moroccan–Pakistani relations. Despite strong Islamic ties and similar orientations in the world spectrum of policies, relations are not intense. The reasons are clear:

other than on a global level of generality, the two countries have few common interests, and in specific terms can do little for each other. Yet again, Morocco's relations with Pakistan simply reinforce the conclusion that Islam certainly takes its place among other criteria of foreign relations, but that its role is not primary.

The nature of relations, however, is not enough to provide a full answer to the question of Islam in Moroccan foreign policy. Just as many different things can be done for the same reason, indicating the difficulty of identifying one single foreign policy behaviour that is 'Islamic', so many reasons can be given for the same action. It is therefore important to return to the language of Moroccan foreign policy speeches to ascertain the role of Islam in presenting and justifying what Morocco does.

The most striking aspect of the general referent values used in these speeches is their standard nature. Morocco is for good and against evil, defined in terms of the niceties of international relations. Independence and unity are prime values; hegemony, ideology, and aggression are prime negatives. In relations among states, peace and cooperation are by far the most frequent referents, followed by *détente* and dialogue. On the other hand, the conflicts, tensions, instabilities and threats to the positive exercise of international relations always come back to the twin ills of hegemony and aggression, as manifested by such orientations and practices as hegemonic tendencies, the desire to impose one's own ideology, the struggle to gain influence and benefit, the destruction of peoples and their identity, etc. One other source of problems among states which does not fall within this nexus is economic disparities and their burdens, the gap between prosperity and poverty, and the ensuing weight of international indebtedness.

Although there is nothing exceptional in this balance sheet at first glance, a deeper look shows a very distinctive view of international relations. Morocco's world is an arena of pluralism, tolerance and cooperation; not of warriors and revolutionaries, true believers and oppressed peoples, dependents and dominators. It is a world in which problems arise when actors stray from the principles of equity which, in Moroccan calculations, they do, not because of objective factors such as size or levels of development, but because of political will, desires for power and aberrational tendencies. Moroccans thus seem to suggest that if the component units of the world are recognized and treated with proper respect and tolerance, the positive values of international relations will emerge.

In this world, Morocco is a historic monarchy: Arab, Muslim, African,

non-aligned, Mediterranean, in that order. The King stated the hierarchy of identities succinctly when he described a Palestinian solution:
'une patrie ... reconnue par la Ligue arabe, reconnue par le monde
islamique, reconnue par l'OUA, reconnue par les non-alignes ...'.[13]
Except for 'non-aligned', these are ascriptive identities and have no
specific functional value.

In general, Morocco believes that Arab, African and Mediterranean
states should take care of their own affairs in their respective regions,
and so the identity means above all the right to participation, *mutatis
mutandis* an international relations corollary of self-determination. However, the exclusive aspects of self-determination are not carried over
into regional participation; short of alignment (which implies domination
and loss of the primary value of independence), Morocco will cooperate
with other states including those outside the region in dealing with
regional matters. It should be noted that this notion of regional participation is merely another translation of the Moroccan idea of equity, with
regional affairs handled by sovereign peers through cooperation.

Of all the identity terms, the one that implies some value content
is 'Islamic', yet the content is never spelt out. 'Islamic' is used less
frequently than 'Arab', but more than other descriptive terms. 'The
teachings of Islam and the principles of peace', Morocco as a 'repository
of an important part of the Islamic heritage and defender of its eternal
identity', 'assuming the persistence of the values of Islam', and seeking
the 'liberty, glory and dignity of our Arab and Muslim Nations', are
all typical references to Islam which presuppose that the audience will
fill in the blanks behind the notion of 'Islamic' with the same meaning.
When pressed, Islam is given a specific content of tolerance and piety,
but not meaning as rules of conduct. Thus, rare reference to the content
of Islam reinforces the Moroccan notion of a *laissez-faire* world.

To pursue the point to the extent of a digression, one may ask of
Hassan II what it means to be a Muslim, for he made a number of
statements on the subject during the 1982 meetings of the al-Quds Committee. Thus, he contends that Islam as a religion 'is true, eternal, and
universal, and its five major moral virtues are tolerance, conciliation,
mutual aid, solidarity and equality'. Moreover, 'Islam is above all a
religion which advocates the reign of peace and security, of dignity and
liberty.' He further advises that before 'being political, our responsibility
is moral', and that religion 'as the Prophet has emphasized, is above
all a matter of social relations. However, in our times these relations
are essentially international. If our international relations are good, so
will our future be too.' And therefore, 'you see, Gentlemen, that the

problems hold together like links on the same chain. We cannot be Muslims at al-Quds and impious with regard to the Iran–Iraq conflict . . . The duty to intervene to reconcile Iraq and Iran is incumbent on each of us. It is a religious duty.'[14] The thought progression is quite clear, starting with personal moral commitments and ending at prescribed international behaviour. Despite the compelling language of the sermons, it is not likely that Hassan ben Mohammed is a saint nor is there any indication that he accomplished much, if he tried at all, to terminate the Gulf war. But there is no evidence either that he is a hypocrite and these words are not a fair translation of his thoughts, even if not an absolute guide to his actions.

In this world of many worlds, Morocco is a link. The image may seem fitting for the extreme geographic west of the Arab world, but it is notable that it is frequently used: 'a dynamic bulwark in the interplay of civilizations between Africa and Europe', 'a decisive role in links between Muslim and Christian civilizations', 'linked in friendship and cooperation with the Soviet Union', 'linked across the straits of Gibraltar to Spain', etc. The metaphors sometimes stumble over their feet in portraying the position of Morocco in a pluralistic, cooperating world of many civilizations and regions. Linking, too, is a way of participating, on the basis of equity: Morocco is not only tied to others but is also the tier, hyphen as well as hyphenated.

One final ingredient in Morocco's international relations, which is not subsumed under the previous images, is the notion of the roles of heads of states. Particularly in the speeches of Hassan, and also in the foreign policy behaviour of Morocco, there seems to exist the almost pre-Grotius idea that the real decisions of cooperation are only taken in meetings on the heads-of-state level. Where others might refer to the actions of a state, Hassan refers to actions of its head, not acting arbitrarily or out of touch with its people, but representing a level of responsibility that none other can equal. 'Decisions could only be taken validly if all the heads of state, without exception, were meeting together,' said Hassan at the Fez summit of the Arab League. The same sentiment has been echoed in OAU meetings since 1978 on the Sahara, and in various Islamic Congress meetings. This leads to a very personalized notion of diplomacy quite the opposite, for example, of the faceless state diplomacy as viewed by the Algerians. Clearly, this is a royal rather than a collective leadership approach.

In summary, on the level of images, values and linkages among them, Morocco uses Islam as a symbol of identity, second in importance to its Arab identity, but the content of the symbol merely reinforces in the most general way the general image of the world of international relations in which Morocco operates. Islam also provides Morocco with an alliance group, participatory membership in a region larger than the Arab world and smaller only than the non-aligned movement, about whose cohesion Morocco has some doubts. This Islam gives Morocco an area of concern; 'our homeland is affiliated with the Muslim nation and our civilization adheres to Islam, so we follow with special interest anything that goes on in the Muslim world', but its interest is naturally attenuated by the very breadth of the area. Furthermore, since the psychologically closest part of this vast area is Arab, covered by a higher term of interest and identity, 'Islam' in a sense is robbed of its appeal by being called on to cede to 'Arab' on matters of importance. For example, although Jerusalem should be restored to its position 'as cross-roads for believers of the three revealed religions', this is to be accomplished by restoring *Arab* sovereignty over the holy city, through the efforts of the Arab community and the Islamic community.

There is much congruence between the world as Morocco sees it and the roles which it has assigned itself. Although Morocco has important goals to accomplish, they do not include a change in the structure and practices of the international system. Instead, to the Moroccans, it is the aberrational motives of a few ideological states which threaten to upset the world order, or at least world peace and cooperation. One system of world order, colonialism, has receded in Moroccan eyes as the powers have come to reconsider policies on the basis of a more tolerant ethical system and a comprehension of the aspirations of the people (a very detached view of the victory of the anti-colonial struggle). Unfortunately, *détente* in the bipolar system has also receded in recent years; the effects of this situation on Morocco are regrettable for it threatens conflict and cataclysm, but as an area of foreign policy activity it is beyond Morocco's reach. Great power disarmament (probably rather arms limitation or arms control) is a goal toward which Morocco would like to work, notably within the non-aligned movement, but it is distant from Morocco's immediate concerns.

Morocco's images of its role cover four different levels: national, Arab, African, and global. Morocco's foreign relations are dominated by the issue of national integrity, in which Morocco conceives of its role as defending and asserting its historic existence. Morocco has been a historic state 'since the day when, under the reign of Moulay Idriss I, it was established as an independent entity among the states',[15] and so has had a longstanding duty to defend its territorial integrity, national unity, and faith. Since this has been accomplished, Morocco now fears those states, presumably Algeria, trying to foster secession, impose balkanization, and extend hegemony. While the defence of national integrity is a standard role for sovereign states, it does raise a specific issue with regard to the Saharan provinces (Western Sahara). There is nothing particularly Islamic about it, especially since the opponents, for all their ideological pretensions at hegemony in Morocco's eyes, are as Muslim as Morocco. Islam has no special appeal in relation to this role, nor can it unambiguously rally a potential alliance group when used as a slogan of support. It is true that the Green March of 1975 was propelled under Islamic banners as it constituted a sort of 'bei'a-investiture of power by popular acclaim',[16] but there the enemy was Catholic, colonial Spain, not Algeria or the Polisario. Morocco achieved the decolonization of the Western Sahara from Spain 'by all legal and diplomatic standards', and Morocco continues to insist that its major and basic preoccupation remains the care and protection of its Saharan population within the national community.[17]

The second role involves participation in regional problems of the Arab Muslim world, from Iraq and the Gulf problems to Mauritania. But the Arab world is only a place, and the Moroccan role in that place is less explicit. For all the large number of references to the identity image there are few that give it content, and even those that do depend on the Islamic image to provide a more precise sense of a role. 'Arab' is usually associated with 'unity', and the means to unity is the Islamic value of reconciliation. One might expect this conceptual emphasis on Arab Muslim unity to make Morocco a more frequent mediator in Arab disputes, and in fact the role may be more real than apparent. The characterization makes Morocco's sense of the role not one of active mediation but of providing a venue where a meeting will constitute the basis for reconciliation. Morocco has been active in this sense. It has been true to this role image in its insistence on a face-to-face meeting with Algeria over the Sahara, but less consistent in the case of the missed OAU meetings in 1979. Thus, although it has no mediations to its credit, unlike some other Arab League members, Morocco's role image of a link and a conciliator in the Arab Muslim world does give it the basis for some specific policies.

Morocco's image of its role in Africa during the early 1980s has not been too positive. To begin with, Moroccans have been bitter over the way in which the procedures of Africa's international organization, the OAU, have been manipulated over the Saharan question. Then, too, there is generally less of a sense of identity in Morocco with the African world than with the Arab Muslim region; the characterization of

'African' appears less frequently and it has no strong content that would indicate any type of behaviour. As in the Arab world, 'unity' is an important attribute of Africa but it does not exist on the political level and is largely inconsequential on the organizational level. The difference with the Arab world is striking: disunity appears to be an aberration in the Arab world, but a characteristic of Africa, and Morocco's role, in Nasir's terms, is to seek unity of ranks among Arabs and unity of forces among Africans, even though some of the same states are involved, along with Morocco, in both regions. Finally, some of the African issues tend to be rather distant from Morocco's immediate concerns. Thus, Morocco constantly cites the Namibian problem, but without much effect; otherwise Morocco's main African concerns tend to be Arab, Muslim or Maghrebi. Unlike the situation of the late 1970s, when Ethiopia, Shaba and Angola were boiling, there is little to bring out a Moroccan sense of role in the continent in the early 1980s. At that time, however, Morocco's African role was seen in the same terms as identified above: defence by countries which Morocco supported against aggression and hegemony by ideologically oriented, mainly communist, states and movements.

The fourth role area is the vaguest and the most intriguing, as Morocco seeks a role image for itself in the global arena. Vagueness is the first characteristic; the subject is little discussed and there is no notion of leading the assault on the barricades of the international political order and its core club, as is usually found in the imagery of some other Arab and African states. Since Morocco's world view is made up of equity among states and regional participation, the bipolar conflict falls into a region of its own that is of little direct concern for Moroccan participation. However, regions are not hermetically sealed. Some problems, such as disarmament and indebtedness, are not only trans-regional but also imbalanced in their power implications. There is little indication of a Moroccan role in these situations. A second way in which regions permeate into each other is through the interest of great powers in the affairs of regions other than their own, even if the reverse does not obtain. Morocco does not withdraw from the world; while its spokesmen regularly cite their good relations with the Soviet Union, they also defend vigorously the country's right to single out the United States as Morocco's erstwhile friend and ally.[18] In this case, the Moroccans seem pleased to discover an 'identity of views and a convergeance of preoccupations'.[19] One other matter of related interest is the Conference on Security and Cooperation in Europe, where Morocco would like to participate as a member of the Mediterranean region.

How can all these elements be brought together into a notion of role on the global level, in the absence of explicit statements by Moroccans themselves? It would seem that the best key is the notion of equity. Morocco is an ancient historic unit; a country which achieved statehood prior to some of the European countries. It thus wants to be treated equally and be granted access to great power regions as its interests dictate. Its purpose is to maintain relations as they are required by the other roles and interests of the state. Moreover, Morocco sees itself as part of the West as much as it is part of the Muslim world. In Moroccan perceptions, the West is a loose non-ideological pluralistic group of states characterized by equitable participation by all, but not by regimentation. The King is quite explicit in his view of these characteristics:

As a Westerner, as a Muslim, I am very worried about what can happen after the inevitable, if the inevitable occurs in Iran ... For the Muslim, for the Westerner that I am, that is, the free liberal democratic man that I am, I realise simply that we are undergoing a state of events which is programmed ... the Soviet Union and its friends form a coordinated [*solidaire*] team, we in the Western world live in a club without any ties of solidarity.[20]

In conclusion, we can return to the question of explanation. Why is it that Islam has such a small role in Moroccan foreign policy? First, it should be recognized that the question is somewhat of a straw-man, in that Islam is neither a basic parameter of analysis nor a guide of behaviour in any state, let alone a state that is among those least touched by the phenomenon of Islamic revival. This is true because of the ambiguous content of Islam on the subject of foreign relations; because of the overriding imperatives of national interest; and because of both broader and sharper applicability of international politics concepts for both analysis and behaviour. Islam does not always tell us what to do unambiguously, and when it does do so, national interest and systemic dynamics tell us better. 'Reconcile,' says Islam, but imperatives of international politics tell us when, how, why and when not to do so. Islam is not a good predictor of foreign policy behaviour, primarily because its predictions are not particularly precise. Nor does Islam seem to be a valid explanatory tool for the motivations of Moroccan foreign policy. Otherwise how could the analyst explain Morocco's support, in some issues, for the United States against Libya or for Spain against Algeria.

Second, Morocco has not been rocked by the revival of militant Islamic fundamentalism to the same degree as others have been – indeed, if anything Morocco can point to a decreasing use of Islamic symbolism to emphasize that difference. This is not the place to go into the question of fundamentalism in Morocco,[21] but state control of religious personnel, the position of the King as *emir al-mu'minin*, and the less disruptive effects of modernization all contribute to a moderating effect. Islamic language[22] and a certain degree of Islamic content are therefore expected but are not subjects of rending debate. The sharpest judgement in all the May 1982 religious discourses of the King, in which much time was spent on decrying the split in Islam between Sunni and Shi'i, was the very Sunni pronouncement that 'No Muslim can tear himself away from his obligations in this life on the pretext that he is imam, sheikh, 'alem, qadi or mufti ... In Islam, there is no clergy, neither sunni or shi'i.'[23] That speech was not particularly addressed to Moroccans, but in Morocco it was scarcely controversial.

Third, Islam has little relation to Morocco's major issues. It is not a relevant differentiating and unifying force in the Sahara; it does not legitimize a balance of power with Algeria and Libya in the Maghreb; it does not designate a peace or a war strategy in Palestine; it does not even help win friends and influence nations over the future of al-Quds; it does not prescribe how to keep the Libyans out of, and the Chadians in, Chad; it does not put backbone into the structures of the O A U; and it gives no guidance on positions to take or partnerships to make on global issues such as facilities, indebtedness, and disarmament.

Moroccan foreign policy is a horse painted green, but it is still a horse. Whether to groom or to govern, the same word is used. But it is best to analyse and understand it by its nature than by its colour.

Notes

1. There are few good sources on Moroccan foreign policy as a whole. On an earlier period, see I. William Zartman, *Problems of New Power* (New York, Atherton, 1964) and I. William Zartman, 'North African Foreign Policy', in L. Carl Brown (ed.), *State and Society in Independent North Africa* (Washington, Middle East Institute, 1966). On the Western Saharan problem, see John Damis, *Conflict in Northwest Africa: The Western Sahara Dispute* (Stanford, Hoover Institute, 1982); Richard Parker, *The United States and North Africa* (forthcoming); I. William Zartman, *Ripe for Resolution: Conflict and Intervention in Africa* (New Haven, Yale University Press, 1983); and Francisco Molar, *El Proceso de Autodeterminación del Sahara* (Valencia, Fernando Torres, 1982). On Islam and North Africa, see Dale Eickelman, *Moroccan Islam* (Austin, University of Texas Press, 1976); Clifford Geertz, *Islam Observed* (New Haven, Yale University Press, 1968); Ernest Gellner and Jean-Claude Vatin (eds.), *Islam et politique au Maghreb* (Paris, CNRS, 1981); and Jean-Claude Vatin, 'Revivalism in the Maghreb: Islam as an Alternative Political Language', in Ali Hillal Dessouki (ed.), *Islamic Resurgence* (New York, Praeger, 1981). On Moroccan politics in general, see John Waterbury, *The Commander of the Faithful* (New York, 1970) and Remy Leveau, *Le Fellah marocain, défenseur*

du trône (Paris, Fondation nationale des sciences politiques, 1976). On problems of dealing with the phenomenon of Islam, see Edward Said, *Covering Islam* (New York, Pantheon, 1981), esp. pp. xv, 53–5, 59.

2. See Robert Axelrod (ed.), *Structure of Decision: The Cognitive Maps of Political Elites* (Princeton, Princeton University Press, 1976), and Robert Axelrod, 'Argumentation in Foreign Policy Settings', in I. William Zartman (ed.), *The Negotiation Process* (Beverly Hills, Sage, 1978); Jack Snyder, 'Rationality at the Brink', *World Politics* (1978), 345–65.

3. See Kai J. Holsti, 'National Role Conceptions in the Study of Foreign Policy', *International Studies Quarterly* (1970), 233–309.

4. Speeches are found in UN General Assembly records, in Moroccan newspapers, and also in Ahmed Osman, *Discours, declarations et interviews 1972–79* (Rabat, Prime Ministry, 1981) and Hassan II, *Discours et interviews 3 Mars 1978 – 3 Mars 1979* (Rabat, Ministry of State for Information, 1980).

5. Al-Fassi died in 1973. Note that one of the authoritative statements on Istiqlal principles, 'Abdulkrim Ghallab, *Al-Istiqlaliya: 'Aqida wa madhhab wa burnamej* (Casablanca, 1960), contains one line about 'Islamic solidarity' on its penultimate page (p. 166); and another, 'Abdulhamid 'Awad, *Al-Istiqlaliya* (Rabat, c. 1960) contains nothing on foreign policy.

6. *Maroc Soir*, 4 June 1973.

7. See *Maghreb*, November 1969, pp. 28–33.

8. See *Maghreb-Machrek*, July 1979, pp. 23–5.

9. Hassan II, *Discours et interviews*, p. 293.

10. *Maroc Soir Hebdo*, 1 July 1973.

11. *Maroc Soir*, 2 June 1973.

12. On Libya and Morocco, see I. William Zartman and Aureliano Buendia, 'La Politique etrangère libyenne', in M. Flory (ed.), *La Libye nouvelle* (Paris, CNRS, 1975); John Cooley, *Libyan Sandstorm* (New York, Holt, Rinehart and Winston, 1982); and John Damis, *Conflict in Northwest Africa*.

13. *Le Matin*, 18 March 1982.

14. See especially *Le Matin*, 8 May, 9 May 1982; also Hassan II, *Discours et interviews*.

15. *Le Matin*, 4 March 1982, speech from the throne.

16. Mhamid Boucetta, *UNGA A/36/PV21ff*, 5 October 1981.

17. *Le Matin*, 4 March 1981. See Jerome Weiner, 'The Green March in Historical Perspective', *Middle East Journal* (1979), 20–33.

18. *Le Matin*, 18 March 1982.

19. *Le Matin*, 4 March 1982.

20. Hassan II, *Discours et interviews*, pp. 295, 306, 308, 9 and 23 February 1979.

21. See Gellner and Vatin, *Islam et politique au Maghreb*.

22. See Vatin, 'Revivalism in the Maghreb.'

23. Hassan II to ISESCO, *Le Matin*, 7 May 1982; see also Hassan II, *Discours et interviews*, pp. 292ff, 9 February 1979.

8 Invoking the Spirit of Arabism: Islam in the Foreign Policy of Saddam's Iraq

ADEED DAWISHA

In the middle of the Middle East lies Iraq; a country 95 per cent of whose population is Muslim, but which is ruled by the Ba'th Party, a mass organization which purports to be secular. Ba'thist principles began to penetrate the ideological orientation of Iraqi society after the Second World War, and by 1958 when the monarchy was overthrown the Ba'th Party had established itself as a major political force in the country. By 1963 it had gained enough strength to take over control of the government, albeit for a period of months before it was overthrown by non-Ba'thist nationalist officers. Its ideological appeal, and correspondingly its underground activities, continued to grow until in July 1968 it engineered a series of *coups d'état* which made it throughout the 1970s the undisputed governing party of Iraq.

In the personalized political world of the Middle East, however, it is not so much the party itself, even one as prestigious as the Ba'th, but the key person within the party who directs the country's ideological orientation. This is not to suggest that the Ba'th Party has no influence, for it certainly sets certain limitations on the Chief Executive's freedom of manoeuvre. Yet power, including political, and even in certain cases ideological, direction, resides in the final analysis with the Chief Executive; for to set limitations is not to formulate or reverse policies, and to argue a point is not to make the argument stick.

In analysing governmental values and policies, therefore, the focus of attention ought to be directed towards the 'man at the top'. Since the Ba'th Party's assumption of power in 1968, the man who has filled this central role has been Saddam Husayn. First as Assistant Secretary-General of the Party and Vice-President of the Republic, and later on and more authoritatively after July 1979 as President, Secretary-General of the Party and Commander-in-Chief of the armed forces, Saddam

Husayn has dominated the decision-making process, determining the country's foreign policy orientations.

Husayn's centrality could be explained by a number of reasons. In the first place, he entrusted a number of sensitive positions within the political leadership to members of his clan from the town of Takrit. The efficient and brutal internal security machine is headed by his half-brother Barazan Ibrahim. With his cousin and brother-in-law 'Adnan Khayrullah in charge of the defence portfolio, and another member of the clan, Sa'doun Shaker, acting as minister of the interior, Husayn has been well in control of the state's instruments of coercive power.

But the reasons for his political control extend beyond the simple mechanics of state coercion. Since 1976–7, Husayn has been the architect of a variety of social welfare programmes aimed at broadening his own personal support base in the country. With an eye towards bridging the gap between rich and poor, he vigorously pursued policies that included massive and rapid improvements in housing, education, and medical services; and enacted legislation on social security, minimum wages, and pension rights. Tirelessly he endeavoured to change his image from that of the ruthless party man of the mid-1970s to one of a meritorious and accessible popular leader.

By the time he had assumed the presidency in 1979, ridding himself in the process of any possible danger to his authority, he had certainly achieved a position of clear dominance over the party. This was more than evident in the changing attitudes of the other members of the party's command, who came to accept him as a leader rather than a mere colleague. For example, in an article in the official party newspaper, Mr Tariq 'Aziz, Vice-President and senior member of the party leadership, wrote in an almost embarrassingly eulogistic tone:

As for the leader of the movement, Saddam Husayn, he is not a politician who attained political authority through heredity or through rigged elections. He was the 'youth' who started his political struggle ready to martyr himself for the sake of liberation from the dictatorship of 'Abd al-Karim Kasim, and he is the struggler who was sentenced to death, and who led the secret military and civilian organizations of the Ba'th Party until the victorious revolution of July 1968. He is the struggler, the organizer, the thinker and the leader.[1]

Husayn, therefore, has been the dominant political personality within the party and the country as a whole. Nevertheless, for ideological and psychological reasons relating to the party's perceived legitimizing role in Iraq's system, and to the president's own adherence to Ba'thist ideology, Husayn tends to operate within Ba'thist overarching ideological parameters. The relation between the two is symbiotic: the president's power and authority are enhanced by the party's perceived legitimacy and its organizational responsibilities within the country, and the party's control is aided by the population's acceptance of presidential authority. But in all this there is little doubt that the presidency is the dominant institution.

To what extent therefore does Islam influence presidential, and to a lesser extent party, action in the foreign policy sphere? The example of the Iraq–Iran war is illuminating. At 1.30 p.m. on 22 September 1980, as Iraqi military units began to pour into Iran, Saddam Husayn in his capacity as Chairman of the Revolutionary Command Council made an emotional appeal to the 'masses of the Arab nation', urging his soldiers onward in the following terms:

> Descendants of 'Ali bin Abu Talib, 'Umar, Husayn, Salah al-Din al-Ayyoubi and Muthana; valiant Iraqi army, pride of Iraq, pride of the Arab nation; descendants of Muthana, Sa'd bin Abu Waqqas, Qa'qa and Khalid bin al-Walid, it is the banner of Qaddisiya and the honour of the mission once again which Iraq and the Arabs have placed in your hands and on your shoulders. We are confident that you are worthy of this mission and will discharge and protect the sovereignty, honour and traditions of your land, people, nation and glorious history.[2]

The appeal was consciously and unashamedly nationalist rather than religious. The president and his colleagues urged the 'Arab' population of Iraq to recreate the battle of Qaddisiya, when in AD 637 the Muslims of the Arabian Peninsula defeated Sassanid Persia and proceeded to capture Ctesiphon, the Sassanid capital on the Tigris near contemporary Baghdad, and to expel the Persians from all of Iraq. While part of the explanation for this relates to the conditions and peculiarities of the war itself (which will be examined in detail later in this chapter), the minimal utilization of religious symbolism in war rhetoric and propaganda throughout the duration of the conflict is indicative of a much broader and more fundamental system of values held by the president and the party leadership.

In a series of addresses in 1977, Husayn expounded his attitudes on the role of Islam in Arab politics and society. In one address, he asked rhetorically whether the Arab characteristics of integrity, truth, and honour came into being before or after Islam. His own answer was unequivocal: these values existed before Islam but naturally changed and were modified with the development of society. Therefore, he himself believes fundamentally that 'our party is not neutral between faith and atheism; it is always on the side of religion, but it is not a religious party, nor ought it ever to be'.[3] In another address, he drew the logical conclusion:

We are a nation. And in order that this nation does not appear as though it had been created by Islam, which would strengthen reactionary religious conservatism, and which would mean that we constitute a religious party, we have to emphasize that the history of the Arab nation extends to the ancient ages, and that all the major civilizations which were born in the Arab world are expressions of the characteristics of the inhabitants who themselves have emerged from one root.[4]

Why therefore this consciously minimal emphasis on religion? In the first place, as has already been noted, Saddam Husayn is a life-long member of the Ba'th Party, and seems genuinely to adhere to the ideological tenets and orientations of the party. Consequently, he is bound to minimize the role of Islam in politics. According to Michel 'Aflaq, the Ba'th's philosopher, the party is a revolutionary movement based on an ideology emanating from the spirit of Arab nationalism and concerned with overcoming the regression and degeneration of the Arab world. 'Aflaq, a Christian, acknowledges the debt of Arab nationalism to Islam, but stresses only those aspects of Islam that are moral and spiritual in nature, and pointedly disregards its political and constitutional implications.[5] To 'Aflaq, Islam is important in so far as it is one of those objective characteristics that make up the Arab nation, and is therefore an important part of the Arab heritage. However, 'Aflaq insists that Islam was created out of the Arab essence, and therefore must be subordinate to Arab nationalism. No independent ideological status is accorded to Islam in 'Aflaq's scheme of things, and the references to Islam are all secondary to the mainstream of his thought.[6] As an adherent of Ba'thist ideology, Husayn concurs:

Our ideology is not a reproduction of a religious philosophy. It is the ideology of life for the Arabs and carries the spirit of their mission ... including the spirit of Islam, but within a new context which is open to continuous development. As such, although it contains the Arab spirit in Islam, our ideology is neither a religious ideology, nor is it contradictory to religion ... It is an existential ideology that directs the Arabs to build a new civilization in a revolutionary spirit, while at the same time connects them to their history and heritage.[7]

In addition to his own ideological orientation, Husayn has also been very sensitive to the sectarian divisions within Iraq.[8] The majority of the Arab population in Iraq belongs to the Shi'i sect of Islam, whereas political power has traditionally rested in the hands of the Sunni minority. And Husayn himself is a Sunni from the small town of Takrit, from which a number of the present leadership originate. He therefore is suspicious of 'some opposition forces who seek under the cover of religion to entice the regime into interfering in religious matters which would plunge the party into the various sectarian interpretations of Islam'. Husayn warns that such an interference would 'divide the Muslims in accordance with their varying sectarian beliefs'. He then asks rhetorically: 'Is this not an entry into a doomed policy through its most perilous opening?'[9] There can be no doubt, therefore, that Husayn's clear appreciation of Iraq's sectarian divisions has reinforced his own ideological leanings into endeavouring consciously to minimize the role of Islam in Iraq's political activity.

The conduct of Iraq's foreign policy over the last decade has been consistent with these views. The primary foreign policy concerns of Iraq between 1968 and 1978 centred on the Arab world, the Arab–Israeli conflict, and Iraqi–Iranian relations. In inter-Arab relations, Iraq's behaviour reflected the radical credentials of its ruling party. Its rhetoric and policies were aimed at undermining the 'feudal' and 'reactionary' states of the Arab world, particularly those which were close to the United States, such as Saudi Arabia and the Gulf states. Indeed, in December 1972, a road-building crew crossed the border into the neighbouring Gulf state of Kuwait, and, under the protection of an Iraqi military brigade, began to build a road leading to the Gulf in Kuwaiti territory. Later on, in March 1973, Iraqi troops occupied a Kuwaiti police station at Samitha, with a number of Kuwaiti casualties. During this period, 'radical' Iraq had very little respect for the sovereignty claims of what it considered to be mere 'reactionary entities'.

On another inter-Arab level, Iraq's most venomous attacks, physically and verbally, were directed at the rival Ba'thist regime of Hafiz al-Asad in Syria. To the Iraqis, the Syrian regime was an 'illegitimate entity which would soon be swept out of power by the will of the oppressed Arab people of Syria. The principled Arab people of Syria will soon get rid of the deviationist clique in Damascus who have shamelessly trampled upon all Arab values and principles.'[10] The Syrians were no less venomous. To them, the government in Baghdad was 'a fascist regime of executions, blood and gallows; a regime drowning in isolation'.[11] Perhaps similar to the Sino-Soviet conflict, Iraqi–Syrian hostility reflected a generous dose of personal animosities and jealousies, as well as an acute ideological rivalry between the two regimes: which of the leaderships should be seen by the Arab populace as the true representative of Ba'thist ideology, and which of the two capitals ought to be regarded as the centre of the Arab nationalist movement.

On the Arab–Israeli front, Iraq was again firmly placed on the radical spectrum of Arab opinion. The Iraqi leaders rejected the United Nations resolution 242; they continued to emphasize and encourage the notion of 'Palestinian struggle' and the concept of a Palestinian secular state. Throughout the 1970s, they were against any compromise, or negotiations, with the 'Zionist enemy'. The Iraqi government encouraged Iraqi citizens to join the Palestinian commandos by decreeing that public employees who joined the guerrillas would not lose their rights or salaries. Moreover, Palestinians would be given equal treatment in employment, and Palestinian students would not be treated differently from Iraqi students. In the 1973 October war, Iraq, not having been consulted about the joint Egyptian–Syrian preparations for war, nevertheless did dispatch some 20,000 troops to the Syrian front. Having been involved in the fighting, the Iraqi forces withdrew to Iraq as a sign of displeasure with Syria's decision to accept the United Nations' call for a ceasefire. In the following years, Iraq persisted with its unbending hostility to any compromise with the Jewish state.

Perhaps the most immediate concern of Iraqi foreign policy was its relations with neighbouring Iran. Border disputes, particularly over Shatt al-'Arab, had bedevilled Iraqi–Iranian relations for decades. And when the Shah unilaterally abrogated a treaty signed in 1937 which gave Iraq complete control over the waterway separating the two countries, the relations between the two regimes plunged to a new low. Further deterioration occurred in November 1971 when Iran seized the two Tumb and Abu Musa islands in the Gulf. Ba'thist Iraq could hardly afford to remain silent on what it perceived as a usurpation of Arab lands, so the Baghdad government broke off diplomatic relations with Iran. Only in 1975, after Iran had vigorously supported the Kurdish uprising in the north of Iraq which was beginning seriously to undermine the security of the country and the stability of the regime, did Saddam Husayn and the Iraqi leadership acquiesce to the demands of the Shah. A treaty was signed in March 1975 which settled border disputes to the satisfaction of the Iranians.

The point about this phase of Iraqi foreign policy is that the role of Islam as a motivator, or an instrument, of policy was negligible. Iraq's relations with other countries in its region were motivated by geostrategic interests and ideological concerns relating more to Ba'thist pan-Arabism than to Islamic sensitivities. In the post-1978 period, particularly after Husayn's assumption of the presidency in July 1979, this trend continued, with the regime consciously projecting an Arabist rather than an Islamic orientation. The major change in Iraq's behaviour in the post-1978 phase was its seeming abandonment of the 'radical' image that characterized its regional and international activities in the earlier period. The change could probably be traced back to the 1978 Baghdad summit of Arab heads of state, held to discuss concerted Arab action after the Camp David agreements. As the host, Iraq had a great stake in ensuring the success of the conference, but realized at an early stage the difficulties involved in reaching a position acceptable to all states. In bringing the various Arab positions onto a common platform, the Iraqis themselves were forced to temper their hitherto 'radical' position.

The Baghdad summit seemed to whet the appetite of the Iraqi leadership for diplomacy as an effective instrument of policy. Making a bid for Arab leadership, Husayn embarked on vigorous diplomatic activity during 1979 and 1980 aimed at establishing Baghdad as the core of Arab political action and himself as the central figure among Arab leaders. In a speech in April 1980, Husayn declared that Iraq had 'always had a unique historical position within the Arab nation' and that 'the Iraqi army will remain strong to defend the honour of all Arabs fighting foreign forces'.[12]

In the government's emphasis on the Arab world, Husayn proclaimed in February 1980 an Arab National Charter, which set out and communicated to other leaders in the area the president's ideas on future political action. The Charter is interesting as a document for it embodies the ideological orientations of the Iraqi leadership. It thus emphasized the commitment of Iraq to the following principles:

(1) The presence in the Arab homeland of any foreign troops or military forces shall be rejected and no facilities for the use of Arab territory shall be extended to them in any form or under any pretext or cover. Any Arab regime that fails to comply with this principle shall be proscribed and boycotted both economically and politically, as well as politically opposed by all available means.

(2) The recourse to armed force by one Arab state against another Arab state shall be prohibited, and any dispute arising between Arab states shall be resolved by peaceful means in accordance with the principles of joint Arab action and the higher Arab interest.

(3) The principle embodied in Article 2 shall apply to the relations of the Arab nation and its constituent states with neighbouring countries, with recourse to armed force in any disputes arising with these countries prohibited except in the case of self-defence or the defence of sovereignty against threats that affect the security and vital interests of the Arab states.

(4) All the Arab states shall collaborate in opposing any aggression or violation by any foreign power directed against the territorial sovereignty of any Arab state or the waging of war against any Arab state. All the Arab states shall

act together in facing up to and repelling such aggression or violation by every available means including military action, collective political and economic boycotts, or action in other fields as the need arises and in accordance with the dictates of the national interest.

(5) The Arab states reaffirm their adherence to international law and practice in so far as concerns the use of air space, waterways and land routes by any state not in a state of war with any Arab state.

(6) The Arab states shall steer clear of the arena of international conflicts and wars, and shall maintain strict neutrality and non-alignment *vis-à-vis* any party to a conflict or war, provided that none of the parties to such conflicts and wars shall violate Arab territorial sovereignty or the established rights of the Arab states as guaranteed by international law and practice. The Arab states shall prohibit any involvement by their armed forces, partially or totally, in wars or armed disputes in the area or outside it on behalf of any state or foreign party.

(7) The Arab states undertake to establish close economic ties between each other in such a manner as to make possible the creation of a common foundation for an advanced and unified Arab economic structure.

(8) In putting forward the principles of this charter, Iraq reaffirms its readiness to assume the commitments implicit in it towards all Arab states or any party that adheres to it, and is prepared to discuss it with the other Arab states and would welcome any suggestions that would reinforce its effectiveness.[13]

What is revealing about the Charter is that throughout the text there was not one mention of Islam, nor was there any effort to undertake a parallel charter for the Islamic world.

Beyond the Arab circle, the Iraqi leadership seemed to move towards the non-aligned rather than the Islamic world. Iraq worked hard internationally, but as it turned out unsuccessfully because of the persistence of the Iraq–Iran war, at bringing the non-aligned meeting to Baghdad in September 1982, a move that would have bestowed on the Iraqi president the mantle of leadership of the non-aligned world for the following three years. In order to pave the way for all this, President Husayn invited, and indeed received, during 1980 more than thirty Third World heads of state and prime ministers. Out of these, 14 were leaders of Muslim countries, but even with these leaders the statements issued at the end of their visits hardly mentioned Islam, but invariably referred to problems of the Third, non-aligned, World. True, after the Baghdad summit in November 1978, Iraq became an active member of the Organization of the Islamic Conference (OIC), and President Husayn certainly used the Organization's summit meeting in Mecca in January 1981 to forcefully plead Iraq's case in its conflict with Iran. However, there are no indications that Iraq considers its membership of the OIC to be either politically more important or ideologically more significant than its membership of the Arab League or the non-aligned movement. On the contrary, Iraq's diplomatic offensive throughout the 1970s, and certainly since 1978, clearly shows a conception of the country's national role more akin to that of India, even Tunisia, than to Pakistan or Libya. Similarly, Saddam Husayn himself seems to see his own role on the international stage more in the mould of a Nasir or a Nehru than a Zia, Khumayni or even a Qadhafi. Thus, when Iraq joined the other members of the OIC (with the exception of South Yemen and Syria) in condemning the Soviet invasion of Afghanistan, Iraq's action was due more to Afghanistan's non-aligned and Third World status than to its Muslim affiliations. And, for example, unlike countries like Saudi Arabia or Libya, whose sympathies have consistently been on the side of Muslim Pakistan, Iraq has remained neutral with regard to Indian–Pakistani relations.

The seeming lack of a clear and conscious Islamic foreign policy orientation can also be discerned from examining Iraq's foreign aid. In 1979, for example, Iraq's disbursements totalled $861.5 million, representing about 3 per cent of the country's Gross National Product. Most of this was channelled through the Iraqi Fund for External Development, which in 1979 had a capital of $677 million, and which had a clear mandate to direct funds to poor Third World countries generally. The criterion for the disbursement of funds was the particulai country's need for financial and economic help rather than its ideological or religious affiliations. In mid-1979, Iraq decided to compensate poorer customers for its oil for any future oil-price increases by granting them long-term, interest-free loans. Under this system, twelve developing Muslim and non-Muslim countries (Bangladesh, India, Madagascar, Morocco, Mozambique, Pakistan, the Philippines, Senegal, Somalia, Sri Lanka, Tanzania and Vietnam) received over $200 million in the second half of 1979.[14] In its foreign aid activities, Iraq's one concession to Islam seems to be an annual subvention of $2 million to the Islamic Development Bank.[15]

Iraq, therefore, has been following what could even be termed a 'secularist' foreign policy: a foreign policy that does not consciously distinguish between Muslim and non-Muslim. For a country whose population is 95 per cent Muslim, and which is susceptible to sectarian Sunni–Shi'i divisions, a secularist orientation could become a risky political option. However, in the past, Islamic radicalism has been contained by the party's ideological penetration of the populace, by efficient internal security and surveillance, and by the regime's vigorous social policies – that is, until Ayatollah Khumayni returned triumphantly to

Tehran to scenes of hysterical adulation from the Shi'i Muslims of Iran, and proceeded to upset the delicate balance of Iraqi society and to undermine the hitherto careful calculations of the secularist Ba'thist regime.

The immediate appeal of the first truly grass-roots revolution that succeeded in overthrowing a 'secularist' monarch was considerable among the Muslim populations of the Arab world. Iran's revolution seemed to be a living proof and lesson of what Muslims could achieve if they clung doggedly to their faith. Many Muslims saw the Iranian revolution as the first Muslim victory over non-Muslims since the sixteenth and seventeenth centuries when the Ottoman empire was at its zenith. To the Arab Muslims, the victories of the *ayatollahs* during 1979 and 1980 represented the advent of a new heroic age of Islamic assertion and power. For Muslims, including the Arabs, who had suffered for centuries under Western intellectual, technological and military superiority, the eclipse of the Shah's, and by definition the West's, might in Iran simply emphasized to them that it was through Islam, rather than through nationalism and secularism, that the Muslim world would emerge triumphant.

If the Arab regimes everywhere were to feel the impact of the Iranian revolution, Iraq, it seemed, was particularly vulnerable. Not only did the country border on a revolution that had ominously rejected the concept of borders within the Islamic world, but it was also the only other country where Shi'i Islam happened to be the faith of the majority of the population. And when the new Tehran leaders resolutely dismissed Iraq's frequent overtures for friendly relations, preferring instead to mount increasingly hostile verbal onslaughts against Ba'thist secularism, the Iraqi leaders realized that their response to this new, almost uncontrollable, phenomenon would have to be vigorous and resolute. For implicit in Iran's Islamic message was the obvious bond that existed between the *ayatollahs* in Iran and their co-religionists in Iraq. Thus throughout 1980 reports of disturbances in the Shi'i-dominated area of Southern Iraq were rampant. Terrorist acts increased, and a semblance of an effort at Shi'i organization appeared in the form of al-Da'wa Party. In March 1980, a bomb was thrown at Tariq 'Aziz, the only Christian member of the Iraqi leadership, by members of al-Da'wa who, according to Baghdad, had been receiving arms, training and equipment from Tehran. This incident and another bomb attack a few days later prompted President Husayn and the Ba'thist leadership to execute the most influential Iraqi Shi'i Ayatollah, Baqir al-Sadr, and to expel some 35,000 Iraqi Shi'is, supposedly of Iranian descent, to Iran. This naturally only served to fuel the hostility already existing between the two countries and to increase the vehemence of Iranian appeals to the Iraqi Shi'is. By summer 1980, a conflict between the two neighbouring countries had become unavoidable.

The reasons for Iraq's military invasion of Iran on 22 September 1980 were many, but there can be no doubt that a main cause was the mounting exasperation felt by the Iraqi leadership in the face of Iran's continued efforts to incite the Shi'i population in Iraq against the Baghdad government. In his speech on 17 September 1980, abrogating the 1975 Iran–Iraq treaty, Husayn declared:

The ruling clique in Iran persists in using the face of religion to foment sedition and division among the ranks of the Arab nation despite the difficult circumstances through which the Arab nation is passing. The invocation of religion is only a mask to cover Persian racism and a buried resentment for the Arabs. The clique in Iran is trying to instigate fanaticism, resentment and division among the peoples of this area.[16]

As in all wars, the battles on the front were accompanied by vigorous propaganda campaigns. And it is in an examination of the latter that the different ideological orientations of the two conflicting parties are clearly apparent. At the first sound of Iraqi tanks moving on to Iranian soil, the Tehran government alluded to unashamedly mystical and religious symbolism. At the very beginning of the war, the Iranian clergy confidently predicted the downfall of the 'worthless infidel who opposes Islam'. The message to Saddam Husayn from Tehran was confident and to the point:

God will defeat your devices. In the coming days you will learn how the Muslim people and army of beloved Iraq will respond to you, and how the Muslim Iranian army and people will respond to you. You will know how you have dug your own grave – the grave of shame and humiliation in this world, and the grave of hellfire in the hereafter.[17]

Saddam Husayn and the Iraqi leaders, ideologically nationalist and aware that they had no hope of competing with the Ayatollah's Islamic status, countered Iran's verbal assault with a deliberate invocation of pan-Arabist symbolism. As has already been pointed out, Iraqi references were to the Arabs' battle of Qaddisiya, emphasizing in the process the ethnic divide between the 'Arab' Shi'is of Iraq and the 'Persian' Shi'is of Iran. For example, the government made a point of placing an official banner at the entrance of the Imam 'Ali Mosque in the Iraqi city of al-Najaf – the holiest mosque and city in Shi'i Islam – which declared: 'We take pride at the presence here of our great father 'Ali, because he is a leader of Islam, because he is the son-in-law of the Prophet, and because he is an Arab.'[18] The repeated emphasis on Arabist symbolism and the ethnic divide between Arabs and Persians was actively pursued by the Iraqi leaders throughout the war to counteract, and hopefully overcome, the undoubted religious affinity existing between the Shi'is in the two countries.

And indeed as the months passed, and what looked at first to be a runaway Iraqi victory soon became a stalemated war of attrition which was slowly, yet surely, turning Iran's way, an important consolation was that Iraqi unity seemed to be able to withstand the pressures of war and the enticements of the *ayatollahs*. By the middle of 1981, it had become obvious that the Iraqi Shi'is were not going to revolt against the Baghdad government. Vigorously using religious symbolism, the Iranians failed in their efforts to induce the dislocation of Iraq. National ethnic unity proved a more potent force than religious affinity. This time, a clearly relieved Husayn was confidently to declare:

There are Sunnis, Shi'is and other religions and sects in Iraq. All of them have been fighting obstinately for six months. Why all this obstinacy and all these sacrifices, especially as we keep telling them that the land they are fighting on and dying on is not their land. It is very easy to tell the Iranians: 'This is your land, the Iraqis are on it, so you have to fight to retain it.' But it is difficult to tell the Iraqis to fight on a land which is not theirs. The Iranians have to understand, therefore, that it is not Saddam Husayn who is fighting them, it is the whole unified Iraqi people who are fighting to safeguard their values and their new spirit.[19]

A year later, when it had become clear that the Iraqi army was heading for certain defeat, and Iranian power, revitalized by the great patriotic war, was again becoming the major threat in the area, Husayn, in a speech in the Iraqi Shi'i city of al-Najaf, pointedly touched on the subject of Iraqi demographic unity. He belittled the efforts of the 'enemies of Iraq' who 'suffered from illusions when they believed that Najaf could be part of Iran'. He could not imagine why they should believe such a thing. After all, 'Najaf is Iraq; the territory and people of Najaf are Arab' and 'the sons of Najaf are the same as the sons of Basrah, Qaddisiya, Nineveh and Baghdad'. He went on to insist that 'Iraq is one; Iraq has become one governate, one city, one village and one family from the north to the south.' In Husayn's perceptions, Iraq's national unity bound by the spirit of their Arab being was 'the real and great triumph'.[20]

The *ayatollahs* naturally did not concur. As the tide of the war turned Iran's way, Khumayni's enthusiasm for setting up an Islamic republic in Iraq correspondingly increased. In a speech on 21 June, the Imam explained the purpose of Iran's war effort: 'When Iran defeats Iraq, Iraq will be annexed to Iran: that is, the nation of Iraq, the oppressed people of Iraq, will free themselves from the talons of the tyrannical clique and will link themselves with Iranian nation. They will set up their own government according to their own wishes – an Islamic one.'[21] For this purpose, Iran had a team of Iraqi divines ready to go into Iraq and set up an Islamic government. The man who seemed to have been entrusted with the task of forming the government was 38-year-old Hojatilislam Mohammed Baqr al-Hakim, who is the son of Iraq's late grand Ayatollah Muhsin al-Hakim, the man who brought Khumayni to Iraq when the latter was expelled by the Shah in the early 1960s.

The Iranian invasion of Iraq on 13 July 1982 was meant to bring about the swift demise of the 'tyrannical Saddam' and his Ba'th Party while simultaneously ushering in a popular uprising amongst the Iraqi Shi'is which would sweep al-Hakim into power in Baghdad. Immediately after Iran's invasion, as the 'martyrs of Islam' were walking on Iraqi minefields, Ayatollah Khumayni went on the radio to address the 'beloved Muslim people of Iraq':

Beloved Iraqis: rise up, and with inspiration from the great religion of Islam attack the enemies of Islam, because with the valuable help of you beloved ones, your Iranian brothers will excise these cancerous tumours from the body of your Islamic country and will make the noble Iraqi nation govern their destiny. You the zealous inhabitants of Basrah, welcome your faithful brothers and cut short the oppressive hands of the blasphemous Ba'thists from your land. You the respectable inhabitants of the holy shrines of Najaf and Karbala – you zealous youths who have attacked these filthy ones at every opportunity, use the opportunity offered to you by God and rise up in a manly manner and fulfil your own destiny ... I beg the Almighty for the victory of Islam and the Muslims.[22]

This messianic conviction that the Muslims of Iraq would rise against Saddam Husayn and the Ba'th Party the moment Iran's armed forces set foot on Iraqi soil must have been severely dented when the Iraqis, in fierce fighting throughout first the month of July and later the months of October and November, successfully contained and then beat back the Iranian advance. And the *mullahs* of Iran must have become a little wiser about their religious influence inside Iraq, for indeed the expected Shi'i uprising never materialized, and the hoped-for coup against Husayn never occurred. In Iraq, religion as a motivating force was simply not powerful enough to dislodge the secularist Ba'thist leadership from power.

This did not mean that the Iraqi leaders were consequently dismissive of Islam's influence among the Iraqi people. While always emphasizing the Arab character of Iraq rather than the regime's Islamic zeal, the

Iraqi leadership nevertheless alluded increasingly (and particularly after the eruption of hostilities between Iraq and Iran) to the religious instrument as a factor for government legitimization. As the war progressed, the president and other party leaders were to be seen attending mosque prayers more regularly than in the period before the war. The streets began to be filled with pictures of Husayn with Qur'an in hand or reverently kneeling in humble prayer. The frequency of Qur'anic recitals, as well as of religious discussion, on radio and television was increased. More significantly, government disbursements towards the building of new mosques were raised considerably.[23] This was particularly the case with the regime's funding for the Shi'i holy places in Karbala, which between 1974 and 1981 had received $80 million. In 1982 alone, however, the regime's allocation for Karbala amounted to $24 million, while a further $24 million were earmarked for the other Shi'i holy city of Najaf, where, for example, the inner shrine of al-Haydariya Mosque was lavished with gold and silver leaf. Moreover, in addition to marble work and crystal chandeliers, the two big mosques in Karbala, where the tombs of Imam Husayn and Imam Abbas lie, have been promised power generators and air-conditioning.[24] In the light of all this, *al-Thawra* attacked the Iranian leaders for accusing Iraq of being anti-Islamic. The paper retorted:

We tell yout that Iraq is a true Islamic state, and the people of Iraq, as well as its leaders, believe in God and in the teachings of Islam as a religion and as a heritage. Indeed President Husayn's regular visits to the holy shrines and his continuous efforts to provide for these shrines is a clear proof of his deep and unequivocal belief in the glorious message of Islam. Moreover, Iraq's recent donation for the purpose of building a new mosque in Yugoslavia is a living manifestation of Iraq's efforts to spread the values of Islam all over the world.[25]

All these activities were efforts on the part of the Iraqi leaders to appear as good Muslims to a population which might have been heavily imbued with Arabism yet nevertheless still adhered strongly to its Islamic faith. This is why Husayn regularly invoked the memory of the Muslim, yet Arab, leaders of early Islam. Moreover, aware of his Sunni affiliations, he consciously and frequently referred reverently to the early leaders of Shi'i Islam, Ali and Husayn. In a speech in April 1982 he said:

We shall never tire of making sacrifices as long as we know that right is on our side; as long as we know that God is with us. Today, our great ancestor, the father of all martyrs, Husayn, may God's peace be upon him, stands as a lofty symbol of heroism, glory and firmness in defending right ... We his descendants are proud to be connected with him; we are proud to be tied to him in soul and blood. We are fighting to defend right, justice and the holy land of Iraq which harbours the remains of our ancestor Ali, may God brighten his face.[26]

In this passage, Husayn skilfully counteracts Iranian claims that he is an 'infidel' and an 'enemy of Islam' by his deference to Iraq's Islamic heritage; by his respect for, and loyalty to, the two main symbols of Shi'i Islam, and by reminding his listeners that it is they, the Arabs, and not the Iranians, who are the descendants of Ali and Husayn.

It is clear that, even through their deference to Islam, Husayn and the other Iraqi leaders always endeavoured to invoke Arabist symbolism that exists within the heritage of Islam. It is thus more upon the spirit of Arabism than on the spirit of Islam that Husayn's foreign policy is conducted, explained and justified. It is significant that as late as May 1980, at the height of the feud with the Damascus regime, the Iraqis continued to pay their share of the financial aid to Syria in its capacity as the main confrontation state with the Arabs' enemy, Israel. When the tables were turned, and the war with Iran was beginning to turn against Iraq, the Baghdad government expected other Arab countries to rally to its support. As the mounting cost of the war led to a rapid diminution of Iraqi financial reserves from $35 billion to $13 billion in just over one year,[27] the Iraqis had no qualms about requesting and receiving about $10 billion from Arab oil states.[28] However, united Arab political and military support never materialized. With Syria, Libya, South Yemen and Algeria supporting Iran, there certainly was no closing of ranks behind the Iraqi position. President Husayn was naturally unhappy at the general Arab response to the war. How could he be happy, he declared, for if any other Arab was waging this war, 'the blood of the Iraqi army would have been spilling next to that Arab'.[29] The Iraqis had expected plainly, and erroneously as it turned out, that the 'bond of Arabism' would prove strong enough to pull the Arab world together against the 'racist Persians'.

The problem for the Iraqis here was that while the invocation of Arabism in Iraq and in the Arab world as a whole could counteract the Islamic appeal of the non-Arab Iranians, it proved singularly in-effective when used against other Arab countries and leaders. Thus the Syrians, for example, were contemptuously dismissive of Iraq's invo-cation of Arabism in its appeals for help from other Arab countries. The Syrian leaders pointed out that the Gulf war had, if anything, retarded the cause of Arabism. In the first place, the Syrians argued, the Iraqis had attacked an Islamic country which, while non-Arab, had become, since the revolution against the Shah, one of the most implacable enemies of Israel. President Hafiz al-Asad of Syria thus asked rhetorically: 'Given the large, broad significance of this revolution and the huge gains it achieved for us Arabs, is it not our duty to ask why was war launched against this friendly revolution?'[30] And secondly, the Syrians and their allies stressed that the war had diverted attention from what ought to have been the real focus of concern for Arabism and Arab leaders, namely the Palestinian cause and the Arab–Israeli conflict.

Whether successful or not, Saddam's Iraq has laid greater emphasis on Arabism than on Islam. Its rhetoric has been generally Arabist rather than Islamic, and in invoking the 'glorious' heritage of the great Islamic empire, the Iraqi leaders have been at pains to emphasize the Arab essence of that empire. And this declaratory dimension of Iraq's foreign policy was consistent with the actual conduct of policy. Iraq's main focus has been directed much more firmly at the Arab world than at the Islamic world. Indeed, if anything, the wider non-aligned movement has proved to be a more active domain for Iraq's foreign policy than the realm of Islam. And, what is more, the war with Iran has led to even greater emphasis on the ethnic dimensions of 'Arab Iraq'. It is difficult to ascertain how permanent or how deeply engrained in the psyche of the Iraqi population these basically Ba'thist principles are. One thing is certain: as long as Saddam Husayn and the Ba'th Party continue to rule Iraq, then the values that have governed their foreign policy so far will remain unchanged.

Notes

1. *Al-Thawra* (Baghdad), 9 May 1980.
2. British Broadcasting Corporation, *Summary of World Broadcasts, Part 4, The Middle East and Africa* (hereafter cited as *SWB*), ME/6531/A/6, 3–4, 24 September 1980.
3. Saddam Hussein, 'Nadhra fi al-Din wal Turath' (A Look at Religion and Heritage) in Saddam Hussein, *al-Turath al-Arabi 'al-Mu'asarah* (The Arab Heritage and Contemporary Life) (Baghdad, Dar al-Huriyah, 1978), pp. 4–5.
4. Saddam Hussein, 'Hawla Kitabat al-Tarikh' (On Writing History) in Hussein, *ibid.*, p. 28.
5. See Adeed Dawisha, 'The Transnational Party in Regional Politics: The Arab Ba'th Party', *Asian Affairs*, 61 (1974), 23–31.
6. Leonard Binder, *The Ideological Revolution in the Middle East* (New York, Wiley, 1964), pp. 167–72.
7. Hussein, *al-Turath*, pp. 11–12.
8. See Hanna Batatu, 'Iraq's Underground Shi'a Movements: Characteristics, Causes and Prospects', *Middle East Journal*, 35 (1981), 578–94.
9. Hussein, *al-Turath*, p. 9; see also Batatu, 'Iraq's Underground Shi'a Movements' p. 591.
10. *Al-Thawra* (Baghdad), 23 March 1974.
11. *SWB*, ME/5021/A/1, 1 October 1975.

12. *Al-Thawra* (Baghdad), 17 April 1980.
13. Hassan Mohammed Tawalibah, *al-Kadhiya al-Qawmiyah bein al-Manhaj al-Kifahi wal Tadhlil al-Maqsood* (The Nationalist Question Between the Programme of Revolutionary Struggle and Conscious Falsification) (Baghdad, Wizarat al-Thaqafa wal l'lam, 1980), pp. 101–5.
14. *The Middle East and North Africa, 1981–82* (London, Europa Publications, 1981), p. 432.
15. *Qaddisiyat Saddam* (London), 2 October 1980.
16. *Al-Thawra* (Baghdad), 18 September 1980.
17. *SWB*, ME/6531/A/7, 24 September 1980.
18. Adeed Dawisha, 'Iraq: The West's Opportunity', *Foreign Policy*, No. 41 (Winter 1980–81), 142.
19. *Al-Thawra* (Baghdad), 3 March 1981.
20. *Al-Jumhuriya* (Baghdad), 25 February 1982.
21. *SWB*, ME/7059/A/8, 23 June 1982.
22. *SWB*, ME/7079/A/10–11, 16 July 1982.
23. *Qaddisiyat Saddam*, 24 September 1982.
24. *The Guardian* (London), 5 October 1982.
25. *Al-Thawra* (Baghdad), 16 January 1982.
26. *Al-Thawra* (Baghdad), 2 April 1982.
27. *Al-Mostaqbal* (Paris), 9 January 1982, p. 41.
28. *Middle East Economic Digest* (London), 19 February 1982, p. 10.
29. *Al-Anba* (Kuwait), 19 January 1981.
30. *Al-Thawra* (Damascus), 7 November 1980.

9 Islam and Nigerian Foreign Policy: Tradition and Social Criticism

SAM C. NOLUTSHUNGU

Nigeria has a substantial Muslim population whose strength, like other Nigerian demographic facts, is not exactly known, but it is probably between 40 and 50 per cent of the total population. It is concentrated in the northern part of the country where, throughout the colonial period and during the First Republic, there existed a kind of theocracy: a colonial and later post-colonial subordinate state dominated by a privileged stratum who had some traditional and religious claims to rule which the secular constitutions, both before and after independence, recognized and upheld.[1] The image of the Islamic North is very largely the image of these political facts – and their social and ideological consequences.

However, the North is by no means wholly Islamic – it has substantial animist and, to a lesser extent, Christian minorities. Nor is the South solidly non-Muslim: there are significant Muslim communities, both from the North and indigenous, in virtually all the major cities, particularly in Ibadan and Lagos which like most Yoruba cities have Muslim majorities. Northern Nigeria, as a political region, was, broadly, a successor to the Sokoto Caliphate which the British had subdued and incorporated in an adapted form into the structure of colonial rule.[2] Yet, the Northern Islamic community has no history of belonging to a single Nigerian Muslim state; the political boundaries of the community were both less definite and more changeable, as were the patterns of ethnic dominance and the forms of class domination within Islamic states before the colonial period. What came to be the Northern Region during colonial rule included areas that had never succumbed to the hegemony of Sokoto. The notion of an inherently cohesive Islamic political entity is, therefore, false. There exists no Northern, Muslim, political monolith in Nigeria.

Constitutional development since the civil war has served to reduce the tendency towards the emergence of a unitary Northern bloc that could become a state-within-a-state. Significantly, the process of breaking up the North into various states was not only carried out by military regimes that had a preponderance of Northern officers but was also generally quite popular in the North as well. Furthermore, that development has favoured a secularization of politics at all levels even though at a somewhat cautious pace.

Nigeria is, therefore, not a Muslim state, nor even approximately so. Yet, Islam does represent an important social force. Politicians have used it in the past in sectarian ways and may do so again. Those who deplore such manipulation of religion, or who prefer a secular politics, nevertheless have to come to terms with the strength of religious belief among the people. Through Islam, ordinary people in the North are open to influences from outside the country's borders and to moral sentiments that may conflict with those of the secular state. International boundaries in West Africa are still not impermeable – to migration as well as trade. Moreover, substantial numbers of believers make the Pilgrimage to Mecca and Medina every year – in 1981, some 100,000 souls, the largest number from any single country.

Yet, for the entire period since independence, it would be hard to find any trace of Islamic influence on foreign policy; and in the inter-party debate on external relations questions of religion have featured only marginally. Even on the question of Palestine, or of Arab–Israeli conflict more widely, or the Middle East generally, Nigeria's position has been no more Islamic than that of most African states and was, at one time, decidedly more accommodating to Israel than to the Arabs.[3] Both during the first civilian administration and under the present one, Israel has had bold champions among some of the older Southern leaders, reflecting a vigorous diplomacy that openly plays upon their fears of 'Northern', 'Islamic', domination – or their willingness to conjure such a spectre in the minds of their followers. The Federal government, though undoubtedly sensitive to Muslim opinion in Nigeria and the continent as a whole, has not advanced a religious defence of its policy of continued avoidance of relations with Israel, but has pointed to the continued occupation of Arab lands and to Israel's close collaboration with South Africa. That the two countries are indeed ideologically linked in Nigerian politics was perhaps also shown by the fact that when Jaja Wachuku, then Senate Foreign Relations Committee Chairman, called for re-establishment of relations with Israel, he also urged a dialogue with South Africa. He lost his chairmanship for his pains, as well as the Senate leadership of his party.[4]

The Middle East is not an important preoccupation of Nigerian foreign policy, though some have tried to make it so. Indeed, taking account of how limited are its economic relations with Middle Eastern countries, Nigeria is undoubtedly over-represented diplomatically in the Middle East; that may well be a concession to religion but it is equally likely to be another example of bureaucratic growth whose roots are in the nature of the state and the uses to which it is put which are ultimately economic. Nigerian foreign relations are mostly with two areas, Africa and the West. Economically it is tied to the West, principally Britain and the United States, but increasingly also with the major countries of the EEC as well. Ideologically, those who have made Nigerian policy have, in common with most of the elite, felt themselves irresistibly drawn towards the West; emulating its economic ways, and somewhat more superficially, its political forms as well. It is also from the West that Nigerian governments have obtained their arms – except during the brief period of the civil war when Western equivocation forced them to buy Soviet arms – and it is in the West that military training is obtained.[5] Except during moments of disagreement over specific issues, Nigeria's Western orientation is taken for granted by the elite, and most certainly by the higher bureaucracy who dominate foreign policy. Africa, by contrast, has consciously been selected as the major focus of Nigerian foreign policy, for various reasons.

Relations with West African neighbours are, for obvious reasons, attracting increasing concern. In addition to the desire for greater economic cooperation and even integration to facilitate economic development, there is an awareness that the problems of neighbouring states may sometimes spill over into Nigeria itself, whether in the form of communal conflict in border areas, border violations by officials and troops of neighbouring states, illegal migration, smuggling, or religious movements.

There is also a sense of a continental role with much talk of Nigerian leadership in Africa. Some states and political movements have been recipients of Nigerian aid, most notably Angola during its civil war.[6] The idea of shouldering responsibilities in Africa, with its pan-Africanist resonances, may function as part of the myth of legitimation, hold out to the Nigerian leadership an image of themselves which cannot displease them, and provide an ideological alibi in the face of demands for a more radically nationalist and non-aligned position in world affairs. Given the leadership's attitude to the West, the idea of such leadership, whether in southern Africa or in Chad, is one that Western powers, for their part, have every reason to encourage. On the other hand, the more credible that pretension becomes the more it will enhance Nigeria's standing in the area of external relations that matters most: that of its dependent interaction with the Western economies. For radicals, an active African policy has the attraction that it might involve Nigeria more deeply in the anti-racist and anti-imperialist struggles of the continent, particularly in southern Africa, and thereby, hopefully, achieve two ends at once: introduce an element of suspicion and resistance into Nigeria's relationship with the West which is generally considered a major source of the country's woes, and help sustain pan-African sentiment within the country with its still surviving, though somewhat faded, radical associations.

Might not Islam have some role to play in the African theatre? So far even African states with much more homogeneously Islamic populations have not sought to push religious issues into continental politics. Shortly after independence, the leading scholar in the field, Trimingham, put forward an explanation that has some bearing on politics and Islam in Nigeria as well:

After the formation of these states the universalism of Islam, the way it can transcend tribal particularisms, might have been expected to appeal to nationalists. In fact, the new men associated Islam with conservative and backward elements, whilst the conservative and clerical classes were frequently dissatisfied with the status quo, distrusted the new tendencies, and were lukewarm or opposed to the new order.[7]

In a footnote, Trimingham added: 'In Northern Nigeria ... where the British fostered the Fulani ruling classes, the privileged were lukewarm to the appeal of nationalism, particularly since it came from despised southerners.'[8]

The conservatism of the Northern ruling class and its effect on Nigerian foreign policy is well documented, particularly by Akinyemi and Idang, but, significantly, and in the view of this author, quite rightly, neither scholar attributes it to the influence of Islam.[9] On the general point, it is because there were different nuances to African nationalism, and it had different relations to tradition and religion in different areas, that nobody thought it prudent to introduce an Islamic cleavage into the already strife-torn relations of African states.[10] In a country like Nigeria, such a use of Islam would have been sectarian rather than universalist. At the same time, the generally accommodative and tolerant character of Islam at the popular level meant that there was no pressure from the masses of the faithful for the imposition of an Islamic imprint upon the state. There are two further qualifications to Trimingham's observation which need to be made and which bear directly on the view of the role of Islam which this chapter attempts to put forward.

First, it is not that the post-independence ruling classes in Northern Nigeria were lukewarm toward nationalism that explains their attitude to Islam, but that their nationalism was not directed against the imperial power (for the obvious reason that they were, indeed, fostered by the British), and it was not essentially inclusive of Nigeria as a whole. The most illustrious of all British-fostered conservatives, Alhaji Sir Ahmadu Bello, the Sardauna of Sokoto (capital of the erstwhile Caliphate of that name), championed a Northern nationalism which combined religious and ethnic chauvinism. He created a pseudo-Islamic order, the Usmaniya, in a reactionary invocation of the founder of the Caliphate, Usman dan Fodio, which ignored his attributes as a militant reformer and purifier of the community but not his spawning of a lineage with dynastic aspirations.[11]

Secondly, it is misleading to imply that Islam as such was, or was considered to be, conservative and backward-looking even by Muslim leaders; or that those who were suspicious of the new leaders were neces-sarily of a conservative tendency. Both in the South, where the Ahmadiya order is strong, and in the North where two rival brotherhoods pre-dominate, Qadiriya (mainly of the Fulani ruling class) and Tijaniya (more popular among the Hausa *talakawa* or common people), there was a strong impulse toward reform and modernization. In the North it led to the growth of the Reformed Qadiriya and the Reformed Tijaniya which were viewed with some suspicion by the 'British-fostered' Fulani ruling class.[12] In addition, there have always been sporadic grass-roots movements within Islam, always in some tension with the 'establish-ment'. Thus, Islam was not unitary, either in religious doctrine and practice, or in its political leanings. Indeed, if there was a reactionary nationalism, its principal aim was to overcome these divisions, to neutral-ize the dangers which they contained for the established order of privilege as well as to mobilize a united North against Southern political forces in the competition for state power and economic resources at the federal level. Even within the Sardauna's political party, the Northern People's Congress (to some extent now resurrected as the ruling National Party of Nigeria, though now much more moderate on ethnic and regional questions), conservatism had many meanings. For Balewa, it signified cautious reform in an increasingly secular state accommodating Western values; for the meritocrats and businessmen, it had an equally secular meaning – maintaining the conditions under which their alliance with the Fulani ruling class would be most effective politically. That conservatism was reflected in their special relationship with the colonial administration before independence and, subsequently, in their strong inclination to follow its leadership in international affairs as well.

With the political and constitutional changes that have occurred since the passing of the Sardauna, with the emergence to social and political pre-eminence of a new middle class that owes very little to the traditional ruling class, but above all through the creation of several states out of the original Northern Region, the image of a Northern, Islamic unity is much less credible. Undoubtedly there is one dominant party in the area that was formerly the Sardauna's domain, but without a charismatic leader, with regional chauvinism much discredited, and a more 'plural' institutional framework, old cleavages have become more evident. The old 'ruling class' is much less assured of its support among the masses. The political opposition to the dominant elite has expressed itself in two ways: an attack upon their class privileges and particularly those associated with feudal extortion and ethnic dominance, as, for example, in the attack on such taxes as *haraji* and *jangali*,[13] and the hereditary principle in the appointment of religious and secular leaders; and demands for greater local autonomy at various levels, sometimes reflected in the demand for the creation of new states, emirates, and local government structures. The demands for a breaking up of large political entities and the creation of more bureaucratic and semi-bureaucratic (e.g. traditional) positions reflects a process that is going on throughout the Federal Republic. It does not necessarily challenge the established order, although its effects could weaken that order, but represents, essentially, a competition for recognition and eminence within that order and, most important, an attempt to gain access to state power, however limited, for all the advantages which that may confer both in economic life and in society generally.

It is more than likely that the balance of power within the ruling alliance in the North has changed markedly since the first civilian government – with businessmen and non-Fulani meritocrats gaining greater influence. Likewise, traditional concerns probably count for much less than material objectives related to the process of accumulation and the emergence of a bourgeoisie. Yet the ideological defence of the alliance still rests on a 'tradition' of which the Fulani ruling class are still the bearers. At the heart of that 'tradition' is their conception of the *Dar al-Islam* and their hereditary pre-eminence within it. While even among the ruling elite there are clearly rival conceptions of 'tradition' and the role of Sokoto, it is politic in the struggle for popular legitimacy to suppress those rivalries, especially in the face of more radical challenges to the whole structure of dominance, modern and traditional, religious and secular, from which they all benefit.

Popular and populist oppositions do not, however, tend to be stated in opposition to tradition. Quite the contrary, radicals legitimate their demands for justice and democracy and even socialism in terms of the 'true' traditions of Islam. The same is, of course, true of localist oppositions – they also invoke tradition. The whole significance of Islam as a political force lies precisely in this: that it forms not only a basis of legitimation but also accessible terms for the interrogation of claims to legitimacy. Babs Fafunwa, a Southern Muslim intellectual, expressed a widely felt view when he claimed that Islam is 'a democratic religion for it has no special place for princes, kings and the nobility'.[14]

The presently ruling NPN is the party of the Northern ruling elite so that the class oppositions to that elite in the North are of direct significance for federal politics as well. There is a further reason why this is so. Although Nigeria is notorious for its regional and 'ethnic' divisions, the Northern ruling elite does not differ in any important way in ideology, material aspirations and external orientation from ruling elites of other parts of the country. The problem of the Nigerian ruling strata lies not in their lack of consensus but in the *articulation* of that consensus, of common if competitive aspirations of regionally based power groups. It is the difficulty, within a context of rapid accumulation and a plural political framework, of conducting intra-elite competition within limits that reflect and serve the real, underlying consensus.[15] Some of these features may also be seen in elite orientations to foreign affairs.

There is very little disagreement within the Nigerian ruling elite about the country's external orientation. From time to time controversy has erupted about particular, limited issues, or over the style and image of policy. In the early days there was some acrimonious debate – initiated outside the elite, by students – about the relationship with Britain which seemed much too close when the Balewa government was seeking to maintain a defence pact with the UK after independence. On Rhodesia and South Africa, too, Balewa was seen to be too moderate.[16] But there was, so far as the elite debate showed, no question of any radical alternative to the policy of leaning West and maintaining a special post-colonial attachment to Britain. It was the subsequent military governments which began to sound a nationalist tone with a much more definite involvement with OAU politics, and within Nigeria, seeking to indigenize foreign enterprises. There was more support given to African liberation movements but this stopped short of allowing them to open offices in Nigeria – until 1975 when Murtalla Mohammed became head of state. Indigenization, much more 'moderate' than the nationalizations which had become all too familiar in the Third World, was not likely to affect Nigeria's business relations with the West adversely. These had, in any event, shifted heavily toward the supply of oil to the West which financed a phenomenal increase of imports of all kinds and the award of contracts in construction – more than adequate compensation for a Nigerian participation in expatriate companies. Only under Mohammed's populist leadership did the relationship with, first, the United States, and later with Britain, come under threat.[17] That was in part a reaction to the perceived closeness of the ousted Gowon regime's relationship with the British, and in part a response to a popular nationalism that was shaping up against an evident alliance between an increasingly unpopular regime and foreign business interests. The radical nationalist posture in foreign policy led to the decision to support the MPLA in the Angolan civil war which put Nigeria in direct opposition to the West. Subsequent regimes inherited from this one an active involvement with southern African liberation but it did not remain informed by 'anti-imperialist' sentiment for long.

There has, to be sure, been vocal and persistent opposition to the elite consensus on foreign policy but seldom from among those who had any realistic chance of holding state power. It has come mainly from young intellectuals and small opposition parties who are critical of the internal social order with which the foreign policy is associated.

No party feels that it would be sensible to impose a religious character on the Federal state or its policies. That could involve dangerous division and bloody conflict, and, besides, the elite, in foreign policy as in other spheres of politics, have other, more pressing, more worldly, concerns. For those who might have favoured a more Islamic stance on such questions as Palestinian–Israeli conflict there has always been a dilemma. Such policies would bring them into conflict with the West while at the same time bringing under popular scrutiny and criticism their own relations with the West. Furthermore, the Islamic camp has always contained radical nationalist states of a kind that the elite is uneasy with, but which have greater popular sympathy within Nigeria than the more 'moderate' Islamic states like Saudi Arabia who are alien in every respect except religion to Africans. Latterly, conflicts among Muslim states have sometimes been bitter and intractable, and not only in the Middle East. It is difficult to see what advantage Nigeria could derive from plunging itself into the maelstrom of Islamic international relations. Therefore, its participation in Islamic summitry – as a state – has been nominal and infrequent.

In the day-to-day implementation of Nigerian foreign policy, there is very little appeal made to Islamic sentiment. The foreign policy bureaucracy is predominantly manned by non-Muslims, and indeed all the foreign ministers have been Christians. At Islamic political meetings Nigeria tends to be represented by the ambassadors in the area in which the meeting is taking place and always with observer status since the country does not have membership in any of the Islamic intergovernmental organizations. Yet the fact that Nigeria has the largest Islamic population in sub-Saharan Africa and has longstanding cultural links with the Arab world may create a presumption of amity between itself and Muslim countries which is helpful in diplomacy. Likewise, because it contains both Christian and Muslim populations, both strongly represented in the state and in business life, Nigeria has a certain advantage in Africa as well; in Sudanic Africa as well as coastal West Africa, culture can support diplomacy while in the rest of Africa the secular, plural character of its state does to some extent facilitate communication. If there are cultural difficulties as between Nigeria and other African states, they would appear to derive from the particularity of *Nigerian* life rather than any of its religions. To other Africans, especially in a political and ideological sense, the differences among Nigeria's cultural and religious groups are far less apparent than their similarities.

It is through internal politics that the influence of Islam might come to bear on foreign policy and, principally, through the dialectic of legitimation in the relationship between the power bloc and the masses. As has already been observed, its primary significance is in legitimating the position of the ruling elite *vis-à-vis* their power base in the North, where, however, it may also form a basis of opposition. At the same time, it can be part of the ideological self-defence of the lower classes in the North – smaller traders, and even workers – against encroachments, real and imagined, from Southerners as well as from emergent intermediate strata. Thus, even within the urban modern context, the old ruling classes could still present themselves as the defenders of the interests of the common people against the palpable burdens of that emergent order. At the federal level, Southern responsiveness to 'Islamic' interests functions as a test of the worth of the still evolving political institutions for Northern interests. One example of this latter manifestation of religion in politics occurred during the debate on the new constitution in 1977, when some Northern delegates to the Constituent Assembly called for the creation of Federal Shari'a Appeal Court – a matter which was debated with some acrimony with fears of a North–South split. Curiously enough, the idea of the Shari'a Appeal Court probably had no foundation in Islamic law and, more important, it was objectively a rather technical matter which did not involve any modification of existing rights or those proclaimed by the constitution (even though there was a group of Muslim intellectuals who advocated an extension of the scope of application of Islamic law and who continued to do so afterwards). However, it became a troublesome issue, probably for two reasons: one, positions in the state machinery were at stake; and two, it was a claim on behalf of strata who had eminence in the North which was threatened by 'modernity' or 'Westernism' in the wider federal context. A 'crisis' arose because of the militant way in which the issue was debated on both sides, and because it raised the spectre of the popular Northern fury which could be provoked by the appearance of Southern dominance and disdain for 'Northern' things.[18]

Yet the Northern conservative leadership did eventually adopt a conciliatory position under pressure from the military regime then still in power. The dangers of religious sectarianism and of militant regionalism are too clearly understood by the ruling elite as well as by the populace at large. What the episode showed was that no one could rule out the possibility that less cautious aspirants to power and pre-eminence, or even, perhaps, a substantial part of the elite, could, in response to provocative opposition, or in the heat of political controversy, or in moments of unguarded populism, sail dangerously close to the wind. Equally, an anti-Islamic, anti-Arab, and anti-Northern demagoguery in some parts of the South is a perpetual possibility. It would seem that some of the demands for friendlier relations with Israel – including the quite extraordinary suggestion that Christians in Nigeria would like to go on pilgrimages to Israel as the Muslims do to Saudi Arabia – were made in this spirit, though there may have been some practical considerations as well. If a Christian *hajj* to Israel could be organized with state support like the Muslim one there would be economic gains for many: for tour operators and traders as well as the travellers themselves, who would thereby gain access to foreign exchange and foreign consumer goods both for personal use and for retail in the luxuriant small trade of Nigerian cities.[19]

The fact that the South contains substantial Islamic communities, in the case of Yorubaland, mostly ethnically identical with the non-Muslims, inhibits the use of religious prejudice in political campaigns against the North. Moreover, in the South the Ahmadiya sect, regarded as heretic by Northerners who are Sunni, remains very strong, although it is impossible to estimate its relative strength in the absence of census data. Although the Ahmadiya sect has legally ceased to exist many believers among the ordinary people in the South still identify themselves as belonging to it. Too strong a religious tone in politics may simply divide a regional power base, and weaken it, with little advantage. It remains to be seen, however, whether the recent growth of revivalist Christianity, of American style and inspiration as well as of the indigenous variety, may not affect the relations among religious groups and the spirit of tolerance which prevails among ordinary people at present.

It seems wholly unlikely that demands for significant Islamic influence on foreign policy will arise among the masses who, in any event, pay little attention to foreign policy. The popular challenge to the established international orientation of the elite is more likely to be contained in a general repudiation of ruling–class values and practices. In the absence of grass-roots political organization, especially in the rural areas, mass protest tends to be sporadic and ideologically disorganized, religious and political themes being amalgamated in ways that seem obscure, in expectations that seem both millenarian and non-rational. Yet social conflict is evident, and evident too is its origin in the pressures resulting from the process of economic development fostered by the ruling class.

While the growth of capitalism may be no less compatible with Islam than with Christianity, as Maxine Rodinson has eloquently argued,[20] the emergence of new classes and the intensification of inequality under conditions of primitive accumulation undoubtedly place a strain upon the community. It is threatening to many of the clerical strata who cannot make the transition to comparably advantageous positions in the emerging order. It is particularly burdensome to those whose traditional economic rights, limited as they already were, are abrogated in favour of 'development and modernization'; and this has lately produced severe conflict in the rural areas where even the role of the World Bank has come under suspicion as serving the narrow interest of an emerging class of agrarian capitalists at the expense of the peasantry.[21] Finally, the new order of inequality exacerbates ethnic and regional feelings of relative deprivation. Within the larger cities, like Kano and Kaduna, it has produced strong support for radical democratic parties, in the 1960s the Northern Elements Progressive Union (NEPU), led by Aminu Kano and, latterly, the successor People's Redemption Party containing a significant left faction.[22] NEPU attracted a good deal of sympathy among the members of the Reformed Tijaniya.

At present, religious dissent or reformism has been much less clearly defined but a number of important manifestations of disquiet may be considered. Anxiety has been expressed by various members of the elite about the increasing activity of unorthodox preachers. Jama'atu Nasril

Islam set up a committee to investigate the causes of conflict among those preachers in January 1980; following massive religious riots in Kano, the police in Bauchi State decided in January of the following year to ban all public religious preaching. The Sultan of Sokoto called for stricter regulation of preaching throughout the country, claiming that the young Yen Izala preachers 'had now taken over the rural areas where they were introducing new things into Islamic religion'. The most serious outburst of dissent was in Kano, in December 1980.

The disturbances which the Inspector-General of Police described as 'an insurrection on a large scale' resulted in over 4,000 deaths as members of Yen Izala sect, whose followers reportedly included 'aliens' from Niger, Chad and Cameroun, took to arms against their 'enemies' in what they may have seen as a *jihad*. Two features of the incident are of immediate relevance: first, that it drew a following from people who had come from neighbouring states, including Chad, which, subsequently to this, was associated with disturbances in Cameroun as well; second, that this 'fanatical' and 'fundamentalist' movement, as it was variously described, was anti-elite. According to E. J. Okoli, reporting in *West Africa* on 12 January 1981: 'Its stated aim is to strike at materialism and privilege and to purify Islamic practice. It is said to be against compulsory prayer hours, against the need to face Mecca at prayer, against such ostentation as private houses and possession of wrist watches.'

Despite the appalling toll of human life it took, the upheaval was a limited one. There is no reason at all to expect that similar events on such a large scale will soon recur, or to suppose that more widespread discontent might take this form in future. Yet it is a dramatic illustration of one form that disillusion and alienation can take, combining in a very muddled way religious and social criticism. However, even the metaphysical and irrational forms that rebellion takes contain a critique of the political culture and are a symptom that all is not well in the *'Dar al-Islam'*.[23]

It is of considerable interest that speculation among the elite about the causes of the 'insurrection' included allegations of foreign involvement: some accused Israel, others blamed Libya; some blamed Pakistani Muslims, while others still, inevitably, named the Ayatollah Khumayni. In the event, none of these speculations appears to have been backed by evidence. The official tribunal found that only 107 persons involved in the riots had originally come from neighbouring countries.

The divisions of the Arab world find some echo in the cleavages of the Islamic community in Nigeria. Jama'atu Nasril Islam, a conservative pressure group with strong support among certain sections of the Northern intelligentsia, is believed to receive aid and encouragement from Saudi Arabia. It is closely associated with the ruling party. On the other hand, there has been some apprehension in conservative circles about possible links between some of the Northern leftists and Libya. Although Aminu Kano, now one of the *chefs des tendances* (as it turns out, of the least radical faction) of the People's Redemption Party, has visited Libya, there is no plausible sign of financial support from that quarter for this small and fissiparous party. Many believed at the time of the Libyan intervention in Chad that there were Libyan agents in Nigeria who were recruiting Nigerians for Qadhafi's 'Islamic Legion', supposedly designed to destabilize the Sahelian states as a prelude to the creation of that Great Islamic state that Libya allegedly desired. Such fears, never in fact substantiated, had a definite negative effect on Nigerian policy toward Libya and its role in Chad.

It seems unlikely that the various sporadic outbursts and other more conventional forms of popular protest could coalesce into anything like an organizable movement with or without external backing. It is certain they would do little for their protagonists and could do untold harm. But they might tempt others with a clearer sense of modern politics to feature rather more conspicuously their own religiosity in politics. That could open a path, perhaps many false paths, for the elite as well as for the masses, but one of those diversions might conceivably lead to a tone of religious militancy that could have a bearing on foreign policy also. To predict the kind of international relations that might be favoured in such a case is a task for prophecy, not political science. Yet it is safe to say that in any eventuality, the justice of rule, and the privileges it confers, will be a crucial factor; and in this context, the reference is to justice as the disprivileged classes think and feel it.

Notes

1. See C. S. Whitaker, Jr., *The Politics of Tradition: Continuity and Change in Northern Nigeria, 1946–1966* (Princeton, Princeton University Press, 1970); B. J. Dudley, *Parties and Politics in Northern Nigeria* (London, Frank Cass, 1968).
2. D. M. Last, *The Sokoto Caliphate* (London, Longman, 1967).
3. See O. Aluko, 'Nigeria and Israel: Continuity and Change', in his *Essays in Nigerian Foreign Policy* (London, Allen and Unwin, 1981); B. Akinyemi, *Foreign Policy and Federalism* (Ibadan, Ibadan University Press, 1979), chapter 5.
4. That Wachuku should have secured this post despite his reputation for having held such views in the first administration is, perhaps, significant. On the earlier period, see Akinyemi, *loc. cit.*
5. Recent major arms purchases, mostly relating to coastal defence, have been mainly

from France (including 36 ship-to-ship Exocet missiles), the Netherlands (including 18 Seacat ship-to-air missiles), the United States (6 Chinooks) and Italy (36 Otomat ship-to-ship missiles): SIPRI *World Armaments yearbook 1981*. Arms purchases from the US for the period 1970–9 amounted to $23 million compared to $0.4 million in 1960–9.

6. See Aluko, *Essays*, chapters 1–3; J. Stremlau, *The International Politics of the Nigerian Civil War 1967–1970* (Princeton, Princeton University Press, 1977), Appendix II.

7. J. S. Trimingham, *The Influence of Islam upon Africa* (London, Longman, 1968), p. 114.

8. *Ibid.*

9. Akinyemi, *Foreign Policy*; G. Idang, *Nigeria: Internal Politics and Foreign Policy, 1960–1966* (Ibadan, Ibadan University Press, 1973).

10. See also an early article by V. McKay, 'The Impact of Islam on Relations among the New African States', in J. H. Proctor (ed.), *Islam and International Relations* (London, Pall Mall, 1965).

11. Cf. Dudley, *Parties and Politics*; Whitaker, *The Politics of Tradition*.

12. On Tijaniya and Qadiriya, see J. N. Paden, *Religion and Political Culture in Kano* (Berkeley, University of California Press, 1973), especially pp. 73–189; and on the nature and origins of Ahmadiya in Southern Nigeria, see H. J. Fisher, *Ahmadiyyah: A Study in Contemporary Islam on the West African Coast* (London, Oxford University Press, 1963). Although social and economic change creates new divisions among the faithful, it does appear, however, that in recent years there has been a definite movement toward greater religious unity in Nigerian Islam. See P. F. Clarke, *West Africa and Islam* (London, Edward Arnold, 1982). I am very grateful to Dr. Clarke for his comments on this and other points.

13. Taxes on the use of the common, and on cattle.

14. 'The Islamic Concept of Education with Particular Reference to Modern Nigeria', *Nigerian Journal of Islam* 1 (1970), 15–20.

15. See also my 'Variations on a Theme of Order', in M. Dent and D. Austin (eds.), *Nigeria's Return to Civilian Rule*, forthcoming.

16. On the controversy surrounding the defence pact, see, among others, C. S. Phillips, Jr., *The Development of Nigerian Foreign Policy* (Evanston, Northwestern University Press, 1964).

17. Cf. S. Tyoden's Ph.D. thesis on Nigerian foreign policy for an interpretation of the shifts in policy (Lancaster University, 1980).

18. Cf. Y. B. Usman on 'The Manipulation of the Shari'a Issue', in his *For the Liberation of Nigeria* (London, New Beacon Books, 1979), pp. 65ff.

19. Given the character of Nigerian politics, and the almost assured Northern predominance thanks to their numerical strength, other groups are very watchful of any unfair advantage which the state may accord to Northerners. That became apparent in the *shari'a* debate, and the present controversy over the application of the principle that all public institutions must reflect the country's 'federal character' (i.e. the ethnic and regional balance of population strength) is another illustration. The pilgrimage issue fits into this context. See, among others, the voluminous press correspondence reproduced in W. L. Ofanagoro, A. Ojo and A. Jinadu (eds.), *The Great Debate: Nigerian Viewpoints on the Draft Constitution, 1976–77* (Lagos, Daily Times, n.d.).

20. M. Rodinson, *Islam and Capitalism*, translated by Brian Pearce (London, Allen Lane, 1966); also J. S. Trimingham, *Islam in Africa* (Oxford, Clarendon, 1959), chapter 8.

21. T. Wallace, 'Agricultural Projects in Northern Nigeria', in *Review of African Political Economy*, No. 17 (1980).

22. There was a left–right split in the PRP almost from the start. But attempts are constantly being made to regroup the 'progressive' opposition in one party.

23. The official tribunal led by Justice A. Aniagolu and the Kano State Government, who agreed on very little else, both rejected the suggestion that foreign influences were involved. But the fact that the leader was a Camerounian who had once been issued a deportation order, and that his followers included many non-Nigerians, fed a growing resentment of aliens who are often used as scapegoats for Nigeria's problems of law and order. The Kano state government suggested a link between the rebellion and organized political thuggery on the part of right-wing forces including eminent members of the presently ruling party. It is an ever-present fear in Nigerian politics that bands of thugs and even private armies, organized by political parties, may, with arms supplied from outside, be used against opponents. The 'evidence' of NPN complicity in the *evénements* of 1980 is, it must be said, weak and very circumstantial. A charge of negligence, however, can be made to stick.

10   The Islamic Factor in Indonesia's Foreign Policy: A Case of Functional Ambiguity

MICHAEL LEIFER

Although approximately 90 per cent of Indonesia's population of some 150 million are Muslims in one sense or another, the Republic is not an Islamic state. Indeed, one feature of its foreign policy has been a conscious attempt to disabuse all abroad of such an assumption. Spokesmen for Indonesia have insisted that the Republic is 'neither a theocratic nor a secular state'. Moreover, Indonesian governments, especially from the advent of the New Order inaugurated by General Suharto, have taken great care not to allow foreign policy to be dictated by Islamic considerations. This position has been determined by domestic circumstances which will be discussed below. Islam, however, is not without influence on Indonesia's foreign policy but that influence has been expressed much more in the form of constraint than in positive motivation. To understand the precise relationship between Islam and Indonesia's foreign policy, it is necessary to appreciate the complexity and contentiousness of religious–cultural identity within the distended archipelago. It is essential also to take account of attendant governmental concern that incautious engagement in any international Islamic issue might feed back with adverse consequences into the domestic political process. Finally, it is important not to exaggerate the Islamic factor in assessing, for example, Indonesia's relationship with Arab–Islamic states. Conciliation towards them is as likely to indicate interest in General Assembly votes over East Timor or Kampuchea as in any matter with an identifiable Islamic dimension.

Invariably foreign policy begins at home. To assess the Islamic factor in Indonesia's foreign policy, one is obliged to begin by noting the absence of a single great cultural tradition within the post-colonial state. The national motto, 'Unity in Diversity', constitutes a statement of aspiration rather than one of established fact. The most fundamental source of diversity is the communal division between nominal and observant adherents of the Islamic faith which is most acute on the pivotal island of Java which contains almost two-thirds of the country's population. That division has its origins in the arrival and acceptance of Islam in the archipelago. In many parts of East and Central Java, Islam was only superimposed on a syncretic cultural tradition which drew its inspiration from entrenched Hindu–Buddhist beliefs. The uneven impact and degree of penetration of Islam has left a divided cultural legacy which continues to trouble the cohesion of a state which has enjoyed more than thirty years of independence.

The attendant communal divisions within Indonesian society, as well as divisions within orthodox Islam, have been dealt with ably and at length in the corresponding chapter to this in the companion volume, *Islam in the Political Process*. In that chapter, the point has been well made, that 'For all the overwhelming number of Islam's formal adherents in Indonesia, which makes it on paper the world's largest Muslim nation, Islam in any strict sense is a minority religion.'[1] Nevertheless, Islam's faithful adherents within Indonesia have never accepted that view. Their claim to religious primacy has constituted the principal source of contention over the identity of the state which became a matter of public debate even before the proclamation of independence in August 1945. The protagonists of Islam had sought to entrench an obligation for all Muslims to observe *shari'a* law in the constitution of the embryo state. However on 1 June 1945, future President Sukarno enunciated five principles before the Investigating Committee for the Preparation of Independence, which in effect frustrated Islamic expectations. These principles have served since as the philosophical bases of the Indonesian state.

Sukarno represented an example, *par excellence*, of the alternative Javanese cultural tradition to that of orthodox Islam. Although he acknowledged adherence to Islam,[2] his dominant values were drawn from pre-Islamic spiritual precepts which had taken deep root in East and Central Java. His five principles, or Panca Sila, were intended to provide a harmonizing frame for Indonesian diversity. One of them, above all, was intended to ensure religious pluralism and tolerance expressed in a belief in a single deity which would in turn permit every Indonesian to 'believe in *his own* particular God'.[3] Concerned lest provision for an Islamic state undermine national unity from the outset, Sukarno sought to exclude its prospect through the medium of a syncretic device designed to provide for all forms of religious expression. Muslim reaction was to press for a preamble to the draft constitution which would incorporate Sukarno's five principles but with specific 'obligation for the professors of the Islamic faith to abide by the Islamic laws'. This document, known as the Jakarta Charter, was promulgated on 22 June 1945 but met with strong resistance from Christian denominations who solicited Japanese representation to voice objections on the very day of the proclamation of independence (17 August). The late Vice-President, Mohammad Hatta, has recorded that, 'in order to prevent the splitting of the nation, we agreed to remove the sentence which was causing so much distress to the Christians ...'[4] In the event, the constitution which was promulgated on 18 August included an article which stipulated that, 'the state shall be based upon belief in the One, Supreme God', but the preamble which virtually reproduced the Jakarta Charter excluded the phrase which made mandatory religious obligations for all identifying Muslims.

From that juncture, the protagonists of Islam in Indonesia have harboured a strong and abiding sense of grievance. A feeling that legitimate entitlement has been denied has been based on the belief that the vast majority of Indonesians are Muslims and that lax adherents would become more observant members of the *umma* if only the right circumstances obtained.[5] This view of false consciousness has been sustained despite the outcome of the first general elections in Indonesia in 1955, in which Islamic political parties secured approximately only 43 per cent of the recorded vote. For example, during the course of debates in the Constituent Assembly in 1957 and in 1959, Muslim political parties sought without success to restore the controversial phrase excluded from the preamble to the 1945 constitution. The inconclusive debates about the identity of the Republic were even more divisive than those which preceded the proclamation of independence. They took place against a background of fundamentalist revolt in West Java in the cause of *Dar ul-Islam* (House of Islam) from 1948, which had been joined after independence by affiliated insurrections in North Sumatra and South Sulawesi. In February 1958, more complex regional rebellion in Sumatra and Sulawesi, in which the modern reformist Islamic Masyumi (Consultative Council of Indonesian Muslims) was implicated, had assumed formal expression. Public debate about the identity of the state reached a climax concurrently with a transition from one political system to another. Parliamentary Democracy (1950–7), in which Muslim parties had participated actively, was challenged successfully by forces which represented in the main the Javanese-based alternative cultural tradition to that of Islam.

With the onset of Guided Democracy inaugurated by Sukarno in

July 1959 with the reinstatement of the 1945 presidential constitution, Islam was placed on the defensive. It was also in a divided condition. The accommodationist Nahdatul Ulamma (Muslim Scholars) accepted a client role within the framework of Sukarno's unifying design of Nasakom (an acronym derived from Nationalism, Religion and Communism), which provided an acceptable place for a religious party content to exercise patronage on behalf of the faithful. Masyumi was proscribed because of complicity in regional rebellion. As a result, during the course of Guided Democracy political Islam was domesticated. Its representatives were not in any position to challenge the ideological dominance of Sukarno; they were obliged also to seek allies across the cultural divide in order to cope with the growing threat posed by Indonesian communism. That threat was met within a united front in the wake of an abortive coup in October 1965, in which the Indonesian Communist Party was implicated. Legal and proscribed political Muslims joined forces with the army in a bloody exercise in decimation which left the communist movement shattered. In the wake of successful bloodletting and a major revision of the political system, Muslim parties anticipated political reward. It has been pointed out that, 'with the Communist party no longer a dominating faction in Indonesian politics, Muslims not only confidently looked forward to attaining a political majority but also to the wider practice of an Islamic way of life throughout the country, if not the actual attainment of an Islamic state'.[6] They were to be bitterly disappointed.[7] For example, in December 1966, regional military commanders openly identified Masyumi with both the Indonesian Communist Party and *Dar ul-Islam* as deviants from Panca Sila and the 1945 constitution and refused to countenance its rehabilitation. Nevertheless, the protagonists of political Islam persisted with attempts to modify the constitutional structure of the state to reflect their values. During the proceedings of the People's Consultative Assembly in March 1968 – at which General Suharto was confirmed as president in place of Sukarno – demands were advanced for the full reinstatement of the Jakarta Charter with an obligation for the state to ensure its implementation. Such demands were not represented by their proponents as an attempt to establish a theocratic state, but the military beneficiaries of the abortive coup of October 1965 were not persuaded of the good intentions of political Islam. They were not prepared to make fine distinctions in the case of a communal group which had espoused values alien to those prevailing among the military establishment and deemed a threat to the unity of the republic.[8] As head of that establishment, General Suharto represented the values of those Javanese for whom Islam constituted only a cultural veneer and not a basis for a way of life.

Under Guided Democracy, political Islam was divided and kept off-balance because of the requirement to defer to nationalist ideology in the fight against residual colonialism and neo-colonialism and to seek allies against the communists. Under the New Order, or Panca Sila Democracy, with the communists liquidated and development enthroned as the national preoccupation, in the place of the slaking of romantic political lusts, Islam became more of a unity and less defensive, especially because of its role in disposing of the communists. Moreover, Islam as an international phenomenon began to make a domestic impact in a way that had not obtained during the two previous political systems, expressed in increasing *da'wah* (missionary) activity among the faithful. For the administration of General Suharto, concerned with the priorities of development and unity, a prime objective has been to prevent the mobilization of Islam as an independent source of political power. Indeed, Islam has been kept deliberately under constraint and even made to appear deviant to the national symbolism of Panca Sila.[9] Given the sustained sense of entitlement and political deprivation of Islam, such a policy has given rise to evident tension among a population of some 150 millions, of whom at least a third are orthodox Muslims. For the Suharto administration, domestic political context possesses an evident international dimension. A prime consideration has been to prevent international issues being used or exploited either to advance demands presented by Muslim groups, or to enhance the political standing of Islam *per se* within the Republic.

The object of this extended introduction has been to underline the domestic considerations which govern the relationship between Islam and foreign policy in Indonesia, especially during the administration of President Suharto, which has been obliged to confront Islam as an international phenomenon to a greater degree than any predecessor. In discussing that relationship, it should be pointed out that Islam has never exercised a perceptible influence on the international outlook of the Indonesian state; nor has it enjoyed a place in the formal rhetoric of Indonesia's foreign policy. The seminal statement of its ideal nature was articulated by Vice-President Mohammad Hatta (concurrently prime minister) in September 1948 before the attainment of independence. It was made in response to current contention within the leadership of the nationalist movement over the merits of alignment with the Soviet Union and brought forth the notion of an independent and active foreign policy. It constituted an attempt to give more positive character to the incipient concept of non-alignment then expressed by the term neutrality and later neutralism.[10] This locution was subject to revision by Sukarno during the course of Guided Democracy when he introduced his adversary doctrine of progressive New Emerging Forces ranged against reactionary Old Established Forces which drew its inspiration from anti-imperialism.[11] The concept of an independent and active foreign policy was reinstated formally in July 1966 after Sukarno had been obliged to relinquish executive authority and has been sustained as official doctrine ever since.

In geo-political terms, Indonesia's priorities in foreign policy have been concentrated within its own regional environment of South-east Asia. Its international outlook reflects an underlying paradox. Indonesia combines an acute sense of national vulnerability arising from a combination of physical fragmentation and social diversity with a contrasting sense of regional entitlement arising from revolutionary tradition, geographic scale and location, size of population, and natural resources. Under the administration of President Suharto, there has been an attempt to overcome vulnerability and to express entitlement through an unprecedented exercise in regional association; the Association of South-East Asian Nations (ASEAN). The ideal objective in founding and participating actively in ASEAN has been to promote an indigenously rooted system of regional order based on freely entered cooperating relations and not on the kind of hectoring dominance associated with Sukarno. Despite the setbacks which have been occasioned, above all, by the outbreak of the third Indochina war over Kampuchea, Indonesia's long-term regional design has not been set aside. In this undertaking, there is no identifiable Islamic component. One of its regional partners, Malaysia, does present an Islamic identity, while two others possess politically significant Muslim minorities. Islam, however, does not make any contribution to the practice of a *raison d'état* which has been directed to promoting a structure of regional relations based on an agreed code of conduct and which seeks to exclude the undue involvement of external powers.

In international economic relations, Indonesia's main ties are with Japan and the United States. It is a minor, if active, member of OPEC but has not attracted conspicuous economic attention from oil-rich Arab–Islamic states. International economic policy has been governed by criteria of development which in internal expression has not been of notable benefit to indigenous Islamic entrepreneurs. Such elements have tended to feel that the policy of development which has opened

Indonesia up to transnational corporations has been at their expense. In this respect, one practical dimension of foreign policy has served to reinforce internal tensions.

Foreign policy in Indonesia is in the formal charge of a government department. However, ultimate sanction for its conduct comes from a military establishment whose formative experience has produced a strong disposition against an Islam regarded as a danger to national unity. Heavy military representation in senior diplomatic posts and within the higher echelons of the Foreign Ministry provided visible assurance that the external priorities of the armed forces will not be disregarded. However, the civilian section of the Foreign Ministry has been permitted freedom of initiative in areas where matters of security do not impinge too directly. Relations with Arab–Islamic states fall under this heading but have not proved to be a matter of controversy because the consensus which pervades the armed forces over the issue of Islam extends to the Foreign Ministry.

For the greater part of its independent existence, Indonesia has been governed by administrations which have reflected the alternative pre-Islamic cultural tradition associated with East and Central Java. For short periods during Parliamentary Democracy (1950–7), identifiably Islamic prime ministers from Masyumi led unstable coalition governments within which power was shared with secular parties. There have been three such prime ministers. Mohammad Natsir (September 1950 to April 1951); Sukiman Wirjosandjojo (April 1951 to April 1952); and Burhannuddin Harahap (August 1955 to March 1956). An examination of programmes presented to Parliament by these prime ministers does not indicate any Islamic content. A particular disposition toward the Western constellation of states and a vigorous anti-communism on the part of Sukiman may have derived in part from religious conviction but hardly expressed Islamic interests. Moreover, all governments during the parliamentary period were obliged to cope with the *Dar ul-Islam* insurrection which, by its very nature, placed identifiably Islamic prime ministers in a difficult position. The only period in which Islam has served as a positive element in foreign policy occurred during Indonesia's struggle for independence but only as part of a general diplomatic strategy designed to secure recognition and international endorsement for the embattled Republic. Thus, after attendance at the Asian Relations Conference held in New Delhi in March 1947, a conspicuously Islamic Deputy-Foreign Minister, Haji Agus Salim, who enjoyed fluent command of Arabic, travelled to Cairo where he set up a mission with the object of soliciting recognition from Arab League states. He was successful in his endeavours to the extent that he was able to conclude treaties of friendship on behalf of the Republic with Egypt and Syria and secure recognition from Iraq and Lebanon.

With the attainment of independence in December 1949, no evident Islamic strain was manifested in foreign policy. Indeed, foreign policy as such constituted a secondary priority at the outset; the most important foreign policy issue was the recovery of the western half of the island of New Guinea (Irian Barat) which early governments sought to achieve by quiet diplomacy. Nonetheless, there was a propensity for international issues to penetrate the domestic political process; most dramatically exemplified when the Sukiman government was brought down because its foreign minister, Achmad Subarjo, concluded a military-aid agreement with the United States on terms deemed offensive to national dignity and an independent and active foreign policy. Accordingly, there was no disposition to offend orthodox Muslims who identified with co-religionists in the Arab–Islamic world, especially given the revival of links with Middle Eastern seats of learning and of the *hajj* after the Japanese occupation and the struggle for independence. Recognition was not accorded to the state of Israel, but support for the cause of the Palestinians was extended on the ground of the right to national self-determination. Support for the independence of other Arab–Islamic peoples, for example, in the case of Morocco, was extended on the same basis and not on the ground of co-religionist affinity. At the historic Asian–African Conference in Bandung in 1955 both Nehru and U Nu opposed the inclusion of the Palestinian issue on the agenda but Prime Minister Ali Sastroamijoyo (whose secular nationalist party was a bitter rival of Masyumi) argued successfully in favour.[12] An invitation was not extended to any Palestinian delegation, although the Grand Mufti of Jerusalem was among the invited guests. The final communiqué of the conference called for support for the rights of the Arab people of Palestine and for the implementation of United Nations resolutions designed to achieve a peaceful settlement. Subsequently, Indonesia accorded strong support for President 'Abd al-Nasir during the Suez crisis on the ground of anti-colonial solidarity.

· If no offence was given to Muslim opinion by the practice of foreign policy during the parliamentary period, even less opportunity was provided for criticism during Guided Democracy, given its domination by issues of colonialism and neo-colonialism. The issue of West New Guinea (Irian Barat) assumed crisis proportions and culminated in a successful exercise in coercive diplomacy. Confrontation pursued against Malaysia, where Islam was the official religion, was a failure and contributed to Sukarno's downfall. During the period of Guided Democracy, foreign policy served the evident domestic function of sustaining an unstable political equilibrium but Islam had no special place. In August 1962 a stormy episode occurred, arising in part from the exclusion of Israeli athletes from the Asian Games which were being held in Jakarta. Their exclusion in response to Arab pressure cannot be separated from the concurrent exclusion of athletes from Taiwan. Indeed, the double exclusion fitted easily at the time into Sukarno's representation of the struggle of the New Emerging Forces. If exclusion of Israeli athletes did not constitute deference to a specifically Islamic cause, the action may be construed as a sweetener to Indonesia's Muslim community who, together with the Communist Party and leftist affiliates, had been expected to oppose Israeli participation.[13]

The Indonesian Foreign Ministry's conduct over the Asian Games provided a further indication of a pragmatic approach to any international issue which might provoke or serve to mobilize the Muslim community. With the collapse of Guided Democracy and its succession by the New Order, there was a greater requirement both to contain and take account of domestic Muslim potential and opinion. Political Islam was perceived to pose a major threat to national unity in the light of its adherents' capacity for violence demonstrated in the process of liquidating the Indonesian Communist Party and the revival of claims to incorporate a mandatory obligation for Muslims to practise their faith in the preamble to the constitution. Compared to Sukarno at the peak of his powers, General Suharto was less assured of his ability to contain the Muslims. Muslim mobilization had been affected also by the increasing impact of Islam in the international environment which served to influence the attitude of the Indonesian government. Islamic solidarity had been stimulated by Israel's dramatic victory in June 1967 in which all of Jerusalem, including the temple mount, was captured. The moment for greater self-assertion was seized by Saudi Arabia, especially with the burning of the al-Aqsa Mosque in Jerusalem in August 1969. The first meeting of Muslim heads of government convened in Rabat in September and addressed the wider question of Jerusalem. In March 1970, a meeting of Islamic foreign ministers took place in Jidda, which set up a permanent secretariat. In March 1972, delegates met again in Jidda to compile and promulgate a charter of the Islamic Conference, whose first objective was 'to promote Islamic solidarity among member states'. In respect of membership, the Charter stated that 'every Muslim state is eligible to join the Islamic Conference on submitting an application expressing its desire and preparedness to adopt this Charter'. In other words, membership of the Organization of the Islamic Conference (OIC) was deemed to constitute an affirmation of state identity.

Indonesia sent a delegation to the conference in Jidda in March 1972 but it declined to seek formal membership of the OIC and pointedly refused to sign the Islamic Charter in contrast to its ASEAN partner, Malaysia. Indeed, participation itself was controversial within Indonesia, and Foreign Minister Adam Malik was obliged to issue a press statement at the end of 1972, to the effect that the government was not yet prepared to sign the Islamic Charter and that the Republic was not an Islamic country. His statement attracted mildly critical comment from the influential, newly-formed Centre for Strategic and International Studies, a government-sponsored 'think-tank' known to be unsympathetic to the cause of political Islam. It was pointed out that:

Mr. Malik's statement is thus an important affirmation that Indonesia is not an Islamic country or any other form of a theocratic state directly governed by Islamic or other religious laws. It is, rather, if one rejects the term 'secular', a theo-democratic state, indirectly governed by God's laws through sound human reason and common sense.

On that basis, it can surely be argued that Indonesia should not have sent a delegation to the Jeddah conference in the first place. At least the delegation should have only had the status of an observer rather than a full participant. It is possible, however, that the delegation was sent with the understanding that it represented a Moslem country merely in the sense that it is predominantly Moslem populated, so that the interests of the Moslems in general, which the conference was surely meant to serve, would also be the interests of the Indonesian Moslems.[14]

This comment serves to indicate the dilemma of the Suharto administration which prefers to keep the Arab–Islamic world at a distance lest it establish an unhealthy junction with volatile political forces within Indonesia. On the other hand, it is only too conscious of a requirement to express at least nominal solidarity when appropriate in order to contain those forces and deny them an issue which might mobilize their strength. For example, the Indonesian government cannot divorce itself from a matter such as the status of Jerusalem. Indeed, General Suharto has publicly criticized the government of Israel for its unilateral revision of that status which he acknowledged publicly had 'offended the feelings of the Islamic community throughout the world'. Moreover, it was obliged in April 1982, in the middle of a turbulent election campaign, to heed the late King Khalid's call for a one-day strike in protest at a shooting on the temple mount in Jerusalem by a Jewish gunman. Nonetheless, where it has had a choice, the Indonesian government has sought to restrict involvement in Islamic issues and to maintain a balance in external associations designed to fulfil a domestic function in both positive and negative senses. In May 1981, Foreign Minister Mochtar Kusumaatmadja was questioned during the course of an interview as to why Indonesia as a Muslim country had not signed the Charter of the OIC. Apart from reiterating that Indonesia was 'not a Muslim country in the sense that it is an Islamic state', he indicated satisfaction with the position of ambiguity which permitted Indonesia to participate in the activities of the OIC without being obliged to undertake a commitment to unacceptable principles. In response to persistent questioning as to his government's specific objections to the Islamic Charter, he replied:

You are a South Asian but in South-East Asia we are not nitpickers, I am sorry to say that, because I see this always with my South Asian friends. They love to quarrel about one word and spend hours and waste a lot of time. South-East Asians are more practical. They say that what is this, you want to co-operate in this, what is the objective, all right. We are not so particular about details. I prefer the South-East Asian way. It is more productive. It is more pleasant. It does not involve any recriminations, debates, long waste of time and a big fat zero in the end. So the South-East Asian way has much to commend.[15]

Professor Mochtar was, in effect, engaged in the diplomatic equivalent of 'stonewalling' in cricket. He was unwilling to discuss openly and frankly an issue that exposed could serve only to impair Indonesia's relations with the Arab–Islamic world with attendant adverse domestic consequences. The point at issue is that the administration of President Suharto has committed itself to a syncretic cultural design for the Indonesian state which does not admit a special public place for Islam. Yet, it is conscious of the capacity of Islam for political challenge and disruption and cannot afford to appear to neglect Muslim opinion above all over domestic issues, but also over international ones. For example, Professor Mochtar drew his interviewer's attention to Muslim opposition to any restoration of diplomatic relations between Indonesia and China, pointing out that, 'In fact, there are two important sections in Indonesian political life – the Muslims and the armed forces. We cannot ignore that.'[16] The requirement to pay attention to what has become 'the sole effective voice of opposition'[17] has meant that Islam enters into the foreign policy-making process primarily as a factor of constraint. Because of an abiding concern lest the international and domestic dimensions of Islam fuse and establish a political junction, the Suharto administration treads warily. It engages in Islamic occasions and issues in as far as it is necessary to appease Muslim opinion, but not in a way and to an extent which might arouse it. The objective is domestication and the means adopted take a variety of forms. At the symbolic level, for example, President Suharto and his party, when on overseas visits, always wear the *pici* (Muslim black velvet cap) and are photographed so adorned for domestic consumption.[18] Indonesians are permitted to participate in Qur'an reading contests abroad, in Mecca as well as in Kuala Lumpur; while the *hajj* to Mecca is facilitated under government control. The cities of Jakarta and Jidda entered into a twinning agreement in March 1982. In the same month, the Ministry of Religion extended support for the establishment of an international Islamic university but to be located in Malaysia. In addition, the government has tolerated expressions of solidarity by Muslim organizations with co-religionists in Afghanistan since the Soviet invasion. Where matters of substantive political interest are involved, the government has displayed a pragmatic caution.

There are many recent examples of such caution. When the Camp David agreement was reached in September 1978, Indonesia sought to sustain a neutral position in response to appeals from Egypt and Jordan (representing its opponents). The Indonesian government had been sympathetic to President Sadat's earlier dramatic initiative in November 1977, which President Suharto described as bringing 'a new hope for peace', but was unwilling to indicate its explicit support because of the scale of opposition in the Arab world. For example, in March 1978 President Suharto made the equivocal statement that, 'as a fellow sovereign country, we know that our brothers in the Middle East will adopt the best possible decision for themselves. As a friend, we fully support any decision whatever they make.' The revolution in Iran constituted a disturbing phenomenon for an Indonesian government apprehensive at the impact of an Islamic resurgence which drew strength from the dissatisfaction with the values of development. Accordingly, a formal statement was not issued when the Shah was ousted; nor was one issued on the release of the American hostages, over which Foreign Minister Mochtar had refused to be drawn as to the possibility of Indonesia serving as mediator.[19] It has been pointed out that

In Indonesia and Malaysia particularly, this official silence reflects the dilemma of being caught between the pragmatic considerations of the government's support for the principles of international law and the emotional identification on the part of many Indonesian and Malaysian citizens with the idea of the creation of a just and egalitarian state in Iran.[20]

In the case of the Soviet invasion of Afghanistan in December 1979, Indonesia endorsed the condemnation pronounced by the OIC meeting in Islamabad in January 1980 but there was a conscious effort to avoid defending Afghanistan as a wronged Islamic state. The Indonesia went out of its way to stress that the Soviet Union had invaded a fellow non-aligned state and sought to avoid any commitment to defend Islamic principles which might be exploited by domestic Muslim groups.[21] For many Indonesians, there is a tendency to associate Arab with Islamic. For this reason in part, Indonesia has refused to allow the Palestine Liberation Organization to open an office in Jakarta – by contrast with Malaysia which has accorded it full diplomatic status. Officially, Indonesia supports the Palestinian cause. For example, in his address to the House of People's Representatives in August 1981 on the occasion of the 36th anniversary of the proclamation of independence, President Suharto stated, 'our attitude toward the problems of the Middle East has always been clear from the beginning, that is, we stand on the side of the Arab peoples and that of the people of Palestine who are fighting for their just rights against the arrogant aggression of Israel'. Evidently that clear attitude does not include tolerating a mission for the organization widely acknowledged to represent the interests of the Palestinians. In effect, the position of the Indonesian government toward the PLO has been influenced not only by the possible impact which the opening of its mission might have on the Muslim community. It has been affected also by concern lest intra-Arab rivalries be extended to the streets of its capital city and by apprehension at the communist connections of the PLO. In addition, it would probably not be pleased at the prospect of an office in Jakarta which might be used to monitor unofficial dealings between its military establishment and Israel, whose armed forces are admired for their military doctrine and proficiency. Indeed, in September 1979, Indonesia entered into an agreement with Israel for the purchase of 14 A-4 Skyhawk ground-attack fighter aircraft, together with two TA-4 Skyhawk trainers.[22] Indonesia has been willing to defer publicly to Arab and domestic Muslim sensibilities over the Palestine question only by attending appropriate meetings and endorsing declaratory resolutions. For example, in February 1982, its delegation voted in favour of a resolution before the General Assembly of the United Nations which called on members to 'totally isolate Israel in all fields' as a riposte to its annexation of the Golan Heights. And in the following June, its Foreign Ministry denounced 'Israel's aggression against Lebanon'. Nonetheless, in practical dealings, often of necessity, covert rather than overt, the Suharto administration has sought to pursue alternatives to an association with the Arab–Islamic states which requires an anti-Israeli nexus.[23]

International Islamic issues closer to home than the Middle East have also engaged the concern of the Indonesian government. Muslim-based insurgencies exist in Thailand and the Philippines, regional partners within ASEAN. In both cases, Indonesia does not want to breach the principle of non-intervention, to appear to support separatism, or to impair the cohesion of a regional association which has been represented as the cornerstone of its foreign policy. Yet it has faced domestic pressure to remedy the grievances of co-religionists, especially in the case of the Southern Philippines, which is proximate to Indonesia and where the conflict is most serious. Indonesian Muslims have suggested that their government has not done sufficient to resolve that conflict. In effect, the Indonesian government has sought to engage in mediation while at the same time defending the Philippines in the OIC. Because of the priority attached to ASEAN by Indonesia, it cannot be seen to exercise pressure on President Marcos. At the same time, it sustains an apprehension lest Muslim revolt in the Philippines becomes an issue in domestic politics with the charge levelled that persecuted co-religionists are being neglected. In as far as the viability of ASEAN takes pride of place, the Indonesian government remains vulnerable to such a charge. That vulnerability constitutes a special case of a general condition which arises from domestic circumstances.

The Islamic factor in Indonesia's foreign policy has become more significant over the decades since independence because of the greater convergence of international and domestic Muslim dimensions. Islam within Indonesia has become a bitter, beleaguered force with a sense of denial of rightful political entitlement. Although permitted formal expression within a controlled political system, it has been denied a place in the symbols of state. Indeed, it has been obliged to defer to a state symbolism which arouses resentment rather than an intended sense of harmony. Islamic resurgence is nevertheless a fact of life stimulated by the domestic impact of a development policy based on Western orthodoxies and also by international associations and solidarity. The Indonesian government has been conscious of the need to take account of Muslim feeling in the conduct of foreign policy. As one senior diplomat remarked, 'Do not underestimate Muslim public opinion in Indonesia. If neglected, it will be cultivated by extremists'. Accordingly, the government has sought to strike a balance in foreign policy where Islamic issues are concerned in an attempt to appease that opinion without appearing to enhance the standing of political Islam or to validate its domestic political claims. In that delicate exercise, there is a limit beyond which the Suharto administration will not go. Such a limit has been indicated by its persistent refusal to sign the Islamic Charter and by the conspicuous absence of President Suharto from Islamic summit conferences.

In Indonesia, Islam has entered the foreign policy process more by way of challenge than by way of support. Domestic circumstances have been responsible for this state of affairs. Correspondingly, successive governments have made a conscious attempt to excise a co-religionist dimension from foreign policy wherever possible because of its perceived threat to national unity. Because of these same domestic circumstances, it has been found necessary also to engage cautiously in Arab–Islamic issues internationally as a practical means to neutralize political challenge willing to exploit a co-religionist dimension. In addition, such cautious engagement has been used to secure international support over matters deemed vital to Indonesia's interests. However, Islam does not provide a natural meeting ground between Indonesia and other states. Indonesia prefers to keep the Arab–Islamic world at a distance, because Islam remains a divisive symbol and force within the Republic, the more to be feared because of its international resurgence.

Notes

1. Ruth McVey, 'Faith as the Outsider: Islam in Indonesian Politics', in James P. Piscatori, *Islam in the Political Process* (Cambridge, Cambridge University Press, 1983), p. 200; see also Harold Crouch, 'Indonesia', in Mohammed Ayoob (ed.), *The Politics of Islamic Reassertion* (London, Croom Helm, 1981) and H. J. Benda, 'Continuity and Change in Indonesian Islam', *Asian and African Studies: Annual of the Israel Oriental Society*, 1 (1965), and Michael Leifer, *Indonesia's Foreign Policy* (London, Allen and Unwin, 1983).
2. 'We are Moslems, myself included – a thousand pardons my Islamism [*sic*] is far from perfect – but if you open up my breast, and look at my heart, you will find it none other than Islamic,' *Lahirnja Pantjasila (The Birth of Pantjasila): An Outline of the Five Principles of the Indonesian State*. President Soekarno's Speech. (Ministry of Information, Republic of Indonesia, Jakarta, 1952), pp. 24–5.
3. *Ibid.*, p. 28.
4. Mohammad Hatta, *Memoirs*, edited by C. L. M. Penders (Singapore, Gunung Agung, 1981), pp. 240–1.
5. Note the comment by Allan A. Samson, 'Conceptions of Politics: Power and Ideology in Contemporary Indonesian Islam', in Karl D. Jackson and Lucian W. Pye (eds.), *Political Power and Communications in Indonesia* (Berkeley, University of California Press, 1978), p. 207.
6. See Peter Polomka, *Indonesia Since Sukarno* (Middlesex, Penguin, 1971), p. 187.
7. See R. J. Boland, *The Struggle of Islam in Modern Indonesia* (The Hague, Martinus Nijhoff, 1977), chapter 3.
8. Note, for example, the argument against theocracy by former Prime Minister Mohammad Natsir who, nonetheless, advocated a state in which the life of the community would be pervaded by Islamic principles: Mohammad Natsir, *Some*

Observations Concerning the Role of Islam in National and International Affairs (Ithaca, New York, 1954).

9. See Michael Morfit, 'Pancasila: The Indonesian State Ideology According to the New Order Government', *Asian Survey* (August 1981), and also a speech by President Suharto delivered in Pekanbaru on 27 March 1980, reprinted in *Merdeka*, 1 April 1980.

10. The full statement has been published as Mohammad Hatta, *Mendajung Antara Dua Karang* (Rowing between Two Rocks) (Jakarta, Department of Information, 1951). See also H. Roeslan Abdulgani, 'The Origins of the Concept "Free and Active" in Indonesian Foreign Policy', *The Indonesian Quarterly* (October 1975), and Mohammad Hatta, 'Indonesia's Foreign Policy', *Foreign Affairs* (April 1953).

11. See George Modeliski (ed.), *The New Emerging Forces: Documents on the Ideology of Indonesian Foreign Policy* (Department of International Relations, Australian National University, Canberra, 1963); and D. E. Weatherbee, *Ideology in Indonesia: Soekarno's Indonesian Revolution* (New Haven, Yale University, 1966).

12. Ali Sastroamijoyo, *Milestones on My Journey*, edited by C. L. M. Penders (St. Lucia, University of Queensland Press, 1979), p. 289.

13. See Ide Anak Agung Gde Agung, *Twenty Years of Indonesian Foreign Policy 1945–1965* (The Hague, Mouton, 1973), p. 513.

14. 'Indonesia and the Islamic Charter', *Monthly Review*, Centre for Strategic and International Studies, Jakarta (November–December 1972), 7.

15. *Impact International*, London (22 May–11 June 1981), 9.

16. *Ibid.*, p. 7. Note also his remarks in *Far Eastern Economic Review* (15 December 1978).

17. McVey, 'Islam in Indonesian Politics', p. 205.

18. The *pici* is not an exclusively Muslim symbol. It has long been associated also with the secular Indonesian Nationalist Party (PNI).

19. See Leo Suryadinata and Sharon Siddique (eds.), *Trends in Indonesia II* (Singapore, Singapore University Press, 1981), p. 49.

20. Sharon Siddique, 'Contemporary Islamic Developments in ASEAN', in *Southeast Asian Affairs 1980*, Institute of Southeast Asian Studies, Singapore (1980), 90.

21. See Hans H. Indorf and Astri Suhrke, 'Indochina: The Nemesis of ASEAN?' in *Southeast Asian Affairs, 1981*, Singapore (1981), 63.

22. *The Military Balance 1980–1981*, International Institute for Strategic Studies, London (1980), p. 106.

23. For a discussion of the ambiguity in attitudes toward Israel, see Franklin B. Weinstein, *Indonesian Foreign Policy and the Dilemma of Dependence* (Ithaca, Cornell University Press, 1976), pp. 125–30.

Islam in the Foreign Policy of the
Soviet Union: A Double-Edged
Sword?

KAREN DAWISHA and
HÉLÈNE CARRERE D'ENCAUSSE

Russian rulers, whether Tsarist or Soviet, have never shown any great
affinity for Islam as a religion or as a culture. In the fifteenth and
sixteenth centuries when the powerful Khanates of Central Asia with
their capitals in Bukhara, Samarkand, Tashkent and Khiva stood astride
the silk and spice routes between Europe and the Far East, ancient
Muscovy was little interested in establishing contacts; and indeed the
first traveller to penetrate the region (1558–9) was in fact the English
merchant, Jenkinson. Only with the discovery of the maritime route
between Europe and China by the Portuguese and the resultant decline
in the prosperity of Central Asia did Russia become more interested
in the area – not as partner but as conqueror.

Throughout the next three hundred years, Central Asia was periodic-
ally invaded by Russian troops, but it was not until the second half
of the nineteenth century when Russia, having emerged as a great European power, was finally able to subdue the three remaining Khanates
of Khiva, Bukhara and Kokand and redraw the map of Russia. This
period of colonial expansion, when Russian generals operated under the
motto 'Nos frontières marchent avec nous',[1] led to the incorporation
of the lands of Central Asia into the Russian empire, but not the
assimilation of its peoples or the promotion of their Islamic heritage.
Indeed the dominant view held by the Russians of their conquest of
Central Asia – a view shared by most Western colonial administrators
of Islam – was that it had been a civilizing mission. 'Asiatic peoples,'
it was said at the time, 'respect nothing but visible and palpable force.'[2]

Marxism, born in Europe and focussed on the transformation of
European society, shared with the colonial administrations it sought to
overthrow a fundamental contempt for oriental society, with Marx and
Engels writing, for example, that the 'break-up of these primitive forms
is the condition sine qua non of Europeanization'[3] and commenting

elsewhere that 'certainly there will be sooner or later an absolute necessity for freeing one of the finest parts of this continent [speaking here of the Middle East] from the rule of the mob, compared with which the mob of Imperial Rome was an assembly of sages and heroes'.[4] And Islam, with its strong social basis, was seen as a vestige of feudal and patriarchal society and was considered, in common with other religions, to be a reactionary force impeding the modernization of these traditional societies.

When the 1917 revolution occurred in Russia, the Bolsheviks believed that it had 'built a bridge between the Socialist West and the enslaved East'[5] – an East it must be said they considered to be enslaved equally by Western imperialism and the reactionary dictates of Islam. Nevertheless, for a short period, indigenous communists in Central Asia, the Middle East and South Asia did play a central role in the formulation and implementation of a radical strategy for the Islamic world as a whole; a strategy enunciated by Zinoviev, the head of the Comintern at the 1920 Congress of the Peoples of the East in Baku: 'When the East really starts to move, not only Russia but the whole of Europe will seem but a small corner in the vast panorama. Real revolution will break out only when we are joined by the 800 million inhabitants of Asia, of the African continent.'[6] There was never any question, even at this time, however, but that Islam was unlikely to be harnessed as a force in any way sympathetic to the ideals of communism. Communists of Muslim origin were coopted into the movement in this early phase, but they left their Islamic beliefs behind them.

Within a short time, the early optimism enjoyed by these Muslim and Third World communists like Sultan Galiev and Manabendra Na Roy, that they would be at the forefront of the revolutionary struggle in the developing world, was disappointed. Also disappointed were the hopes of the indigenous Muslim (and Armenian) populations of Central Asia, including Northern Turkey and Iran, who aspired to national independence with the overthrow of the Tsar and the break-up of the Ottoman empire. By the mid-1920s, the incorporation of the Central Asian Republics and the Russification of the leadership both of these republics and of the Comintern had been completed. Opposition to Soviet rule by the indigenous Muslim population in Central Asia led to the Basmachi revolts which were ruthlessly suppressed by Russian troops. And in the rest of the *Dar al-Islam* beyond Soviet borders, by the early 1920s, Soviet concerns turned very much away from fomenting communist revolution and focussed more on the establishment of normal state-to-state relations with ruling monarchs and pashas in Afghanistan,

Iran, Turkey, Saudi Arabia, Iraq, Egypt and elsewhere. Then, as now, however, the Soviet interest in these Islamic countries has been due to the proximity of the Muslim world to Soviet borders, and because of the Soviet need both for access to the Mediterranean from the Black Sea and for good maritime links with Black Sea, Mediterranean and Persian Gulf littoral states, rather than out of any cultural, religious, national or ethnic affinity between the Russian people and the peoples of the Islamic world to the south.

From the 1920s until the mid-1950s, the Soviet leadership's efforts to expand its influence into the Islamic world were undertaken only infrequently, and such attempts almost invariably met with failure, most significantly in Iran in 1919, 1945–8, and 1952. In the mid-fifties, however, the Soviet Union adopted a policy with a more eastward orientation, becoming very active in the Third World, and primarily in the Muslim world. A stocktaking of the Soviet position in the Muslim world after 25 years of activity reveals a complicated picture with many failures and many successes. But, when comparing the present Soviet position to what it was in 1955, and not to what it could have been, the result can hardly be called a failure. Moreover, with the rise of Islamic fundamentalism and the projection of Islam as a major world religious and political force, the position of the Muslims in Soviet Cultural Asia has assumed more importance, with the result that Muslims everywhere have become more alert to the treatment of their Central Asian co-religionists, and now demand of the Soviet Union crucial rights for this minority in return for policy successes in the Middle East. As a result, in 1983, the Soviet Union is a major partner of the Islamic world but with key responsibilities to that world which create problems for the leadership.

Within the context of this change in the Soviet position, a number of questions need to be asked. To what extent have the Soviet decision-makers been able to use Islam as a means of extending their influence over the Islamic world? To what extent has the rise of Islamic consciousness and Islamic fundamentalism been perceived in the USSR as providing new opportunities for a more active policy? Is it likely that there would be an increasing link between the Islamic revival abroad and the ethnic problems within the USSR? And, finally, what would Soviet response be if the revival should spill over into the Soviet Islamic areas?

The decisive departure from a Western-oriented policy took place in 1955, when Stalin's heirs discarded the traditional 'two camps' view of the international system which had prevailed until that time. The new policy-makers quickly grasped the opportunities offered to them by the disintegration of the British and French empires, and Khrushchev developed a new ideological view of the Third World. The new first secretary seemed to understand clearly the trends of the changing world of the fifties: that the central area of confrontation between the capitalist world and the socialist one was no longer located in Europe, but in the non-developed countries; that the growing importance of anti-Western nationalism was a significant development not only in regional, but also in world, politics; and finally that the longstanding Russian tradition of directing its southern policy toward influencing contiguous areas had proved insufficient to its needs, since Iran and Turkey were at that time committed to an American-sponsored regional defence pact designed to contain any Soviet expansion; and that consequently, this necessitated a 'leap-frogging' of Soviet concerns into the Arab world, thereby focussing Soviet policy for the first time on the Islamic heartland. Khrushchev and successive leaderships followed, and expanded, on this perceptual and policy reorientation in basically three distinct periods.

The first period was inaugurated by Nikita Khrushchev in 1955 and continued beyond his removal in 1964 until the June 1967 Arab–Israeli war. During these years, the main purpose of Soviet foreign policy was to sell to the Third World, and primarily to the Middle Eastern countries, the idea that the Soviet Union was the only major country able to support an independent and anti-Western foreign policy and to contribute to their national and economic development. In the first years of Soviet activism in the Middle East, Soviet policy was particularly concerned with the strategic objective of breaking-up the West's military blocs in the region. The primacy of the strategic objective was such that it overshadowed and even dictated the Soviet view of Middle East politics. Soviet statements on the Arab–Israeli conflict, for example, especially prior to the Suez crisis, made it clear that without Western interference in the area there would be no reason why Arabs and Jews should not live in peace, since they had both been involved in the struggle against British imperialism[7] – a view certainly not shared by most Arabs.

This single-minded pursuit of the strategic objective also resulted in the support of any Arab government willing to pursue an anti-Western foreign policy, irrespective of its domestic programme. Certainly all of the countries with which the USSR enjoyed good relations at that time were secular, rather than Islamic, republics, although Islam was of course the dominant religion. This meant that Islam was not a directly intrusive factor in bilateral relations, although there certainly was an Islamic tangent to the complex interaction of the period.

163

Immediately prior to the reorientation of Soviet policy in 1955, Islam had been officially denounced as a fraud deliberately invented by a class society and exploited by the imperialist powers for 'the enslavement of the peoples of the East'.[8] Internally, the Soviet attitude toward Islam, if anything, hardened under Khrushchev. In sharp contrast to his image as a liberalizer in other fields, his attitude to religious matters was antipathetic. Thus, for example, he withdrew most of the remaining wartime concessions to religion, resulting in the decline in the number of registered mosques in Central Asia from 3,000 following the Second World War to only 400 by 1966.[9] This had two main effects on Soviet policy toward the Islamic world.

In the first place, the image of the Soviet Union as a 'godless' power was increased and the perception of indigenous Arab communists as atheists seeking to subvert Islam was enhanced even in those states which enjoyed good bilateral relations with Moscow. As a result, communists were persecuted throughout the Middle East, irrespective of the foreign policy orientation of the regime in power. Khrushchev's reaction was to attempt to keep relations with the progressive regimes focussed on areas of mutual interest – namely anti-Western orientation – and to avoid the obvious clash between Islam and communism, as stressed by the statement he made in 1957:

You know, of course, that many Arabs ... are very remote from communist ideas. In Egypt, for instance, many communists are held in prison ... [But] we do not pursue any objectives but one, that the peoples be freed from colonial dependence ... Is Nasir a communist? Certainly not. But nevertheless we support Nasir. We do not want to turn him into a communist and he does not want to turn us into nationalists.[10]

The second effect of the repression of Islam at the grass roots in Central Asia on Soviet policy toward the Islamic world was the conscious official emphasis on the economic achievements of the area and the effort to develop a Muslim clergy loyal to Soviet objectives. Thus, beginning in the mid-fifties, numerous foreign delegations visited Central Asia, and were invited to inspect all the most modern factories, state farms, and educational institutions there. During this period, Islam played some part in these propaganda exercises, but only a minor one. In the course of such tours, the Soviet authorities used to arrange trips to Muslim shrines in order to convince the visitors that such a dramatic economic and intellectual change could be brought about without destroying the traditional culture of society. The Grand Mufti of Tashkent would in such cases testify that the past, i.e. Islam, and the future, i.e. an all-out development programme, could live together.

When the delegations dropped in on a 'working' mosque, or one of the two Soviet *madrasas* of Mir al-Arab in Bukhara or Imam Ismail al-Bukhari in Tashkent, the Grand Mufti usually presented them with a Qur'an printed in the USSR. The purpose of such visits was not only to demonstrate the religious freedoms 'enjoyed' by Muslims in the USSR but also to impress upon foreign delegations the benefits which socialism had bestowed upon Muslims. Faced with the decline in religious freedoms in Central Asia, the Muslim clergy began in the 1950s to participate in a more active, but still limited, way in Soviet foreign policy, making large contributions to the Soviet Peace Fund and representing Soviet Muslims at various Third World solidarity conferences. In return, a small number of carefully chosen people were allowed to go on pilgrimages to Mecca, and the Muslim hierarchy began to discuss the possibility of sending Soviet Islamic students to al-Azhar in Cairo. But, in short, despite the importance attached by the Soviet Union to its Middle East policy in the period 1955–67, Islam was not an important factor in the policy; the fate of Muslims in Central Asia actually deteriorated during the period; and very few Soviet Muslims were actively involved in the formulation or the implementation of policies, and those that were tended to be tools in the hands of the Soviet leadership.

A marked change in Soviet policy occurred in the aftermath of the 1967 Arab–Israeli war. During the war, the Soviet Union had been put in a very difficult position by its inability to support its Arab clients in the face of a devastating Israeli attack. Violently criticized by Nasir, who accused his Soviet allies of having betrayed him, the new leadership which had succeeded Khrushchev in 1964 was forced to rethink its strategy; a necessarily more imaginative and more active policy was required to restore the confidence of its Arab allies. After 1967 it could be said that the Soviet leaders did try to achieve their maximum objective in the area, namely the setting-up of pro-Soviet socialist regimes particularly in Egypt, but also in Syria and Iraq. Extremely close cooperation between Moscow and the Arab world in military, political, economic, social and cultural affairs was established. In this effort, the Soviet Muslims played a role markedly more active than hitherto. For the first time Moscow began to project the Soviet Muslims as representatives of a different Soviet Union; not an atheistic and Marxist Soviet Union, but one which was partly Muslim. In this respect, the severing of Moscow's diplomatic relations with Israel in June 1967 played a useful part in convincing the Arabs that the Soviet Union really did side with 'the Muslims' against 'the Jews'. In late June 1967, the Grand Mufti of Tashkent, Zinutdin Ibn Ishan Babakhanov, heading a large delegation of the Soviet Committee for Afro-Asian Solidarity, was sent to Cairo to attend a solidarity meeting. Speaking in al-Azhar, he emphasized the solidarity of the Soviet Islamic community with its Arab brothers and demanded the immediate withdrawal of Israeli troops. Three months later, in October 1967, the Vice-President of the Central Asian Spiritual Board, Ismail Mashdum Satiev, toured the Arab countries which had fought Israel in 1967 – Egypt, Syria, and Jordan – and tried to convince them that Soviet solidarity was real; that the Soviet Muslims firmly supported Arab rights; and that Soviet Muslims were speaking in Moscow on behalf of their Arab brothers in order to facilitate the despatch of Soviet arms to Arab countries.

From that moment on, the activities of the Soviet Islamic authorities went far beyond their previous pattern. First of all, the Spiritual Boards and primarily the Central Asian Muslim Board greatly expanded their activities. In the realm of foreign policy, they organized a number of conferences designed to express their support for Soviet foreign policy and to increase the solidarity within the Muslim world for Soviet initiatives. The following are some of the main events:

1970: a conference organized in Tashkent on the theme 'Unity and cooperation of Muslim peoples in the struggle for peace', chaired by Zinutdin Babakhanov and attended by a hundred Soviet *ulema* and representatives of 24 Muslim countries. Violent attacks were made against American, Israeli and South African 'imperialism'.

1973: a conference in Tashkent on the theme 'Soviet Muslims support the just struggle of the Arab people against Israeli imperialist aggression.'

August 1974: an important international congress in Samarkand to commemorate the 1,200th anniversary of Imam Ismail al-Bukhari. High ranking representatives from 25 Muslim countries attended the congress, including representatives from Saudi Arabia, Egypt, Morocco, and Jordan. On this occasion, however, there were no attacks against the US or Israel.

October 1976: a congress convened in Tashkent by Babakhanov to celebrate the thirtieth anniversary of the Central Asian Board. Representatives from Syria, North Yemen, Morocco, Jordan, Tunisia, India, and Pakistan were present.[11]

The Soviets utilize these meetings for their foreign policy purposes. In the Tashkent Directorate there is also a special foreign department in charge of organizing tours that show foreign Muslim delegations the wealth and freedom of Islamic organizations in the USSR. The same department is in charge of sending students abroad, of organizing pilgrimages and even of arranging some cultural exchanges for members of the Muslim community. It is worth stressing that Tashkent has a special connection with three major Islamic centres – Marrakesh, Tunis and Tripoli – and due to that, the city hosts numerous gatherings, not all of which are religious, but on the whole tend to be linked to Islamic issues.

Following on the precedent set in 1967, the Soviet Muslim authorities were particularly active also in representing the Soviet Union abroad. Speaking fluent Arabic and with a better knowledge of the various aspects of Islam than most of the Soviet Union's diplomatic staff, they have been very successful emissaries for the USSR, particularly in those conservative Islamic states where the Soviet Union has poor or non-existent diplomatic relations. Some of the visits made abroad by Soviet Muslim leaders during this period include:

1972: a delegation led by Babakhanov to Morocco.

1974: a delegation headed by Babakhanov to North Yemen.

Summer 1975: an important delegation including Babakhanov to Iraq, Jordan (where it was received by King Husayn) and Egypt (including a visit to the University of al-Azhar).

September 1975: a delegation to a conference in Mecca on the 'Mission of the Mosques' (on this occasion Babakhanov was received by King Khalid of Saudi Arabia).

October 1975: a delegation to the International Symposium on Islamic Education, in Lucknow, India.

October–November 1975: a delegation headed by Ysuf-Khan Shakirov – the Deputy Mufti of Central Asia – to Somalia and Mauritius.

1976: a delegation led by the Deputy Mufti Abdullayev to a Muslim–Christian conference in Tripoli (where they were received by Mu'ammar Qadhafi).

Winter 1977: a delegation conducted by Abdullayev to the international conference on 'Islamic Thought' in Wargla, Algeria.

March 1977: a delegation led by Imam-Khatib of the 'Tilla Sheikh' Mosque of Tashkent, Yunus Abu Turab, to an international symposium in Bangladesh on Muslim preaching.

July 1978: a delegation headed by Babakhanov to an international conference in Karachi on the propagation of Islam.

Summer 1978: a delegation led by Abdullayev to Niger, Mali and Senegal.

September 1978: a delegation headed by Babakhanov to an international conference in Istanbul on the *hijra* calendar.

Winter 1978: a delegation headed by Abdullayev to the twelfth international conference on 'Islamic Thought' in Batna, Algeria.[12]

Between 1967 and 1978, Soviet policy toward the Islamic world tended to associate a larger part of the Soviet Muslim elites with foreign policy, but without trespassing certain limits; since the motivators of such a policy remained the non-religious, Marxist–Leninist Soviet leaders in Moscow. The Islamic elites were supposed to propagate Soviet ideas; basically to explain why the Muslim world as a whole has an interest in cooperating with the Soviet Union. In exchange, these elites enjoyed a large autonomy at home. More and more they were able to travel and send people abroad; to publish their journals; and to propagate their ideas. They enlarged their contacts with the whole Muslim world and acquired an internal status which was exceptionally privileged when compared with the status of other religious elites. In short, the price paid by the Soviet authorities for Islamic cooperation has been very high. The Islamic leaders in the Soviet Union were accorded the right of unifying and regulating their Muslim communities; of shaping a coherent *umma* in the Soviet Union; of being the leaders of the true believers; and of cooperating with the Communist Party in the leadership of the 43 million Soviet people who claim to the Muslims; and of regularly appearing abroad as their representatives.

Finally, this period differs from the first period in yet another significant way. Between 1955 and 1967, the external activity of the Soviet Muslims was restricted mainly to the Arab and sometimes Pakistani worlds. In 1975, when Soviet policy became more active in Africa, the relations between the Soviet Muslims and their brethren abroad were extended to Africa. The Mufti of Tashkent and other Islamic leaders began to visit African Muslim countries, including Senegal, Niger, Guinea, Mali, and Chad. It is possible, yet by no means certain, that with regard to some African countries the Soviet Muslims have been given a particularly active role in fostering positive perceptions of the USSR in preparation for, or in tandem with, the improvement of bilateral relations. It seems that this was the case in Chad and probably also in Guinea, where the first Soviet penetration in the early sixties had left many unhappy memories.

If until 1978 the Soviet Union had used Islam as an instrument of its diplomacy, it also never fundamentally altered its conception of Islam. The 1972 edition of the *Great Soviet Encyclopedia*, for example, while presenting a far more realistic account of the history and development of Islam than the earlier 1953 edition had, nevertheless still firmly concludes that Islam 'is incompatible with the principles underlying a scientific world outlook'.[13] Moreover, while the Muslim clergy and political elites gained in stature and prestige *vis-à-vis* other religious elites during this period; while specific centres were restored as showcases for foreign delegations; and although Central Asia did probably receive, as claimed by Moscow, a disproportionate share of development funds (partially as a result of the Kremlin's desire to hold Central Asia up as an example to the Third World of the Soviet model of development), at the same time religious freedoms for ordinary Muslims did not improve appreciably, if at all. For although the anti-religious campaign lost much of its violence and vigour after Khrushchev's removal in 1964, nevertheless the institutional suppression of Islam as a religion and a culture continued in the 1967–78 period, and it was estimated in one survey in 1976 that the number of official mosques had been further reduced to 300.[14]

It had been possible to project an image of the Soviet Union as a power tolerant and even supportive of Islam primarily, but not exclusively, because the major target of Soviet policy was the Arab world which is not geographically adjacent to the USSR and does not have deep ethnic ties with the turkic peoples of Central Asia. Also during this period Arab Muslim concerns were directed first toward the Arab world and only second toward the Muslim world. By the second half of the 1970s, however, all of this had changed.

The Islamic revolution in Iran, followed as it was in 1979 by a Soviet invasion of Afghanistan, designed to suppress avowedly Muslim rebels, forced the Soviet Union, under the glare of publicity, to rethink and reshape its attitude toward Islam, both at home and abroad. The first major sign of this reappraisal emerged only after the invasion of Afghanistan when Igor Beliaev, writing in *Literaturnaya Gazeta*, claimed that the Soviet Union had never condemned Islam and indeed that Friedrich Engels himself 'had adamantly supported its progressive role'. What the article failed to mention was that Engels believed Islam could play a progressive role only in the transition *to* feudalism. Beliaev continued:

It is a secret to no one that fundamental differences exist between Marxism–Leninism and Islam. But the existence of differences, and even disagreements, by no means rules out mutual understanding. Not everyone in the world holds the same beliefs. When the question of respect for state and national interests arises, one's thoughts keep going back to the idea of mutual understanding.[15]

Going beyond the appeal to mutual understanding, the August 1980 issue of the Soviet anti-religious journal *Nauka i Religiia* stated that the reasons for the revival of Islam 'demand explanation'. Some of the reasons suggested by the author went much further in attributing a positive role to Islam than had ever been conceded:

In societies divided into communities based on caste and ethnic characteristics, religion continues to play an important integrating role ... In conditions of restrictive, traditional patterns of life, for many people it is in fact religion that offers the most accessible explanation of the world and foundations of morality ... In our time, one of the reasons for the influence of religion in the social thought of Asian and African countries is its linkage with the anti-colonial movements, and with the struggle of the popular masses for national independence.[16]

Also in the summer of 1980, Yevgeni M. Primakov, the Director of the Institute of Orientology, examined the relationship between Islam and social development in foreign Islamic countries, and suggested that the Islamic revival, to a certain extent, represented a rejection of the Western model of development, since there was no role for Islam in the political or economic structure of capitalist society. But equally the theoreticians of the Islamic revival did not have an alternative economic model, and therefore, according to Primakov, under these circumstances there were great opportunities for 'progressive' elements to fill the void and shape the developmental strategy of any emerging Islamic republic.[17] This is of course precisely the strategy that was adopted by the Iranian Communist Party (the Tudeh) which cooperated fully with the clergy and in return gained a position of some considerable influence within the middle ranks of the state bureaucracy, particularly in the period 1978–82.

The end process of this period of review was signalled by Brezhnev himself at the 26th Party Congress in February 1981, by which time the Soviet leadership had assessed both the merits of the Islamic revolution in Iran and the demerits of the Islamic resistance in Afghanistan. Brezhnev described the Iranian revolution as 'a major international event' and stated that 'for all its complications and contradictions, it is fundamentally an anti-imperialist revolution'. The broader lessons to be learned from 'recent experience' were that 'a liberation struggle may develop under the banner of Islam. Historical experience, including very recent experience, show this. But it also indicates that reaction, stirring up counter-revolutionary rebellions, also employs Islamic slogans. So everything rests on the actual content of the particular movement.'[18]

This thesis has guided the Soviet view of the Islamic clergy in both Afghanistan and Iran. In Afghanistan, for example, the Soviets now concede that one of the mistakes committed by Babrak Karmal's predecessor, Hafizullah Amin, was that he put into effect radical reforms which 'impinged upon the interests of ... patriotic elements of the clergy', and by doing so unnecessarily increased the size and intensity of the Muslim rebellion against central authority.[19] At the same time, of course, there is no doubt that the Muslim rebels who have resisted Soviet troops ever since the 1979 invasion have been subjected to the most all-round condemnation. But the interesting change of nuance in Soviet propaganda is that the rebels are condemned not because they are Muslims but because they are 'reactionaries'. Thus, typical commentaries stress that, despite the Afghan rebels calling themselves the 'defenders of Islam', in fact they 'do not hesitate to kill mullahs, imams of Mosques and other religious functionaries'.[20] It is the Soviet Union which is the true friend of Islam, Soviet analysts stress, and although the Soviet Union is not a Muslim country, 'it has granted Muslims such rights and opportunities as have never been granted in Muslim countries'.[21] Also predominant is the claim that the US as the major supporter of the Israelis could not possibly be a sincere friend of Muslims, as the following typical commentary from the Russian-language Central Asian daily *Turkmenskaya Iskra* illustrates:

It is highly typical that international imperialism, which professes to be a friend of peoples of the Islamic faith, is in fact giving all round support only to the most reactionary, conservative forces in the Muslim countries. For example, the bandit groups of Afghan counter-revolutionaries who have made their head-quarters in Pakistan are enjoying all round support from the US imperialists and Beijing hegemonists. The cynical hypocracy of the US administration, which professes friendship with Muslim believers, is exposed by the facts of its all-round support for Israel.[22]

The revolution in Iran and the invasion of Afghanistan have brought the Islamic revival to the Soviet Union's very doorstep, involving Soviet Muslims more directly than ever before. They are involved both as emissaries to the northern tier countries with whom they have ethnic, as well as religious, ties and as occupants of Central Asia which itself has become a focus of external Islamic concern and internal Soviet efforts to prevent any spillover of the Islamic revival from abroad.

Dealing first with the involvement of Soviet Muslims in Moscow's external policy since 1978, Muslims have of course been participants as advisers up to the deputy minister level in the three Afghan regimes led by Taraki, Amin and Karmal since the April 1978 revolution.[23] They also played a significant role in the first two months following the December 1979 Soviet invasion, acting as interpreters and liaison officers, and forming a disproportionately large segment of the rank-and-file soldiery. There were widespread rumours at the time of extensive fraternization between the Muslim soldiers and local inhabitants, and reluctance on the part of these soldiers to side with Russians against their ethnic and religious cohorts. It is naturally difficult to verify the accuracy of such reports. However, the vigorous campaign in Central Asia glorifying the sacrifices made in Afghanistan might support this view. The first secretary of the Communist Party of Turkmenistan has himself become involved in the campaign, and in an address to the local Young Communist League (Komsomol) he held up the bloodstained Komsomol card of a young Turkman who had died 'while performing the sacred duty of a soldier ... A son of the Turkman people and a Komsomol member, he was helping to defend the freedom, independence and social progress of fraternal Afghanistan.'[24]

If there is reason to believe that the Muslim rank and file in Central Asia has been less than enthusiastic about the Soviet presence in Afghanistan, such is apparently not the case with the Soviet Islamic clergy who have voiced nothing but public support for all of the Soviet Union's activities in the post-1978 period, including the invasion of Afghanistan. They have continued to be very active in organizing international symposia. In July 1979, a conference was held in Tashkent to celebrate the tenth anniversary of the journal *Muslims of Central Asia* and was attended by representatives of Jordan, Iraq, India, Turkey, Tunisia, Pakistan, Kuwait, Iran, Lebanon, Japan, Bulgaria, and Ethiopia. The final communiqué which condemned 'Israeli, American, South African and Chinese imperialism' testified to its having been more than just a publishing event.

In September of the same year, an even larger symposium was held in Dushanbe on 'the contribution of the Muslims of Central Asia, the Volga and the Caucasus to the development of Islamic thought and to the cause of peace and social progress'. Thirty Muslim countries were represented, as was the World Islamic Congress and the World Islamic League. Although Soviet and Afghan efforts to gain universal approval for the Afghan regime as a defender of Islam were not successful due to the determined opposition of the Arab and Pakistani delegations, nevertheless the usual denunciations of US, Israeli, and South African (but not Chinese) imperialism were issued, and the conference was generally deemed to have been a success for the Soviet Union.

In 1980, the USSR sponsored a United Nations meeting in Tashkent devoted to demographic questions, a sensitive issue which the Soviets manipulated for their own benefit. The topic discussed during the meeting was 'Population Growth and Development in the Underdeveloped World'. During the meeting, Central Asia was presented as an example, even a unique example, of the perfect adjustment of population growth to economic development. The explanation for such a perfect solution to a difficult problem was, needless to say, the integration of Central Asia into the USSR and the wise nationalities policy pursued by the central governments. During the meeting, Central Asian demographers, supported by religious authorities, claimed that their socio-economic development would have been impossible without the help of Soviet society as a whole. The Central Asian pattern was consistently presented as the main and only successful road to development. On the other hand, Central Asian elites were exposed to the failures, contradictions and tragedies of development and population growth in the Third World. This kind of meeting is an excellent example of the subtleties of Soviet policy, which aims at convincing the Muslim world abroad of the qualities of the Soviet pattern, while at the same time convincing Soviet Muslims that, by being integrated into the USSR, they are able to solve the problems of development without suffering the difficulties almost universally associated with the process of development in the Third World.

Another meeting, convened in Tashkent in September of the same year, was not such a success. This clearly shows the extent of the Soviet fall from grace in the wake of the invasion of Afghanistan. It also testifies to the way the Soviet government tends to play its Muslim card. Even if the official *raison d'être* of the meeting was the celebration of the beginning of the 15th century of the *hijra*, its real *raison d'être* was the Soviet need to effect a reconciliation with the Islamic world. Condemned at Islamabad for having invaded Afghanistan, the USSR intended to use the Tashkent meeting as a 'counter Islamabad'. It hoped that the convening of such a big Islamic jamboree on Soviet territory would demonstrate that the USSR was a part of the Islamic world, and that its solidarity with this world transcended occasional disputes.

Despite the efforts of the Soviet official Muslim spokesmen, the Tashkent meeting was, to a certain extent, a failure. In the first place, of the 70 countries invited, only half actually sent delegations, and of these only eleven were Muslim countries.[25] The major Islamic countries refused to be represented in Tashkent, so that only delegations from the peripheral Muslim states or the pro-Soviet regimes such as Afghanistan, South Yemen, Syria or Ethiopia were present. The World Islamic Congress and the World Islamic League also boycotted the Tashkent meeting and were replaced by representatives of the Conference of European Churches and of the Buddhist Conference for Peace. Clearly a major result of the meeting was to demonstrate that the part of the Islamic world ready to communicate with the USSR or to accord a hearing to its international policies was shifting from the prestigious Islamic countries of the Middle East to peripheral and inconsequential countries, such as Togo, Ghana, Senegal, Uganda, and Sri Lanka. And many of the Muslim countries represented must have said things not to Moscow's liking, since after the conference three of the four Soviet Muftis (excluding Babakhanov) were dismissed for their inability to turn the conference in Moscow's favour.[26]

But one should not exaggerate the negative results of the Tashkent meeting, or the lasting effects of the Soviet invasion of Afghanistan on Islamic countries. The summit of Islamic heads of state, convened at Taif in Saudi Arabia in January 1981, only 13 months after the invasion, showed that Soviet Islamic policy had had some success. First of all, the Muslim countries refused to allow the Afghan rebels' delegation to be officially included in the meeting or even to be represented as observers. Secondly, the Islamic community of nations, which was unanimous at the Islamabad conference in January 1980 in condemning the Soviet invasion of Afghanistan, was, one year later, clearly divided on the same issue.[27] If some Islamic countries remained adamant that the Soviet presence in Afghanistan was intolerable, other countries sided with the Algerian resolution naming the USA as the main enemy of Islam. The resolution claimed that no Islamic meeting should be used against the Soviet Union because, in spite of Afghanistan, the USSR remained the primary ally of the Muslim world in the international arena.

Thus, to a certain extent, the USSR has succeeded in improving its image and in propagating the idea, through its Muslim elites, that the USSR is a country which respects its own Muslim minority, and supports Islam. But such an improvement of the Soviet image has been possible only due to the continuous compliance of the Soviet Muslim elite. Babakhanov's new colleagues on the Spiritual Board represent a totally new and different Soviet Muslim generation. The recently elected Mufti of Orenburg, Talga Taziev, and the new leader of the Shi'i community, Pachaev, are young, very well educated, and multilingual (Arabic, Persian, and Turkish in the case of Pachaev). As such, they are well suited to the needs of an active foreign policy. But, in addition, they represent a new generation of clergy, the very product of a purely Soviet training. Certainly the Soviet leadership considers them to be reliable people, strongly committed to Soviet official policy; in short, they are perceived more as Soviet than Muslim.

The new Muslim clergy will have to be reliable because there is every indication that they will face numerous challenges in coming years. The Iranian revolution and the events in Afghanistan created problems for the stability of Soviet control over the Central Asian republics. Religious materials including cassettes of Ayatollah Khumayni's speeches began to circulate on the black market; and the Qur'an, bought by Soviet soldiers in Afghanistan, was smuggled back across the border. According to a report in the Uzbek language daily, *Soviet Uzbekista*, a large-scale illegal publishing house, which had produced, with the illicit assistance of state institutions, thousands of copies of an unauthorized book 'about the Islamic faith', was also uncovered by Soviet authorities.[28] Moreover, with the decline of Soviet–Iranian relations at the beginning of 1982, Iranian broadcasts to Soviet Central Islam became much more inflammatory, leading M. G. Gapurov, the First Secretary of Turkmenistan, to admit that such propaganda did aim to 'breed distrust of the social and political systems of the country. By promoting ... the formation of a single muslim nation, they play on religious feelings ...'[29]

To combat any such feelings, Soviet authorities stepped up their efforts to suppress any sign of Islamic revival in the Soviet Union. Articles and new literature on the Soviet suppression of the Basmachis in the 1920s began ominously to appear. The KGB's activities have been extolled as well; and in 1980, G. A. Aliyev, who was at that time first secretary of the Communist Party in Azerbaijan (having been head of the KGB in Azerbaijan and destined to be promoted by Andropov in 1982 to USSR first deputy premier), reaffirmed the absolute necessity of 'an uncompromising struggle against ... survivals from the past, backward news and customs ...'[30] Soon after, the head of the KGB in Azerbaijan, Yusif Zade, denounced the 'infiltration of foreign agents through our borders, and the anti-social activity of reactionary Muslim clergy'.[31]

It is most unlikely that the USSR would be willing to make any significant concessions to their Muslim population. And the Muslim world is constantly becoming more aware of the restrictions. For example, two of the first three issues of the journal published by the new Institute of Muslim Minority Affairs in Saudi Arabia carried articles on the Soviet treatment of its Muslims. Also the Islamic Council of Europe submitted an official and detailed protest to the Conference on Security and Cooperation in Madrid on 11 November 1980 about the situation in Central Asia. The first sentence reads: ' "Genocide" has become an all too familiar accusation in the latter half of the twentieth century.'

The Soviet Union in the not too distant future will have to reassess its attitude toward Islam once again, and decide the extent to which it can effectively use Islam as an instrument of its foreign policy without shattering the coherence of its own society. By associating its Muslims with its foreign policy, and by presenting itself as a state with an integrated and active Muslim minority, the Soviet Union is playing a very risky game. For years such a game was successful; but the Afghan war and the Iranian revolution demonstrated its limits. In the long run two possibilities might emerge: on the one hand, the Soviet Union, through its Muslim population, could propagate in the Third World an attractive pattern of modernization. But also, and negatively, such a policy could result in, first, expanding the national assertiveness of the Soviet Muslims and, secondly, contributing to the development of strong ties between them and the Muslim world abroad, with possibly dangerous repercussions on the domestic stability of the Soviet Union.

Notes

1. Quoted in Michael Rywkin, *Moscow's Muslim Challenge: Soviet Central Asia* (London, Hurst, 1982), p. 18.
2. A. M. Gorchakov quoted by F. F. Martens, *Rossiia i Angliia v Srednei Azii* (St Petersburg, 1880), p. 22.
3. K. Marx and F. Engels, *On Colonialism* (Moscow, Foreign Language Publishing House, 1960), p. 35.
4. K. Marx, *New York Tribune*, 7 April 1853, as quoted in Walter Laqueur, *Communism and Nationalism in the Middle East* (London, Routledge and Kegan Paul, 1956), p. 290.
5. J. Stalin, *Pravda*, November 1918, as quoted in Karen Dawisha, *Soviet Foreign Policy Towards Egypt* (London, Macmillan, 1979).
6. Quoted in Hélène Carrere d'Encausse and Stuart Schram, *Marxism and Asia* (London, Allen Lane, The Penguin Press, 1969), p. 172.
7. *Izvestia*, 18 April 1956.
8. *Bol'shaya Sovetskaya Entsiklopediya*, vol. 18 (1953 Edition), p. 516.
9. Walter Kolarz, *Religion in the Soviet Union* (London, Macmillan, 1966), p. 432; and *Spravochnik propagandista i agitatora* (Moscow, 1966), p. 149.
10. Khrushchev interview with James Reston, *New York Times*, 10 October 1957.
11. Alexandre Bennigsen and Marie Broxup, *The Islamic Threat to the Soviet State* (London, Croom Helm, 1983), pp. 105–6.
12. *Ibid.*, pp. 106–7.
13. *Bol'shaya Sovetskaya Entsiklopediya*, 3rd edition, Vol. 10 (Moscow, 1972), pp. 484–6.
14. V. Furov in *Chronicle of Current Events*, 41 (1976), p. 7.
15. *Literaturnaya Gazeta*, 16 January 1980.
16. B. Brasov, 'Chto za religioznoi obolochkoi nekotoriie kharakterniie cherti religioznikh protssessov na Vostoke', *Nauka i Religiia*, 21, 8 (1980), 56.
17. Ye. M. Primakov, 'Islam i protsessy obshchestvennovo razvitiia stran zarubezhnova vostoka', *Voprosi Filosofii*, 8 (1980), pp. 60–3.
18. Brezhnev's 26th Party Congress speech, 23 February 1981, in BBC, *Summary of World Broadcasts*, SU/6657/C/8.
19. Ye. M. Primakov, 'The USSR and the Developing Countries', *Journal of International Affairs*, 34 (1980/81), p. 276.
20. *Sovet Turkmenistany*, 4 November 1981.
21. *Pravda*, 14 July 1980.
22. *Turkmenskaya Iskra*, 11 September 1982.
23. See Eden Naby, 'The Ethnic Factor in Soviet–Afghan Relations', *Asian Survey*, 22, No. 3 (1980), p. 252; and Bennigsen and Broxup, *The Islamic Threat*, p. 112.
24. M. G. Gapurov, *Turkmenskaya Iskra*, 27 March 1982.
25. *Izvestia*, 2 October 1980; *Radio Liberty Research Bulletin*, 19 September 1980.
26. Chantal Lemercier-Quelquejay, 'Soviet Muslims and the "Islamic Resurgence"', paper presented to the Carnegie Endowment for International Peace Conference on 'Soviet Muslims and their Political Destiny', New York, 19–20 March 1981.

27. See for example *The Times*, 28 January 1981; *The Guardian*, 21 January 1981; and Zubeida Mustafa, 'The Islamic Conference and Afghanistan', *Asian Pacific Community*, 14 (Autumn, 1981).
28. As quoted in *The Observer*, 21 November 1982.
29. *Literaturnaya Gazeta*, 1 December 1982.
30. *Bakinskii Rabochii*, Baku, 29 October 1980.
31. *Bakinskii Rabochii*, 19 December 1980.

12   Conclusion

ALBERT HOURANI

The subject of this book is an elusive one, and the authors of the various chapters seem to have been engaged in a chase after something which had been found, lost and then found again. Clearly they have started with different ideas about how international relations should be studied, and equally clearly they have shown that the role of Islam in foreign policy differs greatly from one country to another. At least, however, there seems to have been agreement on the questions which need to be asked.

Three kinds of questions have been raised, although the distinction between them is to some extent artificial, and answers to one overlap with answers to the others. First, to what extent can Islam – however defined – provide a direction and content for the foreign policy of a state of which the inhabitants, or a large part of them, are Muslims? The general opinion seems to be that there are only a few issues in regard to which the fact that a state has a Muslim population makes it act differently from other states; the most important of these issues is that of Palestine, and specifically of Jerusalem. Even here however there are some reservations: Muslim states more distant from the Middle East, like Nigeria and Indonesia, are more hesitant in their involvement in the problem of Palestine; and those who support the Palestinians may do so more out of Arab or 'Third World' solidarity than Muslim feeling.

Apart from these few issues, there is only one state which is trying to pursue what can in the full sense be called an Islamic foreign policy, and that is Iran, because of a combination of factors which by now have been fully explained: the special role of the religious class in Iranian society, and the way in which the revolution projected it into political power. Ramazani's chapter has shown how Iranian policy is shaped by a certain conception of an Islamic world order: there is a universal Islamic society, within which differences of nations and governments are secondary; potentially it is a worldwide society, countries now external to it are seen as hostile, but will in the end be converted; Iran as the first fully Islamic state has a special role to play in the process of defence and conversion. No other Muslim state is guided by this conception of an alternative world order, although, as Dessouki and others have shown us, there are parties and movements within them which do look at the world in much the same way.

Secondly, to what extent is the view which a state or a nation has of the world moulded (whether consciously or not) by the social and political values of its inherited Muslim culture? Even if these values do not by themselves define the aims of policy, they can affect its methods, or set limits to what is possible. Here again we must make distinctions. Leifer has shown that in Indonesia, systems of values derived from Islam coexist in tension with other older values and religions; Nolutshungu has given a similar picture of Nigeria, and the situation is much the same in other African countries; in such countries, society is inescapably pluralist. In the central countries of the Muslim world, however, either their pre-Islamic cultures have been virtually erased as living forces by the coming of Islam, or else, as in Iran, they have been absorbed into a cultural system which can be described as essentially Islamic. In these countries Islam serves, at the least, as a way of identifying 'natural' friends and allies and thus as a potential way of creating a bloc. It is not a primary bloc for most Muslim countries, and such conflicts as those of Iran and Iraq show that it can be ineffective when more potent interests are at stake. Nevertheless it has a certain reality, and developments in the last ten years have perhaps increased its importance: not only the Iranian revolution but the growth of Islamic institutions such as those Piscatori refers to – the Organization of the Islamic Conference, the Islamic Development Bank and other aid organizations, and the annual Pilgrimage to Mecca, which draws ever larger numbers of Muslims.

The case should not be overstated, however. The inherited values of Islamic culture are no longer unchallenged. The values of the secular, urban, industrial world also help to mould the lives and minds of the ruling elites which formulate and carry out policy. In most countries, governments rest on some kind of uneasy alliance between rulers and military politicians on the one hand and 'technocrats' on the other. The balance between them varies. Tunisia perhaps is the only country where the highly educated class is also the ruling elite, but in all of them, government cannot be carried on without the help of 'technocrats', who tend to see the world in ways in which the distinction between Muslim and non-Muslim countries is irrelevant.

Thirdly, to what extent do governments or ruling elites use Islamic terms and symbols to explain and justify to their own peoples what they are trying to do in the outside world? This is the question which perhaps has yielded the most fruitful answers, because it is clear that governments do use Islamic language more than before, although not all to the same degree or in the same way. A spectrum of attitudes exists: Saudi Arabia and Libya perhaps stand with Iran at one end of it; Pakistan and Egypt, as Tahir-Kheli and Dessouki show, have moved nearer than before to the same end; Iraq, according to Adeed Dawisha, uses Islamic language more than before, but Zartman shows that Morocco uses it scarcely at all, and Nolutshungu says much the same thing about Nigeria; Indonesia carefully avoids it; Karen Dawisha and Hélène Carrere d'Encausse suggest that the USSR has begun to employ it in a systematic way.

Three different kinds of explanation can be given for the change. Governments may employ Islamic symbols because that is their natural way of expressing themselves, and to be able to justify what they are doing in Islamic terms helps them to be easy in their own minds; or they may do so in order to mobilize support among their own people and to disarm opposition, for Islamic feeling may act as a constraint upon them even when it does not give them a direction; or they may do so in order to appeal to the peoples of other countries over the heads of their governments. This indeed follows naturally from the sense of Islamic solidarity: if in the end all Muslim peoples form a single community, then any government can appeal in the name of Islamic legitimacy to those beyond its territorial boundaries. Since the time of 'Abd al-Nasir this has been the practice of more than one Arab government using the symbols of Arabism, and in the last few years Iran has appealed in the same way to the world of Islam, and not only of Shi'i Islam. In countries where the division between Sunnis and Shi'is exists, it may be that the Iranian revolution has exacerbated the tension between them, but in other Muslim countries Khumayni's regime appears not as specifically Shi'i, but simply as Muslim. Even so secular a regime as that of Iraq has to invoke Islam in self-defence in its war with Iran.

Words and other symbols are never neutral; we use them at our peril, as we can see if we look a little deeper into the nature of the Islamic symbols which are being used. None of the writers has tried to define Islam in simple terms; there is a great variety of interpretations of it as a religion and as a system of social and political values, ranging from Sadat's Islamic vision of alliance with the United States to the USSR's idea of a pattern of modernization for Muslim countries. There is, however, one language which seems to have a greater hold over minds and feelings than any other: that which uses Islamic symbols to express a system of social and political ideas which includes development, social justice, national liberation, and some suspicion of American power. As Scarcia Amoretti has shown, the Libyan government is able to use this language with some conviction, even if the guiding force of its social policy is not necessarily Islamic. Most governments, however, cannot use it in a convincing way. They are caught, as all human governments must be, in the tangled web of self-interest, compromises, and improvizations in order to avoid immediate dangers. By holding out a promise of Islamic justice they may arouse expectations which they will not be able to fulfil, and they can be denounced and declared illegitimate in the terms they have themselves used, for this is a language more easily handled by movements of opposition. Governments are therefore caught in a dilemma: in order to appeal to their peoples in present circumstances they must use Islamic language, but it can be turned against them. The attempt to 'domesticate' Islamic feelings and convictions can be dangerous, even fatal to some regimes, and in some cases – as with the assassination of Sadat – issues of foreign policy may help to provide the catalyst.

This does not necessarily mean that the movements of Islamic rigour will triumph. Khumayni may perhaps be bringing with him the wave of the future, but again he may not. The Iranian revolution was the result of a particular movement at a particular point in time and space. It was a product of a certain political and social situation, of alienated and uprooted urban masses at an early stage of rapid economic development. That situation exists also in other countries, but it is not likely that they will be able to throw up the same kind of charismatic leader; leadership will lie less with individuals than with movements like the Muslim Brothers, which seem likely to be more powerful as movements of opposition setting limits to what governments can do than to be able to provide alternative governments. Even in Iran there may be a reaction against the present regime, if not soon then at a later stage of social and educational change. We should remember how quickly the generations pass in the Third World, where expectations of life are still low and wars and revolutions are fought by teenagers. As they pass, the nature of political discourse may change, and although it seems likely that some kind of use of Islamic symbols will remain, there may be a revival of a kind of Islamic modernism, tending in the direction of secularization, and more easily adaptable to the needs of living in a modern urban society.

Index

In the alphabetical order the Arabic article (al-) is neglected

' Abd al-'Aziz, King of Saudi
  Arabia, 33–9, 45, 51
'Abdullah, King of Trans-Jordan, 37, 38
Abdullayev, Deputy Mufti of Central
  Asia, 167
Afghanistan, 37, 47, 161; see also Soviet
  invasion
'Aflaq, Michel, 115
Afro-Asian Islamic Conference, first
  (1964), 87–8
Ahmadiya sect, Nigeria, 133, 138–9
Akinyemi, A. Bolaji, 132
'Alawi, Ahmed, 101
Algeria, 41, 50, 65, 126, 167; relations
  with Morocco, 101, 102, 105, 107, 110
'Ali, Imam, early Shi'i leader, 122, 125,
  126
Aliyev, G. A., 175
American hostage crisis (1979–80), 10–11,
  12–13, 14, 15, 22–3, 29, 77, 155
Amin, Hafizullah, 170, 171
Andropov, Yuri, 175
Anglo-Italian Treaty (1938), 36
Anglo-Saudi Treaties (1915, 1927), 34, 35
Angola, 99, 108, 131, 136
Anyas, Shaykh Ibrahim, 88
al-Aqsa Mosque, Jerusalem, 90; fire at,
  41, 57, 84, 100, 152
Arab-Israeli wars: (1967), 41, 42, 57, 152,
  163, 165–6; (1973), 42, 43, 45, 89, 117
Arab League, 37, 91, 105, 120, 150
Arab National Charter, 118–19
Arab nationalism, 36, 37, 40, 59, 63, 86,
  114, 115, 116, 122
'Arab Revolution', 24
Arab unity, 33, 37–8, 41, 58–9, 86, 107;

  see also Arab nationalism; Arabism
Arabian-American Oil Company, 36, 38
Arabism, 33, 57, 60, 178, 180; Iraqi
  emphasis on, in war with Iran, 117,
  122, 126, 127; and Palestinian question,
  62–3; vis-à-vis Islam, 51, 59, 91, 101,
  106; see also Arab nationalism; Arab
  unity
ARAMCO, see Arabian-American Oil
  Company
Argentina, 30
Aron, Raymond, 25
al-Asad, Hafiz, President of Syria, 41, 49,
  93, 116, 126–7
ASEAN, see Association of South-East
  Asian Nations
Asian Games, Jakarta (1962), 152
Association of South-East Asian Nations,
  149, 153, 157
Ayub Khan, Mohammed, 69
al-Azhar University, Cairo, 87–8, 90, 165,
  166, 167
'Aziz, Tariq, 113, 121
'Azizi, Ahmad, 28

Babakhanov, Zinutdin Ibn Ishan, Grand
  Mufti of Tashkent, 166, 167, 173, 174
Baghdad Pact, 41, 87; see also CENTO
Bahonar, Mohammad Javad, 13
Bahrain, 20, 27, 47, 50
Baku Congress of the Peoples of the East
  (1920), 161
Balafrej, Ahmed, 99
Balewa, Sir Abubakar Tafawa, 133, 135
Bandung Conference (1955), 87, 151
Bangladesh, 50, 70, 71, 74, 120, 167

INDEX

Bani-Sadr, Ahmed, 11–12, 13, 15, 29
Basmachi revolts, 161, 175
Ba'thism, 41; in Iraq, 23–4, 26, 112–14, 115, 117, 121, 124, 127; in Syria, 116
Bazargan, Mehdi, 10, 12, 15
Beheshti, Ayatollah Mohammad, 11, 13
Beliaev, Igor, 169
Bello, Alhaji Sir Ahmadu, Sardauna of Sokota, 133, 134
Bhutto, Zulfikar Ali, 70, 71, 74–5, 78
'Black September', 42
Bogra, Foreign Minister of Pakistan, 69
Bou'abid, Ma'ti, Prime Minister of Morocco, 98
Boucetta, Mhamid, 98, 99, 100
Brazil, 30
Brezhnev, Leonid, 170
Britain: and 'Abd al-'Aziz of Saudi Arabia, 34, 35–6, 37, 38; and Iran, 13; and Nigeria, 129, 131, 132, 133, 135, 136; see also British Empire
British Empire, 69, 163
Brzezinski, Zbigniew, 10
Buch, Yusef, 75
Buddhism, 93, 145, 173
al-Bukhari, Imam Ismail, 165, 166

Cameroun, 47, 140
Camp David accords, 43, 44, 59, 63, 90, 91, 92–3, 94, 118, 155
Carter, James Earl, President of USA, 13, 20
CENTO (Central Treaty Organization), 76
Central Asia, Soviet, 160–1, 162, 164–5, 166–7, 168, 171–3, 174–5
Central Asian Khanates, 160
Central Asian Spiritual Boards, 166, 174; conferences organized by, 166
Centre for Strategic and International Studies, Jakarta, 153
Chad, 47, 94, 131, 140, 168; Libyan interest in, 56–7, 60, 110, 141
China (PRC), 93, 154; relations with Pakistan, 69, 71, 72
Christians, Christianity, 65, 93, 94, 99, 137, 138, 139, 146, 167, 173
colonialism, anti-colonialism, 57, 63, 64, 88, 106, 129, 148, 151; see also imperialism
communism, 22, 41, 55, 69, 91, 161, 164, 168; in Indonesia, 147, 148, 150, 152, 156; Muslim Brothers' view of, 93;

Saudi antipathy toward, 37, 45; see also Komsomol; Tudeh Party
Conference on Security and Cooperation in Europe, 108
Copts, 94
Crane, Charles, 36
Cutler, Walter, 10
Cyprus problem, 89, 99

Dar al-Islam, 134, 146, 147, 150
da'wa (missionary) activities, 48, 148; see also propagation of Islam
al-Da'wa (Muslim Brothers' journal), 92, 93–4
al-Da'wa party, Iraq, 121
détente, 103, 106
Dhahran Air Base, Saudi Arabia, 39
Dome of the Rock, attack on, 85
Dunshanbe conference (1979), 172

East African Islamic Conference, Nairobi (1953), 87
Egypt, 39, 56, 59, **84–95**, 100, 151, 180; and Iranian revolution, 90; relations with Saudi Arabia, 35, 39, 40, 41, 42, 43, 47, 49, 84, 86, 88; relations with West, 91–2; and Soviet Union, 40, 91, 162, 165, 166, 167; see also Arab–Israeli wars; Camp David; al-Nasir; al-Sadat
Engels, Friedrich, 160, 169
Eritrea, 56, 94, 99
Ethiopia, 35, 44, 65, 108, 173; see also Eritrea

Fafunwa, Babs, 135
Fahd, King of Saudi Arabia, 17, 33, 43, 44, 78, 79
faqih as head of state, 11, 15, 18
Faruq, King of Egypt, 35
al-Fassi, 'Allal, 99
Fayek, Mohamed, 88
Faysal, King of Saudi Arabia, 33, 36, 40–3, 45, 49, 73, 75, 102
Fedayeen-e Khalq, 15
Federation of Islamic Associations, Detroit, 48
Fertile Crescent Plan, 37
Fez summit (1982), 44, 59, 105
foreign policy and Islam, methodological problems in study of, 1–7
France, 73, 100, 163
Fu'ad, King of Egypt, 35
fundamentalism, Islamic, 11, 15, 109–10, 140, 146, 162

Gabon, 47, 64
Galiev, Sultan, 161
Gambia, 47
Gapurov, M. G., 175
Gatoil International, 23
Germany, Nazi, Saudi Arabian relations
with, 36
Ghana, 88, 173
Ghulam Muhammad, Prime Minister of
Pakistan, 87
Golan Heights, annexation by Israel, 156
Gowon, Yakubu, 136
Great Soviet Encyclopedia, account of
Islam in, 168
Greater Syrian Plan, 37
Green Book (Qadhafi), 55
Green March of 1975, 107
Guinea, 47, 50, 168
Gulf Cooperation Council, 27, 44

hajj (Pilgrimage), 18, 35, 37, 40, 102, 130,
151, 155, 179; behaviour of Iranian
pilgrims, 26–7, 45; al-Nasir's
conception of, 86–7; participation of
Soviet Muslims, 165
al-Hakim, Hojatilislam Mohammed Baqr,
124
al-Hakim, Ayatollah Muhsin, 124
Hama, Muslim Brothers' rebellion in, 23
Hamza, Fu'ad Bey, 37
Harahap, Burhannuddin, 150
al-Harakan, Sheykh Muhammad 'Ali, 48
Hasan, Mubashir, 75
Hashimites, 34, 35, 37, 38
Hassan II, King of Morocco, 98, 100,
101, 102, 104–5, 109, 110
Hatta, Mohammad, 146, 148
al-Haydariya Mosque, Iraq, 125
Hijaz, 34, 35, 36, 38
Hojati school, 15, 16
Husayn, Imam, early Shi'i leader, 125,
126
Husayn, King of Jordan, 167
Husayn, Saddam, President of Iraq, 23–4,
112–27 *passim*
Husayn bin Ali, Sharif of Mecca, 34, 35

Ibaban, Nigeria, 129
Ibn Khaldun, 4, 61
Ibn Saud, *see* 'Abd al-'Aziz
Ibrahim, Barazan, 113
Idang, G., 132

Imam 'Ali Mosque, al-Najaf, 122
imperialism, anti-imperialism, 21, 39, 56,
64, 87, 88, 132, 136, 149, 161, 163; *see
also* colonialism
India, 14, 30, 120, 166; Muslim
population, 93, 94, 99; partition, 68, 70;
relations with Pakistan, 68, 69, 70–1,
72, 78, 80, 81, 89
Indo-China war, third, 149
Indo-Soviet Treaty (1971), 72
Indonesia, 92, **144–58**, 179, 180; and
communism, 147, 148, 150, 152, 156;
complexity of religious–cultural
identity, 144–8; economic policy,
149–50; Guided Democracy, 146–9,
151–2; Masyumi, 146, 147, 150, 151;
military establishment, 150, 154, 156;
New Order, 144, 148, 152;
Parliamentary Democracy (1950–7),
146, 150–1; policy on Israel and
Palestine, 151, 153, 156; relationship
with Arab–Islamic states, 41, 47, 49,
50, 144, 150, 151, 153, 154, 155, 156,
158; South East Asia policy, 149, 151,
157; and Soviet Union, 148, 155–6; and
USA, 149, 151; *see also* Suharto;
Sukarno
Institute of Muslim Minority Affairs,
Saudi Arabia, 175
International Court of Justice, Judgement
on Iran (1980), 13
International Islamic News Agency, 42
international law, 2, 13, 155
Iran, pre-revolutionary, 9–10, 25, 37, 41,
73, 74, 75, 117, 161, 162, 163; *see also*
Mohammad Reza Pahlavi, Shah of Iran
Iran, revolutionary, 1, 4, **9–31**, 85, 86,
120–1, 155, 178–9, 180, 181; and *hajj*,
26–7, 45; and Libya, 58, 62; Moroccan
attitude to, 101; Muslim Brothers'
support for, 93; and Pakistan, 76–7, 80;
relations with Gulf states, 25–7; and
Saudi Arabia, 43–4, 45, 50, 51; and
Soviet Union, 14, 22, 27–8, 30, 162,
163, 169–70, 174–5; and USA, 10,
12–13, 21, 30; *see also* American
hostage crisis; Iran–Iraq war;
Khumayni; Tudeh
Iran–Iraq war, 1, 5, 11, 13, 44, 57, 81, 90,
119, 179, 180; attempts to terminate,
78, 105; Iranian use of Islamic symbols,
14, 23–5, 85, 123–4; Iraqi invocation of
Arabist symbolism, 114, 122–3, 125–7

INDEX

Iraq, 35, 37, 39, 112–27, 151, 180; Arabist
  orientation, 114, 115, 117–19, 122–3,
  125–7; inter-Arab relations, 116; and
  Iranian revolution, 26, 120–22; and
  non-aligned world, 119–20; and
  Palestinian question, 117; and Saudi
  Arabia, 41, 44, 50, 116; and Soviet
  Union, 162, 165, 167; see also Iran–Iraq
  war
Iraqi Fund for External Development,
  120
Islam and International Relations
  conference, Duke University (1963), 84
Islamabad: Islamic university, 47; OIC
  summit meeting (1980), 155–6, 173,
  174
Islamic Chamber of Commerce, Industry
  and Commodity Exchange, Karachi, 46
Islamic Circle, 84, 87, 91
'Islamic Congress', 39
Islamic Council of Europe, 175
Islamic culture, export of, 65–6, 87–8
Islamic Development Bank, 42, 46, 74,
  120, 179
'Islamic Legion', 141
Islamic resurgence, 1, 61, 68, 85, 155,
  157, 158, 162, 169–70
Islamic Republican Party, Iran, 11, 13,
  14, 15
'Islamic Revolution', export of, 16, 17–20,
  26, 27, 29; see also universalism
Islamic solidarity, 33, 42, 45, 57, 93, 99,
  152, 180
Islamic summit meetings, see Baghdad;
  Fez; Islamabad; Jidda; Lahore; Mecca;
  Rabat; Taif
Islamic World League, 85, 172, 173
Ismail, Shaykh Salah Abu, 94
Israel, 38, 39, 41, 42, 63, 64–5, 73, 101,
  127; anti-Israel strike called by King
  Khalid (1982), 85, 153; Indonesian
  attitude to, 151, 152, 153, 156; invasion
  of Lebanon, 81, 156; Iraqi policy
  towards, 117; Muslim Brothers' attitude
  to, 93, 94; Nigerian view of, 130; and
  Pakistan, 82; Soviet Union's relations
  with, 165–6; see also Camp David;
  Jerusalem; Palestinian question
Italy, 35, 36
Ivory Coast, 100

Jakarta: Asian Games (1962), 152;
  twinned with Jidda, 155

Jakarta Charter, 146, 147
Jalal, Dr Mahsun, 48
Jama'atu Nastril Islam, 140–41
Jamahiriya, 54, 57–8
Japan, 30, 146, 149, 151
Java, 145, 146, 150
Jawara, Dawda, President of Gambia, 47
Jenkinson, Anthony, 160
Jerusalem, 21, 42, 44, 73, 100, 106, 152,
  178; Grand Mufti of, 151; importance
  to Muslims, 63, 94; Sadat's visit to
  (1977), 90; see also al-Aqsa Mosque
Jidda Agreement (1965), 40
Jidda Conference (1972), 152, 153
al-Jihad Group, 92
Jinnah, Mohammed 'Ali, 70
Jordan, 42, 78, 85, 88, 155, 166, 167;
  relations with Saudi Arabia, 38, 39, 41,
  44, 47, 50; see also Trans-Jordan

Kampuchea, 144, 149
Kano, Aminu, 139, 141
Kano, Nigeria, 139; religious riots, 140
Karachi: conference on propagation of
  Islam (1978), 167; Islamic Chamber of
  Commerce in, 46
Karbala, Iraq, holy shrines of, 124, 125
Karmal, Babrak, 78, 170, 171
Kashmir issue, 81
Kasim, 'Abd al-Karim, 113
Kenyan Muslims, 89
Khalid, King of Saudi Arabia, 26–7, 33,
  49, 85, 153, 167
Khalkhali, Ayatollah Sadeq, 12
Khamenei, Hojatolislam Sayed 'Ali, 14,
  19–20, 21
Khayrullah, 'Adnan, 113
Kho'eniha, Hijatulislam, 10
Khrushchev, Nikita, 163, 164, 169
Khumayni, Ayatollah Ruhollah, 5, 9–31
  passim, 90, 101, 140, 174, 180, 181;
  Kashf-e Assrar, 16, 17; and Pakistan,
  76–7, 82; and Soviet invasion of
  Afghanistan, 27–8, 77; and war with
  Iraq, 14, 23–5, 120, 123–4
Khuramshahr, recovery of (Iran–Iraq
  war), 14
Kissinger, Dr Henry, 70
Komsomol (Young Communist League),
  171–2
Kurdish uprising, Iraq, 117
Kuwait, 50, 65, 74, 116

Lagos, Nigeria, 129

Lahore, 2nd Islamic summit meeting
(1974), 73, 91
League of Arab and Islamic peoples, 91
Lebanon, 17, 45, 46, 47, 50, 151; Israeli
invasion of, 81, 156
liberation movements: African, 135, 136;
Arab–Islamic conference of, Cairo
(1953), 87; Libyan attitude to, 56; see
also Palestine Liberation Organization
Liberia, 87, 88
Libya, 5, 42, **54–66**, 88, 141, 180, 181;
African orientation, 56–7, 60, 64–6;
and Arab unity, 58–9; demonization of
West, 55–6, 64; and Egypt, 56, 59, 60,
65; Jamahiriya, 54, 57–8; and liberation
movements, 56; and Morocco, 65, 101,
102, 110; and Pakistan, 73, 74, 120; and
Palestinian question, 56, 62–6; and
revolutionary Iran, 58, 62, 126; and
Saudi Arabia, 50, 62–3, 65

Madagascar, 120
Maktabi school, 15, 16
Malaysia, 41, 50, 149, 151, 153, 155, 156
Mali, 47, 65, 167, 168
Malik, Adam, 153
Manabendra Na Roy, 161
Marcos, Ferdinand, President of
Philippines, 49, 90, 157
Marrakesh, 167
Marx, Karl, Marxism, 160–61
Marxist Islam, 15
Mauritania, 47, 65, 88, 100, 102
Mecca, 34; conference on 'Mission of the
Mosques' (1975), 167; Muslim World
Conference (1926), 35, 37; occupation
of Grand Mosque (1979), 1, 76; OIC
summit meeting (1981), 119; Supreme
World Council for Mosques in, 48; see
also hajj
Medina, 34, 130
Meer, Khurshid Hasan, 75
militancy, Islamic, 57, 58, 92, 109
Minbar al-Islam, 88
Mir al-Arab in Bukhara, *madrasa* of, 165
Mobilization Force, Iranian (*Basij*), 24
Mochtar, Kusumaatmadja, 154, 155
Mohammed, Murtalla, 135, 136
Mohammad Reza Pahlavi, Shah of Iran,
43, 81, 124, 155; foreign policy, 9–10,
22, 25–6, 29, 30, 117; relations with
Morocco, 101; relations with Pakistan,
73, 76; residence in Egypt, 90, 93

Molotov, V. M., 36
monarchical systems, 26, 101, 102, 103
Morocco, 6, 88, **97–110**, 120, 151, 166,
167, 180; African role, 107–8; and
Algeria, 101, 102, 107; and Iran, 101;
and Islamic summits, 100; Istiqlal
Party, 99; and Libya, 65, 101, 102, 110;
national identity and values, 103–5,
106, 109; and Pakistan, 102–3;
participation in Arab Muslim world,
107; policy statements, 97, 98–9; and
Saharan question, 107; and Saudi
Arabia, 44, 47, 50, 100, 101–2;
and Soviet Union, 100, 101, 108;
and USA, 100, 108; world view,
108–9
mosques: building and administration,
48, 65, 88, 92, 125; decline in numbers,
in Soviet Union, 164, 169
Moulay Idriss I, King of Morocco, 106
Mozambique, 120
MPLA, 136
Muhammed's Youth organization, 92
Mujaheddin: Afghan, 28, 170–1, 174; in
Iran, 13, 15, 76
Mukhtar, Shaykh 'Ali, 48
Musaddeq, Dr Muhammad, 22
Muslim Brothers movement, 23, 37, 86,
89, 92, 93–5, 181
Muslim World Conference, Mecca
(1926), 35, 37
Muslim World League, 40, 48
Muslims of Central Asia journal, 172
Mussavi, Mir-Husayn, 17, 20, 21, 22

Nabavi, Behzad, 12
Nahdatul Ullamma, Indonesia, 147
al-Najaf, Iraq, 122, 123, 124, 125
Namibian problem, 108
Nasakom, Indonesia, 147
al-Nasir, Gamal 'Abd, 39, 40, 41, 64, 108,
151, 165, 180; influence on Libya,
58–9; *Philosophy of the Revolution*, 84;
use of Islam, 85, 86–9, 95
Nassar, Mumtaz, 94
National Democratic Front, Iran, 15
National Front, Iran, 15
National Party of Nigeria, 133, 135
nationalism: African, 132–3, 136;
anti-Western, 163; Muslim, 70;
Indonesian, 148; see also Arab
nationalism
Natsir, Mohammad, 150

Nauka i Religiia (Soviet anti-religious journal), 169
Nayif, Prince, of Saudi Arabia, 27
Nehru, Pandit Jawaharlal, 151
neutrality, notion of, 87, 149; *see also* non-alignment
New Guinea, Western (Irian Barat), 151
Nicaragua, 30
Niger, 47, 140, 167, 168
Nigeria, 65, 88, 94, 129–41, 179, 180; African policy, 131–2, 137; Christian population, 137, 138, 139; fear of external fomentation of unrest, 140–41; interest in Middle East affairs, 130, 131, 136, 138; Muslim population, 129, 137; Northern ruling elite, 129, 132–5, 137–8, 140; religious unrest, 139–40; and Saudi Arabia, 136, 141; Southern Region, 129, 133, 137, 138; Western orientation, 131, 132, 135–6
Nixon, Richard, President of USA, 70
non-alignment: Egyptian, 84, 86; Indonesian, 149; Iraqi, 119, 120, 127; Moroccan, 104, 106; Muslim Brothers' support for, 94–5; Nigerian, 131; revolutionary Iran's policy of, 22, 26
North Korea, 14, 30
North Yemen (Yemen Arab Republic), 40–41, 44, 47, 50, 86, 166, 167
Northern Elements Progressive Union (NEPU), Nigeria, 139
Northern People's Congress, Nigeria, 133
nuclear programme, Pakistan's, 73
Numayri, Jaafar, President of Sudan, 41

OAU, 105, 107, 110, 135
OIC (Organization of the Islamic Conference), 41–2, 46–7, 50, 77–8, 85, 91, 100, 119, 179; Charter, 152–3, 154, 158; and revolutionary Iran, 13, 24–5; and Soviet invasion of Afghanistan, 78, 120, 155–6, 174
oil, 42, 73, 78, 91; Indonesian, 149; Iranian, 10, 13, 14, 23, 30; Iraqi, 120; Nigerian, 136; price rises of 1973–4, 43, 74; Saudi Arabian, 36, 44; *see also* OPEC
Okoli, E. J., 140
Oman, 26, 47, 50, 77
OPEC (Organization of Petroleum Exporting Countries), 48, 149
Organization of African Unity, *see* OAU

Osman, Ahmed, Prime Minister of Morocco, 98
Ottoman Empire, 34, 161
'Oweida, Mohammed Tawfiq, 88

Pachaev, leader of Russian Shi'i community, 174
Pakistan, 5, 68–82, 85, 102–3, 120, 180; and Bangladesh, 70, 71, 74; and China, 69, 72, 75; economy, 73–4; and India, 68, 69, 70–1, 72, 80, 81; and Iran, 14, 30, 73, 75, 76–7, 80; military cooperation with Muslim countries, 78–80; rediscovery of Islamic roots, 70–73, 74–6, 80–81; and Saudi Arabia, 39, 41, 44, 47, 49, 50, 73, 75, 78–80, 120; and Soviet Union, 69, 77–8, 79, 81, 166, 168; and USA, 68, 69, 70, 73, 75, 76, 77; Western orientation (1950–62), 68–9
Pakistan People's Party, 74–5
Palestine Liberation Organization, 42, 156
Palestinian question, 36, 37, 51, 62–3, 104, 110, 151, 178; Iraqi stance on, 117 127; Libyan attitude to, 56, 63–5; Muslim Brothers' position on, 94; Saudi view of, 38, 63; *see also* Palestine Liberation Organization
pan-Africanism, 131, 132
pan-Islamism, 17, 29, 60, 84, 86; *see also* Islamic solidarity; universalism
Panca Sila, 145, 147, 148
People's Redemption Party, Nigeria, 139, 141
Persian Gulf region: concern over Iranian intentions in, 19, 20, 26–7, 117; as market for Pakistan, 74; security in, 25–7, 44; Soviet interest in, 44, 101, 162
Philby, Harry St John Bridger, 34
Philippines, 49, 56, 90, 93, 94, 99, 120, 157
Pilgrimage to Mecca, *see* hajj
PLO, 42, 156
Polisario Front, 56, 65, 102
Primakov, Yevgeni M., 170
propagation of Islam, 66, 87–8; Karachi conference on (1978), 167; *see also* *da'wa*

Qaddisiya, Battle of (AD 637), 114, 122

Qadhafi, Mu'ammar, 43, 45, 55–66 *passim*, 73, 167; antipathy towards Morocco, 102; and Palestinian cause, 64–5; pan-Arabism, 57, 58–9, 60; roots of his ideology, 60–2; support for liberation movements, 56; Third International Theory, 55, 57, 58, 60
Qadiriya brotherhood, Nigeria, 133
Qatar, 50
al-Quds, 100, 104, 110
Qur'an: printing and distribution, 48, 94, 165, 174; Qur'anic precepts, 24–5, 57, 58, 61, 89; recitations of, 88, 125, 155

Rabat summit meeting (1969), 41, 84, 86, 89, 100, 152
Rafsanjani, Hashemi, 11
Rahim, J. A., 75
Raja'i, Muhammad 'Ali, 11, 12, 13
Rajavi, Massoud, 13, 15
Reagan, Ronald, President of USA, 12
Repentance and Holy Flight Group, 92
Revolutionary Guards (*Pasdaran*), Iran, 24
revolutionary potential of Islam, 58, 61–2
Reza Shah Pahlavi, 16, 29
Rhodesia, 135
Rodinson, Maxine, 139
Roosevelt, Theodore, 38
Rouleau, Eric, 95
Rousseau, Jean-Jacques, influence on Qadhafi, 61
Royal Institute of International Affairs, 1
Ruhani, Ayatollah, 20
Russian Revolution, 161

al-Sadat, Anwar, 49, 87; assassination, 92, 95, 181; courtship of West, 17, 92, 180; use of Islamic symbolism, 59, 85, 89–92, 93, 95; *see also* Camp David
al-Sadr, Ayatollah Baqir, 121
Saharan provinces, 107, 110
al-Sa'id, Nuri, 37
Salim, Haji Agus, 150
Sanjabi, Karim, 10
Sariya, Saleh, 92
Sastroamijoyo, Ali, Prime Minister of Indonesia, 151
Satiev, Ismail Mashdum, 166
Sa'ud, King of Saudi Arabia, 39, 40, 87

Sa'ud, Prince, Foreign Minister of Saudi Arabia, 46
Saudi Arabia, 4, 5, 33–52, 85, 152, 175, 180; and Camp David accords, 43–4; contemporary foreign policy, 43–9; and Egypt, 35, 39, 40, 41, 42, 43, 47, 49, 84, 86, 88; foreign aid, 46–9, 65–6; foreign policy of 'Abd al-'Aziz, 33–8; foreign policy of Faysal, 39–43; and Iran, 26–7, 43–4, 45; and Iraq, 41, 44, 50, 116; and Jordan, 38, 39, 41, 44, 47, 50; and Libya, 50, 62–3, 65; and Morocco, 44, 47, 50, 100, 101–2; and Nigeria, 136, 141; and OIC, 41, 49, 50, 85; and Pakistan, 39, 41, 44, 47, 49, 50, 73, 75, 78–80, 120; and Palestinian question, 42, 63; and Soviet Union, 35, 36, 37, 45–6, 49, 162; and Syria, 41, 42, 47, 49, 50; and USA, 26, 36, 38, 39, 40, 43, 44, 45, 79
Saudi Fund for Development, 47–8
Sayegh, Fayez A., 84
Senegal, 47, 87, 100, 120, 167, 168, 173
Senussi expansionism, 57
al-Shafi'i, Husain, 88
Shah of Iran, *see* Mohammad Reza Pahlavi
Shaker, Sa'doun, 113
Shakespear, Captain W. H. I., 33
Shakirov, Ysuf-Khan, 167
shari'a, 3, 59, 61, 75, 85, 89, 145; Shari'a Appeal Court, Nigeria, 137–8
Shatt al-'Arab, 117
Shi'is, Shi'ism, 76–7, 110, 174, 180; in Iran, 10, 17, 27, 90, 101; in Iraq, 115, 120–26
Sierra Leone, 88
Sokoto Caliphate, Nigeria, 129, 133, 134, 140
Somalia, 47, 49, 50, 88, 120, 167
South Africa, 130, 135, 166
South Yemen (People's Democratic Republic of Yemen), 44, 47, 50, 120, 126, 173
Soviet Committee for Afro–Asian Solidarity, 166
Soviet invasion of Afghanistan, 1, 120, 169, 170–72, 173, 174, 175; attitude of Saudi Arabia to, 44, 45–6; condemned by Iran, 27–8; and Egypt, 91; and Indonesia, 155–6; Muslim Brothers' view of, 94; and Pakistan, 77–8, 79, 81
Soviet Peace Fund, 165

INDEX

Soviet Union, 20, 55, 69, 72, 100, 101, 108, 131, **160–76**, 180; activism in Middle East, 39, 40, 91, 163–6; attitude to Islam, 160, 164, 168, 169, 175–6; and Iranian revolution, 14, 22, 27–8, 30, 169–71, 174–5; and Saudi Arabia, 35, 36, 37, 45–6, 49, 162; treatment and activities of indigenous Muslim population, 161, 162, 164–9, 171–3, 174–5; visits made abroad by Soviet Muslim leaders 1972–8, 167; *see also* Soviet invasion of Afghanistan

Soviet Uzbekista newspaper, 174

Spain, 107

Sri Lanka, 120, 173

Stalin, Joseph, 36

Strait of Hormuz, 26

Subarjo, Achmad, 151

Sudan, 41, 47, 50, 56–7, 60

Suez crisis (1956), 39, 151

Sufi orders, 88

Suharto, General, President of Indonesia, 144, 147–8, 149, 152, 153, 154–5, 156, 157–8

Suhrawardy, Husein Shaheed, 68

Sukarno, Ahmed, President of Indonesia, 145–7, 149, 152

Sukiman Virjosandjojo, Prime Minister of Indonesia, 150

Sulawesi, South, 146

Sullivan, William H., 10

Sumatra, North, 146

Sunni Islam, 34, 76, 110, 115, 125, 138, 180

Supreme Council for Islamic Affairs, Egypt, 88

Supreme World Council for Mosques, 48

Syria, 37, 41, 59, 93, 117, 151; and Iran, 14, 23, 30, 126–7; and Iraq, 116, 117, 126–7; and Saudi Arabia, 41, 42, 47, 49, 50; and Soviet Union, 120, 165, 166, 173

Taif summit meeting (1981), 174

Talal, Prince of Jordan, 38, 48

Tanzania, 88, 99, 120

Taraki, Nur Mohammed, 171

Tashkent, 165, 166–7; Central Asian Board conferences in, 166, 172; meeting to celebrate the *hijra* (1980), 173; Mufti of, 164, 165, 166, 168; UNO meeting (1980), 172

Taziev, Talga, Mufti of Orenburg, 174

Tehran university, disturbances at (March 1981), 11

Thailand, 93, 157

al-Thawra, 125

Third International Theory, 55, 57, 58, 60

'Third World', 178, 181; Iran's links with, 30; Iraqi hope for leadership of, 119; Pakistan as link between oil-rich Muslim states and, 72–80; and revolutionary potential of Islam, 62

Tiganiya order, 88, 133

Togo, 173

Trans-Jordan, 35, 37, 38

Trimingham, J. S., 132

Tripoli, 167

Trucial Coast *shayks*, 34; *see also* United Arab Emirates

Truman, Harry S., President of USA, 38

Tudeh Party, Iran, 15, 30, 170

Tunis, 167

Tunisia, 46, 47, 50, 56, 60, 100, 166, 179

Turkey, 14, 30, 34, 47, 50, 99; and Soviet Union, 37, 161, 162, 163

Turkmenskaya Iskra newspaper, 171

'twin revolution', concept of, 9

U Nu, 151

UAE, *see* United Arab Emirates

Uganda, 47, 64, 94, 173

umma, 58, 91, 146, 168

United Arab Emirates (UAE), 50, 65, 74

United Nations Organization, 13, 15, 77–8, 99, 117, 172

United States of America, 93, 94, 163, 166, 174; and Indonesia, 149, 151; Libya's attitude to, 55, 63, 64; and Morocco, 100, 108; and Nigeria, 131, 136; relations with Pakistan, 68, 69, 70, 73, 75, 76, 77; relations with Saudi Arabia, 26, 36, 38, 39, 40, 43, 44, 45, 79; revolutionary Iran's attitude to, 10, 12–13, 20, 21, 30; and Sadat, 92, 180; Shah of Iran's policy towards, 9, 26; *see also* American hostage crisis

universalism, Islamic: of Khumayni, 17–18, 23, 29, 62; of Qadhafi, 57–9, 62, 64, 65

Usman dan Fodio, Shehu, 133

Usmaniya order, 133

USSR, *see* Soviet Union

Vatikiotis, P. J., 86

190

Velayati, Ali Akbar, 21
Vietnam, 120
'Voice of Islam' radio, 88

Wachuku, Jaja, 130
Wahhabis, 4, 35, 38, 63
Western Sahara, 107, 110
World Bank, 139
World Islamic Congress, 172, 173

Yazdi, Ibrahim, 10, 20
Yemen, 35, 36; see also North Yemen;
    South Yemen
Yen Izala sect, 140

Yorubaland, Nigeria, 129, 138
Young Communist League (Komsomol),
    171–2
Yunus Abu Turab, Imam-Khatib of
    'Tilla Sheikh' Mosque, Tashkent, 167

Zade, Yusif, 175
Zaïre, 100
Zanzibar, 89
Zia ul-Haq, General Mohammad, 75–6,
    78
Zinoviev, G., 161
Zionism: Iran and, 21, 23; and Islam, 63,
    99; linked with communism, 45